# A DIFFERENT DEGREE



*Memoirs of an Indo-Soviet Doctor*

HARI KUMAR

INDIA · SINGAPORE · MALAYSIA

No.8, 3rd Cross Street
CIT Colony, Mylapore
Chennai, Tamil Nadu – 600004

First Published by Notion Press 2020


ISBN 978-1-64919-933-1

# CONTENTS

# ACKNOWLEDGEMENTS

I dedicate this book to my parents, V.P. Nayar and Lalitha P. Nayar, who are my inspiration, to my beautiful wife, Padmaja, and my lovely daughters Meenakshi and Gayathri, who gave me the strength and support to write it. Professor Radhamony, my favourite aunty, had the patience and perseverance to read and correct the first manuscript. She made invaluable suggestions and encouraged me to tidy it up and publish it. Sadly, she did not live to see the book in print. I will never forget her. T.V. Sree Kumar, my good friend and schoolmate, politely kept on pushing me to proceed with the book. If it weren't for him, I suspect it may have never seen the light of day. Doreen Newlyn amazed me with her boundless energy, sharp memory and observation skills. Ignoring age and frail health, and even as the coronavirus terrorised the world, Doreen kindly went through the manuscript, picked up salient points and guided me in the right direction. I am ever grateful to her. Special mention has to be made of my good friends Jima, Carlos and Shyam, who are essential characters in the book. My school mate, Mohan Sivanand deserves full credit for writing a 'foreword' from the heart.

It is impossible to name all the other people who helped in realising my dream of writing the book, as they are too many to mention individually. Hence a big collective thank you to all of them. I will fondly remember colleagues from my group at the Peoples' Friendship University of

Moscow, USSR who made the course fun, and the teachers who imparted knowledge and wisdom and helped develop empathy. Patients helped me learn the simple philosophy 'Do unto others what thou shall have others do unto you.' I remain eternally grateful to them.

I am indebted to the great people who graciously agreed to read my memoirs. Their names and opinions are on the back cover of this book. I cannot thank them enough.

Finally a word of appreciation for the staff of Notion Press Publishers. Their professionalism and dedication made the last part of my work, which an obstetrician would call 'delivery' smooth and pain-free.

The names of some of the characters have been changed to protect their anonymity.

# INTRODUCTION

Memoirs are written by people with extraordinary achievements. This is the memoir of an ordinary person who got an extraordinary opportunity to study medicine behind the Iron Curtain – in the Union of Soviet Socialist Republics (USSR).

The nine years I spent in the USSR from 1971 to 1980 went by quickly. The unique experiences I had shaped me into the man I am today. I returned to India and started practising medicine. It took a while to adapt to the practice of medicine in India, which was very different from that in the Soviet Union. I specialised in orthopaedics and got a job as a lecturer at the university teaching hospital in Kottayam, Kerala. Then it was marriage and kids. After a few years, I travelled to the UK for higher training in orthopaedics and settled there with my family.

Thirty-five years after leaving the USSR, something incredible happened. I was invited to a reunion of the classmates who had studied in Moscow. By this time, the USSR had been wiped from the map of the world. Moscow was now the capital of a different country – the Russian Federation. Memories that flooded back while walking the streets of Moscow gave me a chance to reflect and take stock of the fascinating bygone era.

History is written by historians. It is no secret that they tend to distort facts deliberately when it suits them. I can honestly say that what I have written in this book is what I have seen and experienced myself in the USSR and later on my return to the Russian Federation.

– Dr. Hari Kumar

# A SHORT APPRECIATION BY JOANNA LUMLEY

Like Hari Kumar, I visited the USSR when I was very young. I was there five years before he went as a medical student; but the Moscow we saw behind the Iron Curtain was the same. It was vast, cold, struggling, under-supplied: but hidden beneath this bleak exterior was warmth and friendliness.

Like Dr Kumar, I too returned many years later and was stunned by the immense change that had taken place since the Soviet Union had been dissolved and a glittering new Russian Federation had risen from the disintegration.

That is where the similarities end: Dr Kumar went on to speak the language fluently, to study medicine there for eight years and to get under the skin of the people and their way of living. His wide experience as a doctor in India and in the UK has put him in a strong position to scrutinise varying politics and regimes, customs and prejudices, communism and capitalism. This fascinating book starts with vivid recollections of his student years, when to an Indian boy the USSR was as alien as Mars: and gradually reveals his understanding and acceptance of a new world, causing him to re-examine the doctrines we absorb depending on where we live. Always the same question comes to the fore: Was communism a better system to live under than capitalism? Like Dr Kumar, I asked people I met from Siberia to Moscow: was life better then? And the answers were the ones he heard as well: many people preferred the certainty of the old days of Soviet Socialism and felt that personal freedom was the price worth paying for security. The one unifying factor over the years was a sort of universal kindness: friendliness and generosity greeted him everywhere he stayed.

Dr Kumar writes with admirable dispassion on the endless dichotomy of the polarising systems of communism and capitalism, and that debate will go on long after we are all gone. Until then, A Different Degree puts us all under the microscope: we are left to draw our own conclusions, guided by his benevolent observations.

# FOREWORD

During the late 1960s when Hari Kumar, the author of this book, and I were at our Catholic boarding school, set in the picturesque former Portuguese seaside enclave of Tangasseri, in Quilon, South India, I reckoned that Hari would become a doctor. He'd opted for the biology stream. Yet, never would I have imagined him getting his MD in Moscow – after learning the Russian language from scratch! Likewise, this memoir too is filled with surprises.

Being a born liberal, I was no admirer of the erstwhile USSR. I'd assumed it was all KGB, communism and brainwashed citizens who had no fun – Ronald Reagan called it "Evil Empire". And Bertrand Russell, the mentor author of my youth, had painted an equally bleak picture. So, I rejoiced when the USSR dissolved in 1991. Now, having read this book, I feel delightfully re-educated. Hari got to know warm-hearted people everywhere in the USSR, describes its high standards of education, sports, art and architecture; its citizens living good lives without having to worry about food and shelter, or even crime, despite the controls and the queues. There are innumerable little-known facts, like why Red Square has nothing to do with the colour. Soviet citizens, remarkably, kept their humour and this book is sprinkled with moments of merriment and characteristically understated Russian jokes.

Another revelation is how Dr. Hari Kumar, who's worked as an orthopedic surgeon in the UK over three decades, recalls his youth in such detail – talking about unforgettable people he came across in the Soviet Union and in India. Scenes of a forgotten era are relived with many heartwarming anecdotes. This book is true to the generous Russian spirit. It walks us simply and plainly through a distilled Russian history from Peter the Great to Gorbachev, Yeltsin and Putin. Hari does not forget some of the USSR's other personalities: like its great renegade poets who were banned, a chess grandmaster, or the celebrity radio newsreader, who like all others, stood in queues. Hari did not get himself brainwashed, as he'd been warned before he left India, nor did he embrace communism. He describes Soviet life as an impartial observer who enjoyed his six student years there and returned briefly to a changed Russia 35 years later.

*– Mohan Sivanand*

*Former Editor-in-Chief of Reader's Digest, India*

## *Chapter 1*

# THE TELEGRAM

I am going to tell you a story. It is a true story that started on a sunny day in June 1971 with the unexpected arrival of a telegram. The telegram was short and sweet, and it simply read 'Selected for Peoples Friendship University, Moscow. Proceed to Delhi at the earliest to go to Moscow.'

It was the happiest day of my life.

I got my passport in a hurry. Dad and I travelled all the way from our little village, Sasthamkottah, in the state of Kerala in South India, by train to the capital of India, Delhi, up in the north.

The Soviet Embassy stamped the visa on my passport, and I arrived at the Safdarjung International Airport in Delhi, ready to board the Aeroflot (Soviet Airlines' flag carrier) evening flight to Moscow.

I was a bundle of nerves as I checked in. The closest I had come to an aeroplane until that day was seeing one up in the skies. I had dreamt of travelling by plane someday, but until this trip to Delhi I had not travelled further than Quilon, our closest town in Kerala, on my own. I was only seventeen and I was waiting to board a plane to take me to a faraway, mysterious country – the Soviet Union. Leaving my family and friends behind was difficult enough, but going to do a professional course without knowing even a word of Russian was genuinely daunting. There were looks of surprise when I told my friends that I was going to the Soviet Union to study medicine. Some considered me fortunate to go to the land of Lenin, which they imagined as paradise on earth. Others were convinced it would be worse than living inside a freezer. I was told that if I survived I would be hounded and brainwashed by the KGB and would end up a die-hard communist. I had no clue who 'the KGB' was.

My dad once had a Russian friend, Mr Golomazov, a basketball coach, whom he had met years earlier in Delhi while serving as a member of the Indian parliament. A few years later, Dad visited Moscow as a part of the parliamentary delegation from India. There, he met up with Mr Golomazov and stayed with him in his apartment for two days. I asked Dad who the KGB was. He explained that it was the plain-clothes secret police of the Soviet Union who helped the regular police maintain law and order in the country. Dad assured me that Moscow was the safest place and Russians the most hospitable people and that I would have the time of my life there.

I went to check in at the Aeroflot counter at 5 p.m. After the security checks, I was directed to the waiting area. In the seventies, security checks at airports were much simpler and the number of people travelling by air was far fewer. I sat in the lounge, staring at the monitor without blinking, determined not to miss my flight details when they came up on the screen. I also kept listening attentively to the intercom for the announcement of my flight. Suddenly, I was overcome with a deep sense of sadness, as I had not said a proper goodbye to my father before checking in. I was unaware that once you go through the security gates, there is no going back.

The thought of my first flight and the new life that awaited me the following day made me nervous. Out of the blue came an announcement: "Passenger Mr Kumar, travelling to Moscow by Aeroflot flight number 567, kindly report to the security desk."

It caught me by surprise. Could my first plane journey have ended even before taking off? The officer at the security desk looked at my passport carefully and put it aside. His deputy led me back to the check-in counter.

My dad had persuaded the officials to let me out for a couple of minutes to say a proper goodbye.

Dad was a hard man with a big moustache and a soft heart. He gave me a great big hug and kiss and said, "Son, you are a young man now and capable of looking after yourself. Take care." I saw tears gather in his eyes for the first time, and it moved me. My eyes filled up, despite my best efforts to keep a brave face, as I was led back into the waiting lounge, but I felt a lot happier inside.

## *Chapter 2*

# FLIGHT TO MOSCOW

My first plane journey was smoother than anticipated. When the air hostess distributed sweets, I took a handful, as a friend who had travelled by plane before warned me to keep chewing during the ascent and descent to avoid earache. My prayers were answered as I had been allocated a window seat. The aircraft moved up the runway, the engines roared, started slowly, warmed up and then, with a sprint, it took off. I was glued to the little window. As the plane gained altitude, Delhi beneath us looked beautiful, with millions of lights like fireflies. They gradually faded and disappeared into the distance below. I was tired and hungry after three hours of waiting at the airport. It was still difficult to believe that the next morning I would wake up in a foreign land. It was surreal.

My ambition was to study medicine, but even in my wildest dreams, I had never imagined that it would be abroad. My grandmother lived with us in the village. She was disabled and doubled up with arthritis and only walked indoors. She often had breathing difficulties and was on medication prescribed by the village Ayurvedic doctor. Grandma had blind faith in this doctor and had many tales to tell about him. He had made the paralysed walk and cured cancer. In Grandma's mind, he was the reincarnation of Jesus.

When I first saw the doctor with my grandmother, I was very impressed. He was a gentle, soft-spoken and likeable person. His patience was limitless, and he was the greatest listener. He was never in a hurry, even when many patients waited impatiently outside to see him. He still had all the time in the world to listen to you. Grandmother used to say that merely speaking to him made her feel fifty per cent better. I used to pull her leg by saying, "Let us see him again tomorrow, and you will become one hundred per cent better."

It was common knowledge that Ayurvedic medicine was not ideal for acute illnesses and was effective only if taken regularly over a long period. One Saturday morning, my grandmother's health took a turn for the worse, and she was struggling to breathe. We had to summon the local Western medicine doctor (general practitioner) from the village. I was sent on my trusted mode of transport, the bicycle, to request a home visit.

The doctor was a tall, plump man with an imposing personality and a high-pitched voice. He reached us in ten minutes. He got out of his car, hung the stethoscope around his neck, picked up his briefcase and walked confidently into our home. He was ushered into my grandmother's room. He placed the stethoscope on my grandmother's chest and listened carefully. There was pin-drop silence in the room. We watched in awe and admiration.

After a brief pause, he turned around to my mother and said calmly, "Nothing to worry about. It is only a mild asthma attack. I will give her an injection, and she will get better soon."

The doctor administered the injection, wrote out a prescription for tablets, collected the white envelope with the fee my mother had put ready and left. As soon as he left, my grandmother's breathing started improving. I set off to the village pharmacy to buy the tablets. As I rode to the pharmacy, I thought to myself, *What a nice, clever man! I want to be like him someday.*

In the seat next to me on the plane was a pleasant, middle-aged, stocky Russian gentleman who introduced himself as Jim (Dmitry in Russian) and started a conversation. He spoke excellent English as he worked in the Russian Embassy in Delhi and knew India well. Jim mentioned the slogan famous in those days, 'Hindi Russi Bhai Bhai' (Indians and Russians are brothers). I was glad to be seated next to a brother during my maiden flight. He was a delightful conversationalist and kept on talking without pausing. It helped calm my nerves and keep my mind distracted. I only had to listen.

Drinks were served before meals. Jim had vodka, and I ordered a soft drink. I had never come across vodka before. I was expecting him to dilute it with soda or water, as with whisky, but he surprised me by gulping it neat, as a shot. Jim swore that vodka was the best drink under the sun. After his second shot, he began singing a tune from a Hindi movie starring his idol, the famous Indian film star Raj Kapoor. The opening words are, "Mera joota hai Japani, patloon Englishtani, sir pe lal topi Russi, Phir bi dil hai Hindustani" ("My shoes are Japanese, trousers are English, the red cap is Russian, but my heart is still Indian").

A delicious dinner was served on the flight, and Jim nodded off after that. In the pouch in the seat in front there were a couple of magazines in Russian and an English newspaper. CD players to listen to music or DVDs to watch films had not been invented then. I picked up the Russian magazine. It was a strange language, with Latin alphabets mixed with some other odd and funny alphabets. I could not understand a word and just looked through the pictures of beautiful women in its pages. I struggled to sleep. The sound of the jet engines and the anticipation of a new life starting in a few hours kept me wide awake.

## *Chapter 3*

# USSR TIMELINE

To get an idea of the country I was going to, I thought it worthwhile to find out a little about its history. Here's a brief summary of what I found out.

- In the year 1917, the tsarist regime was overthrown in Russia after the October Revolution and Lenin's Bolshevik Party came to power.
- In 1922, the USSR was officially formed, with Lenin as its leader. Stalin became the General Secretary of the Communist Party (Bolshevik) Central Committee.
- In 1941, Hitler attacked the USSR in the Second World War (Great Patriotic War, as it was known in the Soviet Union). The 900-day siege of the city of Leningrad began.
- By 1945, Soviet troops had driven the Germans out of the territory of the USSR all the way back into Germany and took Berlin from the east, helping to end the war in Europe.
- Stalin died in 1953 and Nikita Khrushchev became the General Secretary of the Communist Party of the USSR.
- In 1964, a coup in Moscow removed Khrushchev as party leader. Leonid Brezhnev became the General Secretary of the Communist Party. He was the supreme leader of the USSR from then on.

My research on the USSR made me even more curious and excited about the country I was soon going to be living in.

## Arrival in Moscow

Before long, the cabin crew got busy again, serving breakfast. It was 5 a.m. and far too early for me. I just had coffee. A good cup of coffee always reminds me of my mother. Thirty minutes on the dot after I got back home from college, she would fetch me the tastiest cup of milky, frothy strong coffee, along with freshly made snacks. The snacks were to give me energy and the coffee to stimulate my brain and help me concentrate on my studies. After this treat, I would sit with my books for two hours of uninterrupted study. This routine helped me do well in my exams and get excellent grades. Those grades helped me make it onto this flight.

The captain announced, "All passengers are requested to return to their seats and fasten their seatbelts. We are about to begin our descent into Moscow." My eyes were glued to the little window to catch my first glimpse of Moscow. Buildings like matchboxes began to appear below. Their numbers decreased and sizes increased as we got closer to the ground. As we landed I felt the jolt from the impact of the rear wheels hitting the ground, followed by the front wheels. The plane decelerated, taxied and came to a final halt.

In the arrival lounge of Sheremetyevo International Airport, a Russian gentleman was holding a placard reading PFU (UDN). It was the short form for Peoples' Friendship University, Moscow, in English and Russian. The university was named after Patrice Lumumba, the freedom fighter from Congo. I approached the man and he greeted me with, "Namaste, Zdravstvuite" ("Hello" in Hindi and Russian) as we shook hands. He was Comrade Maxim, the senior teacher in charge of students coming to the university from English-speaking countries. Maxim was fluent in Hindi. He too had worked in the Russian Embassy in Delhi a few years before.

Five students from Nepal had arrived on the same flight from Delhi. The airport was a busy and strange place. No one other than Maxim spoke a word of English. We boarded a minibus and set off on our first trip into Moscow. It was a warm, sunny day and we had a pleasant forty-five-minute drive through woodlands. Buildings gradually began to appear on both sides of the road. There were no skyscrapers but mostly five-storey buildings, which looked similar to one another.

We arrived at the hostel complex in Miklukho-Maklaya Street. It would be easy to recreate a miniature model of this hostel complex with eight matchboxes of the same size. The first and third blocks were parallel, while the second was staggered behind them. This pattern continued until the eighth block. I was eager to take a stroll around the campus, but we were taken straight into the second block with our luggage.

After registering at the reception, we were ushered to our respective rooms. Three people had to share each room. We could choose with whom to share, and there was one exciting choice available. If you wished, you could opt to have a Russian student as your roommate. I teamed up with a Nepalese student, but we were in a dilemma as to whom to choose as the third roommate. I overheard someone say they would never share with a Russian, as all of them would be members of the KGB. However, the great advantage of having a Russian roommate was that you could learn the language faster, as most of them spoke only Russian. We took our chances and opted for a Russian as our third roommate.

Vinod, my roommate from Nepal, spoke good English. Our Russian roommate was to join us in a week, as he was away on holiday. Our room was bright and airy. It was a basic students' room with single beds, a medium-sized desk, three chairs and a small cupboard for each one of us. There were five toilets and washrooms at the end of the corridor for the twenty rooms. If you felt like cooking, there was a kitchen with eight electric hot plates on each floor.

The hostel was very cosmopolitan. Students from eighty-five countries of the so-called developing world came to study at this university. There were students of every description – white, black, short, tall, Asian, African, South American, Arab, Hindu, Muslim, Christian, Sikh and Buddhist. There was even an African albino, a Buddhist monk and a Muslim cleric. I longed to go out and see the city, but we were not allowed out of the building, as we were in strict quarantine for a week. Since students came to the university from all over the globe, the authorities needed to make sure no communicable diseases got into the country with them.

The canteen in our block was a big, spacious, bright hall that served hot meals three times a day. We had to get used to Russian food, which was, frankly speaking, rather bland.

# *Chapter 4*

# QUARANTINE

As quarantine was enforced and there was nothing much to do, a lot of time was spent eating, talking and making new friends. One day, I was sitting at the dining table with a couple of newly made friends from Uganda. One of them, George, was admiring the large portrait of a man adorning the wall of the canteen. It was one of the most recognisable faces in the world – the goateed face of the famous thinker and philosopher, the architect of the Soviet Union, Vladimir Ilyich Lenin.

After studying the portrait carefully, George commented, “That must be Patrice Lumumba.”

Everyone burst out laughing.

“No, George. It cannot be Patrice Lumumba. Lumumba is a black man. That is Lenin, the founder of the Soviet Union.”

I could see the logic in George’s response, “Whose portrait are you most likely to see first in Patrice Lumumba University?”

Patrice Lumumba was a Congolese politician and independence leader who served as the first Prime Minister of the independent Democratic Republic of Congo in the year 1960. He played a significant role in the transformation of Congo from a colony of Belgium into an independent republic. The university was named after him as the symbol of freedom movements in colonies all over the world.

There was a recreation hall with a TV and a mini library with books in all common languages in the block. The boys spent most of the time in front of the TV, watching football. The girls preferred chatting to football but joined in to watch the funny cartoon films. Restricting hormone-charged teenagers to one building for an entire week was in itself inviting problems. Relationships did not take long to develop, sometimes overcoming the language barrier and proving that love is not only blind but can be deaf as well. A few hearts were broken in that short period.

All the new arrivals had to undergo a medical check-up. The language did, at times, pose a problem here, as an interpreter was not always on hand. I was told the story of how a lady doctor was once taken by surprise. She had checked the blood pressure and counted the pulse of a Brazilian student. The next step was to listen to his chest. Using sign language she gestured to the student to take his shirt off so she could examine him. She turned around to wash her hands and prepare the syringe to take his blood. When she turned back, she got the shock of her life. He was standing there stark naked, ready to be examined. The sign language had been misunderstood!

A general knowledge test was also compulsory. It was the most basic test. The questions were standard and the same for every student. A big map of the world hung on the wall. The first question was, "Could you show us the city of Moscow on the map?" The next question was, "Which country are you from? Show us your capital city on the map." Most got the answers right, but a few fumbled even on these questions. If they struggled, the examiner would point out the right place. One can imagine the difficult task of the teachers of the Preparatory Faculty (department), which was the location for the first year common to all students. It was the department that taught all the international students the Russian language.

I could not wait to get out and see Moscow but had to wait for quarantine to be over. However, on the third day we hatched a plan. One of the senior students Thomas, with whom I was chatting through the window of our room on the second floor, promised he would take me around and show me Moscow if I could get out of the building. But this was no easy task, as there was a burly, stiff-faced guard stationed at the entrance to the building around the clock. He spoke only Russian and would not even let a fly in or out without a name badge. We would be given a name badge only after the quarantine was over. All the windows of the ground floor, which housed the little library and medical check-up rooms, were usually locked.

Around 5 p.m. that day I checked out the windows on the ground floor. The window in one of the rooms at the far end was not locked. The last person who left the room had forgotten to close it. I asked Thomas to come round to the back of the building. After making sure there was nobody in the corridor, I got into the room and opened the window. It was a six-foot drop to the other side, but it did not matter then whether it was six or sixty. I had decided to get out to explore Moscow. I jumped out and closed the window gently from the outside so that I could find my way back into the building on my return. It was a glorious day, and the sun was shining brightly. We took a stroll around the campus. Students studying the same speciality were all put up in the same block. My friend and guide for my campus tour, Thomas, was living in block number one, next to the quarantine (preparatory) block, and was studying mathematics. Between blocks three and four was a mini supermarket. It was only one floor and spread out more than the hostel blocks. All essentials could be purchased there. Thomas pointed at block seven and said, "This is the medical block where you will be living next year."

A lot of construction work was going on across the road from this complex, as was evident from the many big machines and tall cranes seen there. Thomas explained that a new main building of the university was under construction. The present university building was an old one situated some seven miles away. The development going on across from the seventh block (medical students' block) was the new medical faculty building.

"Where is the medical faculty at present?" I was curious.

"The classes are held on the premises of another medical school, the first medical school in town for the time being. The plan is to move it over here as soon as this building is completed."

I thought it was great. The idea of having to travel long distances to get to lectures daily in the biting cold of Moscow was frightening. I had heard so many horror stories of Moscow winters. Thomas reassured me that winter was not as much a problem as people made it out to be. "You wrap up in several layers and do not usually spend too much time out in the cold. In fact, after the first winter, you will even come to like it," he said.

Thomas told me an interesting story about a student who came to study in Moscow from one of the African countries. He got on the direct flight to Moscow, fully armed for winter, wrapped in a few layers of woollen clothes, although it was only July. The student even had a fur cap on but took it off on the flight as no one else was wearing one and he had noticed people staring at him. He was hot during the flight, despite the air conditioning. He felt unwell in the arrivals lounge and nearly fainted. The airport duty doctor was called out. The student was taken to a cubicle, asked to remove all the extra layers of clothing and given a cold drink, after which he felt better. The doctor reminded him with a smile that winter was at least three months away.

"How many years will it take to complete this building?" I enquired.

"Maybe a year, or less," Thomas replied.

I prayed that by the time I finished at the Russian Preparatory Faculty, the medical block would be completed, and we would only have to cross the road to get to classes. In Moscow, construction was fast as most of the buildings were prefabricated and assembled on site. New buildings sprouted up like mushrooms. It was not unusual to see entire walls with windows being transported on the back of large trucks to the building sites.

We took a bus to the nearest metro (subway) station, called South-West Station. It was the starting point of the underground transport network that ran from the south-west of Moscow to the city centre. The metro was simply amazing. It was spotlessly clean and beautiful, with marble floors, intricate artistic designs on marble walls and massive chandeliers dangling from the ceilings. The trains were frequent. Our next train was in two minutes. During peak hours, there was a train every minute. We travelled a few stations and got off at Lenin Hills. The station was built right over the Moscow River. It had glass walls, and from the station you could see the river below and the sights around it. The escalator took us to the top of the hill and we walked around. The view of Moscow from the hilltop was breathtaking.

The Moscow River flowed past the foot of the hill. On the other side of the river was the massive Lenin Football Stadium. An impressive skyscraper situated some distance away on Lenin Hill was the Moscow State University building. It was built in 1953 and had forty-two floors. When built, it was the tallest building in Europe. Six other similar buildings were built in Moscow during Stalin's reign. They were nicknamed the Seven Sisters of Stalin.

We walked around, admiring the glorious view from the top of the hill for an hour, and then stopped for ice cream. Thomas told me the ice creams in Moscow are the tastiest as no additives or preservatives are used. It was so true. After the ice cream, we went back down the hill to the station and caught the metro back to the hostel.

It was 7 p.m. and getting dark. We went round to the back of the building to the window for me to get back in. Unfortunately, someone had locked it from the inside. I was stuck. *How do I get back in?* We went to the entrance and hung around there for some time. I was trying to figure out a way to get in when fortune arrived in the shape of a minibus. It was bringing a group of African students from the airport to the university. As they were getting their luggage out, I went up and introduced myself to one of them in English, "Hello, I am Hari from India", and extended my hand.

"Hi, Otto from Kenya," and we shook hands.

"Otto, my friend, let me give you a hand with your luggage, man."

I took one of his two suitcases and walked into the building with the group, as one of the new arrivals. While the guard was checking the passports of the new arrivals, I returned Otto's suitcase and slipped back into the block, unnoticed.

The week of quarantine was finally over, and we were ready to start classes.

# *Chapter 5*

# PREPARATORY FACULTY

The first year of study was in the Preparatory Faculty. Imagine how difficult it was not only to teach us Russian but also to raise the knowledge levels in the basic subjects of over a hundred students from across the world to A-Level standard. As one would expect, the intelligence, motivation and will to work hard were very variable in this diverse gathering of students from across the globe. It was difficult to understand how it was possible – yet it was.

The day before we started in the Preparatory Faculty, our third roommate, Alex, a slim, tall and handsome man with a freckled face and blond hair, joined us in the room.

"Zdravstvuite," he said and extended his hand.

I repeated it after him, and we shook hands. It was one of the few Russian words in my vocabulary then.

"Speak English?" I enquired.

"Net. Hachu uchichsa." ("No. I want to learn.")

From that day, we became good friends. While the international students were learning Russian, the Russian students were learning a foreign language of their choice. Their progress was understandably slower, as we were learning Russian under pressure and out of necessity.

For us to travel, shop and even to communicate with our colleagues from non-English-speaking countries there was only one way – learn to speak Russian.

Alex was from Kyiv, the capital of Ukraine, and had just returned from his two-year stint in the army. Serving in the army was compulsory for every Soviet citizen and the military service could be anywhere in the country. It was rigid and rigorous, but at the end of the day it made you a disciplined and hardworking man. There was a saying, "If you survived the training in the Soviet Army, you could survive anywhere in the world." Alex told me that the army service makes a man out of a boy. Sharing a room with Alex proved useful, as soon I got rid of my English–Russian dictionary, and learning Russian became fun. Alex was pleasant, had a good sense of humour and was always willing to help. I realised the suspicions of all Russians being KGB agents was unfounded.

It was with trepidation that we walked into the Preparatory Faculty for our first lesson in Russian. Our year was divided into fifteen groups of ten students each. While going to the classrooms, I caught a glimpse of a group of Russian language teachers in one room. They were having their briefing before the start of lessons. All of them were pretty, young Russian ladies barring one elderly gentleman. I assumed he was the head of the department.

We were all looking forward to seeing our pretty young Russian teacher when the only male member from the group walked into our class.

"Zdravstvuite," he said with a broad smile.

We replied "Zdravstvuite" in unison. The disappointment was written clearly on the faces of the six boys in the group.

Our teacher's name was Vladimir. In the USSR, you call everyone by their first names. Mister is not a prefix used in Russian. If you want to address someone you are not familiar with, you use the word *Tavarish* (Comrade).

Vladimir introduced himself and then asked us to introduce ourselves in Russian. "Repeat after me," he said, "minya zavoot Hari." (My name is Hari).

As we got to know Vladimir better, we realised how lucky we were. He was an extraordinary teacher. It was difficult to tell how old he was. I guess he was in his mid-sixties, but the furrows and wrinkles on his face, receding hairline and sad eyes made him look older. He was the most patient person I had ever met. Vladimir understood English well, as we gathered later, but he pretended not to know any language other than Russian. It was intentional, to make us learn Russian quicker. He would explain the same things over and over until each one of us had understood. Our group was a mixture of students from South America, Asia and Africa. For a couple of them, explaining things even a hundred times would not suffice. Still, Vladimir would continue explaining a hundred and one times until he was satisfied everyone had understood. When he was confident of having achieved his goal, a broad smile would light up his face and there would be a twinkle in his eye. The pace at which we progressed with learning the difficult language was exceptional. Vladimir's methods and manners were the key factors keeping up our interest in studying Russian. He was liberal with the use of the words *mologets* (well done) and *otlichno* (excellent). Having Alex as my roommate also helped me a lot.

Every group had a second Russian language teacher to teach us phonetics. Our teacher was Natalya and she was a perfectionist. She made sure everyone practised the tongue twisters she regularly gave as homework and gradually we understood how rich and precise the language of Tolstoy and Pushkin was.

We never realised how quickly our knowledge of Russian improved. However, Vladimir pointed out that we could be sure we knew Russian well only when we started to think in Russian. At that time, all we were doing was thinking in English, or our mother tongue, translating it into Russian in our minds and voicing it.

There was a unique method the department used to make learning Russian fun. We were given a different kind of homework. Twice a week, after regular class hours, we had to go back to the department to listen to the homework tapes. There were five spool tape decks in the room. The reels were massive, like the ones that played movies. Small cassette tapes or CDs had not been invented then. We had to borrow the tapes from the librarian and listen to them in one of the stations, on headphones. The recordings were of conversations from everyday life, with the correct pronunciations, and they ended with a little story to make it all the more interesting. The following day, Vladimir would ask us questions on what we had heard. One of us would have to narrate the story in his own words. It was fun. I remember a story about two people going to the cinema. The opening statement was, "My father and I went to the cinema yesterday."

Vladimir asked a Nepali student from our class, "Did you go to the cinema?"

"Yes," he replied.

"Who went with you to the cinema? Was it your father?"

"Yes. It was your father," the student replied.

Vladimir repeated the question and got the same answer once again. He laughed then and said, "No. That can't be. My father passed away twenty years ago. Say 'my father and I went to the cinema' and not 'your father and I'."

The message finally got through and he got the correct reply, "My father and I."

There was a telephone booth inside the hostel block, just past the entrance. It worked on coins and was cheap. This booth was probably the busiest telephone booth in the whole of Moscow. It certainly helped a few students polish their Russian. Usually, there was a queue outside, waiting to make phone calls. The teachers told us that it was good to talk in Russian as frequently as possible to improve our spoken language skills. Many took it too literally. A girlfriend would usually be on the other end of the phone. Understandably, conversations went on and on until money ran out. Every day the phone was in use until well past midnight.

After six months of learning Russian, there was an important event in the department – a concert called 'We Speak Russian', organised by the Preparatory Faculty. Any student of the department could participate, but only in Russian. It could be singing a Russian song, reciting a poem, making a short speech or enacting a short play, but the key was that we had to do it ourselves without any outside help. Since I could not sing to save my life and learning to recite a poem in Russian would be difficult, I chose to do a small skit with two of my friends.

Vladimir asked us whether we had any ideas. I told him we were planning to do a small skit.

"Otlichno" ("Excellent"), he replied. "You must prepare and rehearse it as many times as possible to make it interesting."

He told us of a skit one of the groups had enacted the year before. The actor was a brilliant student who had won prizes for acting back in his school in Sri Lanka (then Ceylon). In the skit, he was to act the role of a man who had spotted a tiger outside its cage in a zoo and was petrified. The guy misunderstood the text and acted as the tiger. The skit misfired badly.

Our skit was simple. A farmer's sheep were stolen. He caught the man whom he believed had stolen them. The man vehemently denied it. So the farmer took him to the village chief, who was the judge for minor disputes in the village. Unfortunately, they met the chief at the wrong time. The chief was partially deaf and had just finished a big argument with his wife. The farmer put forward his case, and the thoughtful chief nodded. Then the man accused of stealing the sheep refuted the allegation. The chief nodded again. The two then waited for the chief to pronounce his verdict. The chief paused for a moment to ponder and then said, "Whatever you say, my friends, I have decided not to stay with that wretched woman any longer."

There were only three actors, and I played the judge. Judging by the audience's response, the skit went well. All the students and teachers from the department were present, except Vladimir. He could not make it due to personal reasons.

The next morning, Vladimir came up to me and with a straight face said, "Hari, you are in the wrong place."

*What have I done now?* I thought.

"You should have been in drama school and taken up acting. My colleagues told me your skit stole the show yesterday. It was funny, the acting brilliant and the Russian near perfect. Everyone enjoyed it. You made me proud. I am sorry I could not come," he said and shook my hand. It really made my day.

Our daily routine began with breakfast in the room. It was simple, with bread, butter, jam and a cup of coffee, before starting Russian lessons at 9 a.m. The bread was always fresh and delivered daily to the local store from the bakery. There were only two types of bread, black and white. Black bread made from rye was the favourite among Russians. It was an acquired taste and you either liked it or hated it. Bread in the shops was never sold sliced, so you had to slice it at home. As it did not contain preservatives, it never lasted for more than two days. Russians drank a lot of tea but without milk. By mixing tea with milk, they believe the taste of tea is lost. However, they did drink coffee with milk. Food was cheap, but the choice was limited, especially if you did not like ham and sausages. Soon, we discovered a new item to add to the breakfast menu and break the monotony – condensed milk. Spreading it thickly over toast made it delicious. There was no fridge in the room or the kitchen, hence we could not buy many perishable items. All of us were too lazy to walk up to the canteen in the morning for a full, hot breakfast.

Alex preferred a lie-in to breakfast. He slept until a quarter to nine, got up, brushed his teeth like lightning and ran to class. Having a lie-in was a luxury he'd missed while serving in the army and he was now making up for it.

Who does not like a lie-in on the weekend? Our senior teacher, Comrade Maxim, frequently deprived us of this luxury. He regularly arranged a coach each Saturday to take us on excursions to the countless places of cultural and historical interest in Moscow. The Red Square, Tretyakov Art Gallery, Pushkin Museum, the Kremlin and the Cosmos Museum were among them. If enough students did not turn up to fill the coach on time, Maxim would go knocking on each door and urging the students to come for the excursion. He knew who lived in which room and would continue to knock harder until he got a response, and would relentlessly coax them to join the excursion.

I remember him knocking on a Sikh student's room and begging him, "In the name of Guru Nanak (the founder of Sikhism), get up and come for the excursion. Otherwise, Guru Nanakji will not forgive you."

If there were still not enough bodies to fill the coach, Maxim even went to the extent of getting the keys to a room from the warden, opening the door, waking up the pretending sleepers and urging them to come for the excursion. The only escape route was to hide in the loo before he came, pretending to have an upset tummy and sitting there until the bus left, and then to go back to bed. The guys who avoided the excursions did not realise what they were missing.

One day, the excursion was to the Moscow Metro. I went reluctantly, as senior students had told us we would be travelling by metro almost every day for the next few years. We were taken to metro stations of historical importance and architectural beauty. The guide started the tour with the words, "Welcome to the beautiful underground palaces of Moscow." Stalin wanted metro stations to be built as palaces for the common man. There is an interesting story behind the development of the general plan of the metro, which is formed from a series of underground lines going across from one side of Moscow to the other in different directions.

The architects placed the master plan on the table in front of Stalin, who was having a cup of coffee at the time. He looked at it carefully and placed his cup at the centre of the plan while discussing it with the architects. When he picked up the cup, there was a circular brown stain on the centre of the plan. This stain put a new idea in the architects' heads. They added a circle line connecting all the other lines and named it the 'brown line.' It was a great idea as it made crossing between lines possible and travel to any corner of Moscow much quicker and easier. The construction of the metro began in 1931, and it became operational four years later. During the war, the metro served another purpose besides transport: over half a million people slept in the stations to escape air raids.

Each station was unique. Revolution Square Station was lined with ornate bronze statues. Mayakovskaya Station had beautiful mosaic pieces on the ceiling that symbolised the different shades of the Moscow sky. Kievskaya Station had beautiful paintings on all its walls. It was the deepest station at forty-eight metres below ground and even had a library during the war for people to use and to distract them from the sound of aerial bombings. The Moscow Metro is really beautiful and certainly worth visiting. It's no wonder when American President Nixon visited Moscow that his wife commented that the Moscow Metro was the most beautiful subway system in the world.

Excursions to the Tretyakov Gallery, which houses masterpieces of Russian art from the eleventh to the early twentieth centuries, and the Pushkin Museum of Fine Arts, with a large collection of European art, left permanent impressions on everyone's minds.

A visit to the VDNKHA (pronounced Vedenha in Russian), the permanent Exhibition Centre in Moscow, was interesting and educational. The centre was built in 1939. The idea of building the massive exhibition complex was proudly to show off the achievements of the Soviet Union. There was a pavilion for each industry. The space pavilion was the most popular one, as the USSR was one of the world leaders in space technology.

They put up Sputnik, which was the first artificial object to go into earth's orbit. Russian Cosmonaut Yuri Gagarin became the first human to go into space. His first words from space when he saw our planet were "The earth is blue. How wonderful. It is amazing". The Lunar Two probe was the first spacecraft in the world to reach the surface of the moon. Regular international exhibitions were held here, and they attracted millions of visitors from all over the world.

One weekend, all the boys from our year were taken by coach to the supermarket GUM (pronounced Goom) to prepare us for the notorious Russian winter. The girls had been there the week before for their winter shopping. The large supermarket, located next to Red Square, was spread across three floors. We went to the readymade garments section on the ground floor. There were racks of woollen suits in grey and black in all sizes for men. Each one of us had to pick a black and a grey suit. There were no other colour choices. We also got a brown fur cap (*ushanka*) that had flaps to protect the ears from the cold (*Ushi* in Russian means ears). We were also provided with two pairs of long-johns (to wear under trousers to protect our legs and privates when it got very cold), four pairs of thick woollen socks and a pair of fur-lined boots. The university paid for all this, but if anyone wanted more, they could buy it themselves later. Thus, we were all armed and ready to face our first Moscow winter.

One Saturday morning, as I got out of bed, I felt unusually cold. I peered through the window and saw a strange sight. It was all white outside. Thin white flakes floating down from the skies, like bits of cotton wool in their millions, had decreased the visibility. I woke Alex up and told him, "Look, Alex! What is happening outside?"

He got out of bed with eyes half-open, looked out through the window, rubbed his eyes with his hands and said, "It f***ing started snowing," and went back to bed. I looked out for a few minutes, feasting my eyes on my first ever snowfall.

Later, a few friends and I went for a walk in the snow. The overcoats and fur caps kept us warm. Everything had changed overnight. The trees were all white, the buildings covered in white and even the tarmacked road was white. Cars and buses capped with snow moved slowly over the roads. It was cold, as the temperature had dipped to below zero overnight. Most of the foreign students were wearing their overcoats and Eskimo caps, while the Russians walked around just in sweaters. Anyone who had never seen snow before was thoroughly enjoying it and having fun, pelting clumps of snow at each other.

As the temperatures became warmer during the day and colder at night, the mornings became trickier, with us struggling to walk on the black ice. Hardly anyone got away without a tumble or two. From experience, we learnt to do the penguin walk to avoid falling. Walking with short steps without lifting the feet high off the ground was the right way to move forward. The leg planted on the ground was then less likely to slip and send you flying. Getting out of bed in the mornings was becoming more difficult, although the heaters in the room were running at full blast. Nobody cared about the cost, as electricity was completely free. Lenin had said, "Communism is Soviet power plus the electrification of the whole country."

My bed was next to the window. One morning, I noticed that a bottle of milk kept next to my bed on the windowsill had frozen. I had to keep it over the heater for hours to thaw it before it could be poured into my cup. That evening, Alex bought some reels of insulating material from the general store in town called A Thousand Trifles. As the name indicates, it sold every little thing necessary for life. Alex showed us how to use butter knives to pack the material tightly into and around the window frame gaps to make it draughtproof. What a difference it made! The room became cosy once again. The windows were single-glazed, and one can imagine how much electricity was required to heat the room, but getting out of bed in the cold mornings was no longer a chore.

We found a way to use the cold weather to our advantage. There was a little window, forty-five by thirty centimetres, at the top left corner of the big window. It had a handle on both the inside and the outside. The purpose of this window was to let some fresh air into the room even in winter, and we opened it at least once a day for a few minutes. I could never figure out why the little window had a handle on the outside, but we put it to good use by hanging the small pyramid-shaped, squidgy white milk packets with blue and red stripes, butter and other perishables in the net shopping bag on it and closing the window. The bag would hang outside and remain frozen as long as the temperature outside remained below zero, which was for about six months of the year. It was easy to access stuff from nature's refrigerator whenever required by opening our little window. It saved us many trips to the shops in the biting cold.

Although I was used to the cold by now, I started getting a sore throat frequently. Some days, it was so bad that my voice became hoarse, and I was barely able to speak. Swallowing liquids became painful. I had to see the doctor at the polyclinic (the Russian equivalent of a GP practice). The university had its polyclinic in the main buildings on Ordzhonikidze Street. To get there from our hostels, we had to travel five miles by bus, cross the road and take a tram going in a perpendicular direction for three miles. Buses, trams and the metro were frequent, and travel was cheap. A universal pass for all the three modes of transport – an *eginnoe* (universal monthly pass) – cost only six roubles. With it, you could hop on and hop off any number of times on any mode of public transport and go anywhere in Moscow.

The doctor at the polyclinic was a gentle and kind middle-aged lady. She took a good look at my throat, diagnosed tonsillitis and prescribed tablets. She told me to take them daily and to go back to see her in five days if I was not getting better. I did what the doctor ordered religiously, and found that not only was I not getting any better, but I had also started getting splitting headaches every evening. I went back after five days and explained the situation. The doctor looked a little puzzled. She examined my throat once again and asked me when I was taking the tablets.

"Swallowing a tablet each day after breakfast and dinner," I replied.

She started laughing. "I don't think you understood," she said, and explained that the tablet was to be dissolved in water to rinse the throat and mouth and not to be swallowed. She walked to the washbasin in the corner of the room, filled her mouth with water, gargled loudly to make me understand clearly what to do, and spat it out. I felt foolish. She gave me more tablets, and this time they did wonders. I realised the need to further improve my understanding of Russian.

At the end of the term, we had our first exams in the Russian language. It was something everyone was dreading. There was no fixed syllabus, and we had no idea how the exams would be conducted and what we would be asked. We all asked each other, "How do you prepare for this kind of test?" Vladimir explained the Russian system of exams to put our minds at rest. He said that the exam was going to be just like a regular class, and mainly a viva. Each one of us would be given an article or a story to read for half an hour. Then, we would be asked questions based on it to find out how well we had comprehended the text. There was nothing to prepare and no need for us to worry.

It was interesting, as I had never heard of an exam that did not need any preparation whatsoever. I also found it difficult to understand the marking system, which Vladimir explained. It was a grading system from two to five. Grade 5 (*Pityorka*) meant excellent, Grade 4 (*Chitvyorka*) meant good, Grade 3 (*Troika*) meant pass, and Grade 2 (*Dvoika*) meant fail. A candidate who got a Dvoika had to resit the exam. It was very different from the marking system in India I was used to, where marks were given out of a hundred.

"When do we get the results?" I asked.

"Straight away," replied Vladimir.

The exams we were used to were written exams, and it would take a minimum of two weeks before we got the results.

We had our first Russian examination. Vladimir and a teacher from another group were our examiners. Each candidate was given a two-page article from a popular magazine to read in fifteen minutes. After having read it, the candidates would be called in one by one and examined. They asked probing questions to see how well we had understood the article. Then, we could also ask about what we did not understand in the text, and they would explain it to us. It was more of a friendly chat than an examination. 'How good was that?'

I had worked hard and felt confident on the day. Besides, Vladimir liked me for being punctual with my homework. When someone was struggling to find a word in Russian in the class, Vladimir would ask me to help out, and more often than not, I could.

The examination, which lasted half an hour, went well. The article was more complicated than the ones we were used to, but I answered most of the questions. At the end, Vladimir took up my progress card (*zachyotka*) and with a smile on his face carefully wrote the grade and handed it back to me. I was sure it was going to be a Grade 5, but to my surprise and disappointment it was a Grade 4.

Seeing the disappointment on my face, Vladimir said, "You can do better. You deserve a Grade 5, but you must work harder and earn it."

Although I felt unhappy then, looking back over the years I feel it was the best thing that ever happened to me. The unexpected grade humbled me. It planted my feet firmly on the ground, and I learnt not to take anything for granted. I realised that I had to work harder as the final statement Vladimir made was genuine and from the heart.

# Chapter 6

# WINTER HOLIDAYS

After the exams, we had our first winter holiday. A group of us decided to spend a week in a *dom otdiha* (rest house) in the suburbs of Moscow. It was a heavily subsidised, all-inclusive holiday. What we liked most about this place was that everything was optional. You could get up if you wanted, or stay in bed all day if you so wished. Breakfast, lunch and dinner were served at fixed times. Although cold, the weather was too good to stay indoors. The ground was covered in a thirty-centimetre carpet of white snow, but the sun was shining brightly. It made everything look brighter, and there was a feel-good factor in the air. We went out for walks, had snowball fights and made a snowman. It was a crude snowman with a carrot for his nose and trimmed cabbage leaves for his ears. Although not a picture-postcard snowman, we felt proud of our creation.

There was a television in the recreation room, a table tennis set and a library. By this time, our Russian was good enough to understand television programmes, although, to be honest, there wasn't much on. There were three channels, and the TV did not have a remote control. One good thing about Russian TV was that there were no advertisements at all. Whenever there was an important football match, ice hockey match (national or international) or any other sporting event with the USSR playing, it would be shown on TV. The cartoon programme *Noo pagagi* (Hey Wait!), the Russian version of Mickey Mouse, was popular. It was about a fox chasing a rabbit. The rabbit always outwitted the fox and escaped narrowly, making a fool of the fox.

The news programme at 9 p.m., called *Vremya* (*Time*), was different. It started with all the news about Comrade Brezhnev, then there was some news about politics, highlighting the achievements of the Soviet Union and other socialist countries of the Eastern Bloc. It would be followed by international news from countries of the so-called Third World, where the Soviet Union had interests. Next would be news about the Western world, led by the USA. All the negative aspects of the countries of the capitalist world – like unemployment, strikes, homelessness, poverty and crime rates – would be highlighted without fail. The listeners would be reminded of the ever-increasing military preparations of the NATO alliance. To sum it up, all news about the USSR and other socialist countries was good, and all the news about the Western world was bad. The programme ended with a weather forecast. The Russians humorously described the daily news programme as "All about him (Brezhnev) and little about the weather."

One day, we had a game of football in the snow. Everyone, other than the Russians, dressed up warmly. The goalposts were made with sticks, but the football was real. It was challenging, but fun to run on the fresh snow. If you fell, it hardly hurt and you were unlikely to break any bones falling on to the thick, soft mattress of snow. Although the weather was cold, we soon began to sweat, and after a while we had to shed a few layers of clothing to carry on.

After the game, a Russian friend showed us how to have a snow bath. He took off his shirt, ran out of the building, grabbed some fresh snow, rubbed it on his body for a minute and ran back into the building. The Russians believed cold conditioning was good for your body, as the blood vessels in the skin contracted in the cold to preserve body heat, and opened up again once you were back in the warmth of the rooms, or better still if you had a hot shower. I tried it and found the experience unpleasant, although the theory behind it sounded logical.

The local culture club invited us on a couple of evenings. Concerts were put on, showcasing the local dance forms and musical talent. Mingling with the local population at these functions helped improve our Russian. A carefree, relaxing week without books and homework recharged our batteries, and we returned to the university fully energised.

Six months of Russian classes had laid the foundation for the start of our studies in Russian of our chosen speciality subjects. We had lessons in basic biology, physics and chemistry in Russian. It was exciting but hard work. I loved the chemistry lessons, as the Russian approach to chemistry was a very systematic one. Balancing chemical equations for A-Levels had been by trial and error, and was mostly hit and miss, but I can remember learning a few critical equations by heart to get good grades. The periodic table (invented by the Russian scientist Mendeleev) formed the basis of balancing chemical equations and made a method out of the madness. You were allowed to keep Mendeleev's table with you during the exams. You only needed to know the principles, and Mendeleev's table made balancing equations child's play. It was like being allowed to take a calculator to the maths exams.

The USSR was a country of talented people, and hence they were one of the leaders of the world, be it in science, sport or space technology. Many of their inventors were not given the credit they deserved by the outside world. Alexander Popov, a Russian professor of physics, invented the radio in April 1885. However, the Italian Marconi, who published the results of his experiments in 1897, is credited with inventing the radio. To understand the depth of talent in Russia, one only needs to look at the list of inventions by Russian scientists. The videotape recorder, television, the solar cell, electrical transformers that run the power grids, the helicopter and petrol cracking (to make petrol out of crude oil) are only a few of the great Soviet inventions that changed our lives. Sadly, many of them were promoted abroad first.

We started learning science subjects in Russian, but the mainstay in the second part of year one remained the study of the language itself. This time around, the teachers changed. Vladimir went to another group, and we got Miss Victoria, a slim, tall and pretty young lady with long, blonde hair, in his place. She was a keen basketball player. Miss Victoria's style of teaching was different from Vladimir's. She was not as strict and demanding but all the same was an excellent teacher. She gave individual attention to each one of us who had a query and took enough time to explain problems and clear our doubts. Miss Victoria had a unique style of clarifying queries. She would stand behind you, to one side, lean over your shoulder, point out the mistakes you had made in your notebook and help you correct them. While doing this, her big, soft breasts would be resting over your shoulder. It was not surprising that this style of hers, along with the smell of her sweet perfume, created more doubts in the minds of the boys and set pulses racing.

I told my roommate Alex that my father once had a friend from Moscow, a volleyball coach, called Comrade Golomazov.

"Do you know where he lives?"

"No, although I remember Dad saying that his flat was on a street called Lermontov Street."

I asked Alex if there was any way of locating him. He looked at the street map of Moscow and started laughing. "Lermontov Street is a big, busy street, at least a mile long and with many buildings, shops, side streets and a countless number of flats. Searching for Comrade Golomazov would be like searching for a needle in a haystack. However, if you are keen to find him, we can give it a try this Saturday. If you don't try, you will not know, will you?"

I thought Alex was joking, but on Saturday his friend Victor joined us on the 'Golomazov hunt'. We started early. Alex had warned me to dress up warmly as it was snowing heavily and was going to be a long, cold day. Lermontov Street was an hour's journey by metro from our hostel. We started from one end of the street. Alex and Victor stopped everyone who vaguely resembled a resident of the street, introduced themselves and asked, "Would you by any chance happen to know a Comrade Golomazov living on this street?" The answers were always the same: "I have lived on this street for (X) years and never heard that name before."

We spent a couple of hours searching and it was beginning to feel cold. I was already thinking of giving up the wild goose chase when Victor spotted a sports complex on one of the side streets. "Let us try there," he said. A young lady stood at the reception, and an elderly woman was seated behind her on an armchair in the corner, reading Dostoyevsky's *Crime and Punishment*. Victor asked the young lady the same question he had probably asked a hundred times that day, "Excuse me! Would you by any chance happen to know a Comrade Golomazov living on Lermontov Street? He is a volleyball coach."

"Sorry!" she replied, "Never heard that name before."

On overhearing the conversation, the elderly woman took her eyes off the book, looked up at us and asked, "Does he have two sons?"

"Does he?" Victor deflected the question to me.

"Yes!" I remembered my father mentioning the Golomazov boys.

"He lives in flat 54 in the fourth building to the left."

In a few minutes, we were in Comrade Golomazov's flat, having a cup of hot tea with biscuits. Golomazov was a big-built Russian with a wicked sense of humour. He was delighted to see me and told me about the good times he had had with my dad. He thanked Alex and Victor for taking the trouble to help me find him. From then on, I was a regular visitor to his flat and even spent a couple of days at his *dacha* (summer house) in the Moscow suburbs.

I never imagined that learning a new and difficult language could be fun. Time passed quickly. Winter gave way to spring, and before we knew it, it was summer. The days got longer and brighter. At last, we could put away the heavy overcoats, woollen socks, fur shoes, woollen scarves, long-johns and *ushanka* caps. The whole world brightened up and reflected the beauty of summer. The snow melted away, and green leaves reappeared on the trees. Flowers bloomed. The girls shone in short skirts and sleeveless blouses with low-cut tops. It was a feast for the eyes for a young man far from home. Everyone was more cheerful and happy. The increase in hormonal levels from the rays of the sun must have been one of the contributing factors.

# *Chapter 7*

# RED SQUARE

The most important of the Saturday morning excursions was the one to Red Square, although we had been with friends for a stroll to Red Square before. People from all over the USSR and different parts of the world went there, to the resting place of the architect and founder of the Soviet State – Comrade Lenin. He was the first in the world to build a socialist state based on the teachings of Karl Marx and Friedrich Engels, which was eventually to transform into a communist state. Hearing more about Red Square from the guide during the excursion helped me gain a deeper understanding of its history.

Red Square separates the Kremlin (the former royal citadel and now the official residence of the President of Russia) from a historic merchant quarter known as *Kitay-gorod* (Chinatown). Red Square is considered the centre of Moscow since all of Moscow's major streets, which connect to main highways, originate here. The entire block paving in the square is red, and a lot of the surrounding structures, like the Kremlin wall, are also built of red brick. However, Red Square did not get its name from the colour and its name also has nothing to do with communism, which the colour 'red' symbolises. In the Russian language, the word *krasnyi* (red) once meant beautiful. That is how the square got its name – *Krasnaya Ploshad* (Beautiful Square). In modern Russian, *krasniy* means red. Either meaning is befitting.

In the centre of Red Square, joined to the Kremlin wall, is the Lenin Mausoleum – the shrine to the great leader. The embalmed body of Lenin is displayed here. In front of the mausoleum, two soldiers stood guard, holding rifles in their hands and barely batting an eyelid. The steel bayonets of their rifles sparkled in the sunlight. Every hour of the day and night, throughout the year, there was a change of guard. This meticulously rehearsed, sleek and swift event was worth watching. Two soldiers with rifles march in unison up from the side gate of the Kremlin, in a straight line. They stand next to the guards who had been standing as still as statues for the past hour. At the stroke of the hour, they swap places with lightning speed and precision. If you blinked, you'd miss it. The relieved guards march back into the Kremlin. Irrespective of the climate and season, this ritual still continues daily.

At the far end of the square stands the magnificent St Basil's Cathedral. It is widely regarded as one of the most beautiful cathedrals in the world. With its red brick towers and multi-coloured swirling onion domes, the cathedral is a symbol of the square itself. The building was designed in the shape of the flame rising from a bonfire into the sky and it was built over 400 years ago by the Russian Tsar, Ivan the Terrible. The lucky cathedral had escaped destruction twice. In 1812, Napoleon ordered its demolition but abandoned the plan when rain dampened the gunpowder. Stalin contemplated knocking it down to facilitate the movement of troops parading across Red Square but later changed his mind. In front of the cathedral stand the bronze statues of Kuzmin and Pozharsky, the two Russian heroes who fought off Polish invaders in 1612. Beyond the square, in the distance, quietly flows the Moscow River, a silent witness to the major historical changes that have taken place in this square over the years.

Usually, the queue to get into the Lenin Mausoleum was a mile long. One Saturday, Comrade Maxim arranged an excursion to the mausoleum. Surprisingly, even those who regularly suffered from the 'weekend diarrhoea' were fit that Saturday. He had purchased tickets in advance for the group so that we could bypass most of the queue. No bags were allowed in the mausoleum. It was a small room with shiny marble flooring. At the four corners of the room were soldiers holding rifles. In the centre of the room lay the body of Lenin in a glass case. His face looked fresh and content, as though he was just having a nap. There was no time to stop and study the body, as the queue had to keep moving around the glass case towards the exit. Photography was not allowed. How the Russians managed to preserve the body, looking so fresh and real years after the soul had departed, is beyond belief.

As we exited the mausoleum, my thoughts carried me far away to another mausoleum, the Taj Mahal in India. I could not help comparing the two. Artistically and architecturally they are no match. The Taj Mahal is one of the seven wonders of the world. Politically, Lenin's little mausoleum has a great significance as it honours the architect of the first nation in the world that aimed at ending oppression and exploitation of man by man and creating an equal and just society. One was inspired by love and the other by a just social system. Lenin's Mausoleum was certainly not as awe-inspiring as the monument of love, the Taj Mahal.

Near the entrance to the Kremlin is the Tomb of the Unknown Soldier. An eternal flame burns in front of it around the clock. It illuminates a bronze inscription that translates as "Your name is unknown. Your deed is immortal." Every foreign leader who visits Moscow comes to this site to lay flowers and spend a moment in silence. The significance of this flame is obvious to anyone who knows the history of the world.

From Red Square, we went on an excursion into the Kremlin. The little city within the Kremlin walls is steeped in history from the days of the tsars. The oldest and biggest cannon in the world, Tsar Cannon, which was built in 1586, and the massive Tsar Bell, which weighs over two hundred tonnes, were on display. We saw many cathedrals inside the Kremlin, but they were all non-functioning as religion was actively discouraged in the USSR. The massive Palace of Congresses was visible from a distance. It was the venue for the yearly Communist Party Congress (parliament) of the

Soviet Union. A Russian friend once asked me, "In which part of the world do people live the longest?" I was struggling for the answer when he replied, "In the Kremlin." The top brass of the Communist Party, the politburo members, lived there. At the time, the average age of the politburo, then headed by Comrade Brezhnev, was around seventy years.

After Stalin's death, his body was laid beside the body of Lenin in the mausoleum (from March 1953 until October 1961). During Nikita Khrushchev's reign, as part of de-Stalinisation, Stalin's body was removed and buried near the Kremlin wall, about three hundred metres from the mausoleum. Initially only a dark granite stone marked Stalin's grave, but in 1970 a small bust was added over it.

A Russian friend told me a joke about why Nikita Khrushchev decided to remove Stalin's body from the mausoleum.

While he was the General Secretary of the Communist Party, Khrushchev used to go into the mausoleum late every evening to report on party matters to Lenin's and Stalin's ghosts and seek their advice. One evening, after reporting, Khrushchev stood back, nervously scratching his head.

Stalin asked him, "What is the matter, Nikita? Spit it out."

Khrushchev said that he was beginning to feel old, his bones were aching and joints creaking. He had a feeling that his days were numbered. Stalin got the hint. Khrushchev was hoping to book his place next to the two leaders in the mausoleum. Stalin yelled at him, "Nikita, this is not a bloody hotel or travel lodge for any Tom, Dick or Nikita to stay."

The following day, Khrushchev removed Stalin's body from the mausoleum.

Stalin, as his name (made of steel) suggested, ruled with an iron hand. He loathed dissent and purged (organised mass killings) anyone opposing him, including many of his comrades from the Communist Party leadership during the years 1936 and 1937. Over a million people are believed to have lost their lives in these purges. One dissident writer mentioned that those suspected of opposing Stalin were taken away in vans that supplied meat around the capital; he sarcastically added that the meat supply of Moscow city increased exponentially in those years.

Stalin, however, is credited with leading the USSR against the attack by Hitler's Wehrmacht and crushing it. The Soviet soldiers' battle cry, when charging forward, was "For the motherland, for Stalin." Rumour has it that Hitler captured Stalin's son Yakov, who was a lieutenant in the Soviet Army. He offered to exchange Yakov for a German marshal captured by the Soviet Army. Stalin's reply to Hitler was short: "I do not trade marshals for lieutenants." At Stalin's funeral, on 9th March 1953, over a hundred people are believed to have died in the stampede when trying to catch a glimpse of the leader's body.

An interesting place we loved to hang out in Moscow was the Gorky Culture Park. It was a massive park with lots of trees and benches to rest. There were giant wheels and many exciting rollercoaster rides. You could go boating in the artificial lakes of the park. At the entrance to the park stood a giant statue of Lenin in his characteristic pose of the right arm extended and fingers pointing straight ahead. 'Onward to Communism' was the message the statue conveyed. Russian friends humorously interpreted it as 'This way to the toilet'.

Before we realised it was the year-end. Our knowledge of the language had improved, and the time had come to put it to test. We had our final Russian language exams. I worked harder as Vladimir's words, "You can do better. You deserve a Grade 5, and you must earn it," echoed in my ears. The week before our exams, our teacher, Miss Victoria, injured her knee after falling awkwardly during a game of basketball and could not come to the exams. It was sad, and our group was nervous. The teachers from two other groups who conducted our exams, however, were delighted with the performance of the group. All of us passed, with the majority making the higher grades of 4 or 5. I got my first Grade 5 and was over the moon.

# *Chapter 8*

# SUMMER HOLIDAYS IN THE SUN

After our exams, we had a month-long summer holiday. The university regularly organised a two-week sun-and-sea holiday in a Black Sea resort in Makopse, near Sochi. This was followed by a two-week sun-and-fruit-picking holiday in the Soviet Republic of Moldavia (now the independent country of Moldova).

We were all glad to leave our books behind and go for a well-earned rest. Sunshine and sandy beaches welcomed us at Makopse, where the university had an exclusive resort on the beach. We met students from other universities across the USSR as well as locals and made many new friends. Needless to say, the interaction with the opposite sex was the best practice to improve our language skills, and when it was time to leave two weeks later for Moldova a few hearts were broken.

There were lots of sporting activities in the resort. Tournaments were organised between different specialities in five-a-side football, table tennis, badminton and volleyball. Every other evening local artists would put on shows in the 'little theatre' of the resort. Students from different countries also had to organise an evening of entertainment to showcase their culture and talent. The wide variety of dance forms and music from different continents made these evenings exciting and entertaining.

For those interested, excursions were organised to the nearby town of Sochi. Kamal, a Sikh friend, and I decided to go on one of these excursions. Kamal's turban was the centre of attraction as the rest of the group were all locals, and none of them had met a man in a turban before. They had seen Sikhs in Indian movies and were curious to meet a Russian-speaking, turbaned Sikh in the flesh. We had to answer a million questions about India and our culture, and everyone wanted to be photographed with us. We decided to have a group photo. There was a professional photographer, Voloja, taking pictures of large groups in the middle of the square. He made the group stand in three rows. To fit everyone in, Voloja kept directing from behind his camera. He repeatedly compressed the air in front of him with his hands, from both sides towards the middle, indicating for people to stand closer. The 'up and down' motion of his right hand was for chins to go up or down. Finally, when satisfied, he showed a thumbs up and took a couple of shots. After that, with a broad smile, he promised it would be a great photo. Anyone who wanted a copy had to pay a small fee and give him their address. Voloja said he would post the photograph within a week. Digital cameras had not been invented then.

The last stop on our excursion was the famous botanical garden in Sochi. We had a couple of hours to go round the vast garden that had specimens from all corners of the world. It was fascinating to see a coconut tree and a mango tree growing there. After walking around in the bright sun for some time, Kamal, who was feeling hot under the many layers of his turban, told me, "I am feeling tired. Let's have a rest." There were no benches to sit on. We found an open, lush green lawn under the palm tree. A gentle breeze was blowing. The pleasant fragrance from jasmine plants nearby filled the air. We decided to sit down on the grass to rest our tired legs, and later to stretch our backs and have a little lie down in the shade.

We dozed off and were woken up by a policeman with his baton. Both of us jumped up from sleep, not knowing what was happening.

The policeman asked, "What are you guys doing?"

"Having a nap," I replied.

"Do you know where you are napping?"

"On the grass."

"This grass?" he asked and pointed to a signboard at the far corner of the lawn. It was some rare species of fragrant grass from South America that was challenging to grow in Europe. The local gardeners, with great effort and care, had managed to grow it there. It is on this grass that we were having a nice nap.

"It is an offence even to step on this grass, and you guys are sleeping on it. You deserve to be punished," he said with a smile. I could see a fine coming as he carried on, "I take it that you are from India. Do you know Raj Kapoor?"

"Yes, very well," replied Kamal, as though Raj Kapoor (one of the most famous Hindi film actors) was his best friend.

The policeman, who was a fan of Indian movies, was satisfied and said, "I will let you off this time. Never repeat it."

"Sorry, Officer; it will never happen again." We thanked him, shook hands and went back to our coach.

We were already twenty minutes late, and the coach was waiting for us. On the way back, we described our friendly encounter with the nice policeman, and everyone on the bus found our misadventure and lucky escape hilarious.

Some students who preferred the sun and sea and those who wanted to spend more time with the new friends they had made stayed back in Makopse for another two weeks. I opted for the active holiday and rest package in the Soviet Republic of Moldavia.

Moldavia was the vineyard of the Soviet Union. The resort was next to a river in a picturesque setting. Sasha, the five-foot-tall, muscular physical education instructor and sports teacher from the university, was in charge of our group. After breakfast, Sasha called a meeting and gave us a short lecture about how to conduct ourselves in Moldavia. He warned us not to wander out of the resort on our own as it was surrounded by acres of vineyards and one could easily get lost. The Moldavians were helpful, friendly people and liked good wine. They took pride in their hospitality and loved to entertain. So we had to be careful! The good news, he told us, was that the canteen would be serving us a glass of local wine with dinner every day.

There was plenty of entertainment in this resort too. We played five-a-side football, badminton and table tennis, and the geeks played chess. There was a little cinema theatre on site, with daily shows. Rare vintage classics like *Battleship Potemkin* by the world-famous Russian director Eisenstein, recent Soviet movies and classic foreign-language films from renowned directors like Kurosawa and Satyajit Ray were shown. Just as in Makopse, local artists would come along and perform at the resort on some evenings. However, there was one big difference from our holiday in Makopse: every day, except Sundays, after breakfast a coach would take us to the fields for fruit-picking. It was tomato season, and we went to the tomato fields. Acres and acres of tomato plants showing off their ripe red fruit in the bright yellow sun was a feast for the eyes.

We were divided into three groups, and each group had a captain. We had to pick tomatoes and gather them in the group's corner into a giant container. In the end, they would weigh the containers to see which group had collected the most.

It was fun, to begin with, and everyone tried their best, swiftly picking tomatoes and sprinting to our corner to deposit them. The good news was that we could eat as many tomatoes as we wished. Tomatoes came in so many different varieties, sizes, shapes and flavours. A special type of small, elongated cherry tomato was particularly sweet. Everyone ate a few until the word pesticide was mentioned. After that, our appetite for tomatoes vanished. The fun of pelting each other with ripe tomatoes now and then, however, continued. Three hours of picking tomatoes were enough to tire us out. The group that collected the most tomatoes was rewarded with a bottle of the best Moldavian wine.

On our third evening in Moldavia, I witnessed a strange incident. We were playing badminton on the floodlit court when I saw the workmen carrying somebody on a stretcher from the gates towards the reception hall. We were curious to see who had been taken ill. As they passed the court, I recognised the face. It was Sasha, our group leader. "Is he okay?" I asked one of the guys carrying him. "No, he is not okay. He is pissed! He will be okay by morning." The next morning Sasha looked sheepish at the breakfast table and apologised profusely, saying how sorry he was for his behaviour the last evening.

Mechanisation and advances in agriculture made planting easy and the increase in the yield of fruits and vegetables was manifold. However, a machine that could pick ripe fruits and vegetables was yet to be invented. It was a pity to see large quantities of tomatoes rotting due to lack of a workforce to hand-pick them.

After the first few days, the thrill of tomato picking began to wane. On the way to the tomato fields one day, I asked Sasha, "Why don't we go apple picking instead, as we are all fed up with tomatoes?" He said he would look into it. The next morning, on the bus, Sasha told us we were going "red apple picking". Everyone was excited. After a ten-minute drive, we arrived at a different part of the same tomato farm to pick more tomatoes. We were unhappy. Tomatoes were coming out of our ears. Tomatoes with breakfast, lunch and dinner along with tomato picking were far too many tomatoes. The following morning, soon after breakfast, before the bus left for the fields, I slipped out quietly through the back entrance to the riverbank with a novel and towel in hand. I lay in the shade and read the novel. At lunchtime, before the bus returned, I went back in. A friend asked me, "Where were you? You missed all the fun. We went apple picking today." He offered me some apples he had brought back with him. This time, they were real apples. They were delicious – crisp, fresh and sweet. I cursed myself for picking the wrong day to skip and miss the fun of apple picking.

On day three of our stay in Moldavia, we were taken to a concert in the capital of Moldavia, Kishinev. It was a packed programme of songs and folk dance and a magic show by local artists. When we arrived there, Sasha asked a girl from our group and myself to go with him to meet somebody backstage. A pretty young lady met us there. She asked us to compere the show, and gave us a printed programme with a brief introduction of each item in Russian. A middle-aged, smartly dressed man in a black suit and bow tie introduced himself as the magician. The young lady was his assistant. He made me sit and asked me to take my tie, coat and shirt off. Then he made me put the shirt back on without my arms going into the sleeves and fasten the collar and the top two buttons on the shirt. The empty sleeves of the shirt dangled outside, over my arms. At the end of the long sleeves of the shirt, there is a slit in the cuff with a button. He buttoned the cuff at the wrist. It looked odd. After this, he made me put my tie back on and wear the coat over the shirt as normal. I looked in the mirror, and everything looked the same as before. The magician asked me to go back and start compering. He told me he would let me know when he needed me for his magic.

The programme of dance, song and humour was entertaining. The magic show was the last item. The magician came out with his assistant and showed a lot of tricks. Then he announced that he needed two people for his next item. Since my fellow compere and I were the closest (standing at the side of the stage), he invited us back on the stage and asked me to sit on the chair in the middle of the stage. He apologised to my fellow compere "Sorry Miss. I cannot do this magic on you as I might end up behind bars" and asked her to watch carefully. He stood to one side so that everyone could see us and said, "You all know this young man. I do not. I am meeting him today for the first time." He loosened the knot of my tie and took it off. Next, he unbuttoned my collar and undid the top two buttons of my shirt and then he went on, "Now, observe carefully." He unbuttoned my cuffs at the wrists. There was pin-drop silence. He took hold of my shirt collar and asked me to count to three. At the count of three, he pulled my shirt by the collar upwards, off my body with my coat still on me. Everyone was surprised. Before the end of the programme, the magician met me once again backstage. He said, "Well done," and informed me that he would be coming to our camp in ten days (on the last day of our holiday in Moldavia). He asked me to be ready with my shirt worn as he had shown me today for a repeat of the 'magic', but to keep it a secret.

The magician came to our camp with a group of artists on the last evening. The programme was different this time. The folk dances were more energy-packed. A local singer with a powerful voice belted out popular Russian and Moldovan songs. The magic show was the penultimate item. The magician performed some new tricks and repeated a couple of the ones he had shown at Kishinev. Towards the end, he announced he needed two people for the next item. One of the guys sitting in the front row, who forever wanted to be the centre of attention, volunteered straight away.

I wondered how the magician would demonstrate the shirt trick on him. He asked the guy to come over to the stage. Then he searched the front rows and spotted me. The magician pointed towards me and said, "Could the young man from the second row wearing the red tie also come over to the stage please?" He made me sit on the chair and asked the other guy to stand close and carefully observe what he was going to do. Under the public gaze he loosened and took off my tie, then unbuttoned my collar and the top two buttons of my shirt. He asked the other guy to watch carefully and to count loudly to three. At the third count, he lifted my shirt off by the collar, with my coat still on. The crowd watched in amazement. *How did he do that!* everyone wondered. No one remembered it was my shirt that the magician had pulled off last time around in Kishinev as well.

Time flies when you are having fun. Holidays soon came to an end, and we were back in Moscow before we knew it. Our first holiday at the

Black Sea resort had been most enjoyable. Memories ought to be saved so that they do not fade and vanish with time. I waited for the group photograph that was taken in Sochi by Voloja the photographer to put into my holiday album, but it never arrived. A couple of weeks later I wrote to him, saying that neither my Sikh friend nor I had received the group photo. He replied, "Comrade, could you send me a copy of your photographs so that I can identify you amidst the hundreds of photographs that I took in Sochi that day?" I did that, and a few days later, his reply came, "Sorry, comrade, I cannot spot your turbaned friend or yourself in my collection of photographs from that day." The cheeky bastard!

## *Chapter 9*

# CHILDHOOD MEMORIES

Our Russian was good enough by now to start studying our chosen specialities in it. In two days, we would be starting our busy medical course. Being away from my parents and brothers for a year made me feel homesick and my thoughts slowly drifted back to when it had all begun.

In 1960, my father finished his term in parliament, and our family returned to Kerala from Delhi. I was too young to remember life in Delhi in detail, but there was one particular incident when I was five years old that did stick in my memory. Dad travelled around the country a lot on official duties. On a day when Dad was away, my brother and I were playing cricket in front of our house. Suddenly, we heard beating drums and a group of twenty people, including a few children, opened the gate and walked into our property. In the centre of the group was a large bear with its mouth tied, feet in chains and the upper limbs free. As soon as they were at our front door, a member of the troupe started singing a Hindi folk song loudly. The big bear stood up on its chained hind legs and started dancing to the tune. It was fascinating and I was gobsmacked. I had seen bears in cartoons but never a real one, and I watched with amazement. Hearing the music and the noise, my mother, who was busy in the kitchen, came out, gave the leader of the group some loose change and told him that it was enough and to leave.

The group left, and my curiosity made me follow them. A few minutes later, my brother, who noticed my absence, ran into the house and informed Mum. She immediately darted out in the direction from which the drums could be heard. Luckily, the bear troupe had only moved a short distance and was performing two houses away. In the front row, with a few other fascinated kids, was her son, watching the bear dance, with eyes and mouth wide open. She dragged me home, and as soon as we entered the house gave me what I truly deserved, the most painful pinch on my left shoulder. My poor brother also got the same for not watching over me. That was the end of our cricket playing for the whole week. In the evening, Mum would read us bedtime stories. That evening she told us tales of wicked people who kidnap kids, gouge out their eyes, disfigure them and use them to earn money by forcing them to beg in faraway places. I found it difficult to sleep that night from nightmares of what could have happened had my mother not reached me in time.

## Village Life

Thinking of the happy days of my childhood in our little village, Sasthamkottah, brought back pleasant memories. The word Sasthamkottah means the 'fortress of God'. My father chose the most picturesque spot upon which to build our house. It was on the slopes of a hill, close to the freshwater lake. Across the lake, on the opposite side, was a barren hill. The nearest electric line to our house was five hundred metres away, and the road with public transport was a mile further away. Dad had to obtain special permission to pull the electricity line down to our house. There were no other houses in the vicinity. The whole place was very peaceful and tranquil.

The ravine near our hill was covered by trees and wild bushes. We discovered a natural spring in an opening, in between some tall bushes. Further down, it became a little waterfall. Dad used to take us to the waterfall every morning for a bath. The water was icy cold, and bathing under the waterfall was incredibly refreshing. On the way back home we picked red and white wild berries that grew in abundance on the bushes along the path.

Dad had planted rubber trees on the slopes of the hill down to the house. Rubber trees were considered as a pension, as they would fetch a steady income once they matured and their sap could be sold for making rubber. These trees needed very little looking after, and most importantly, did not require tilling of the soil. Tilling was harmful as it disrupted soil structure, accelerating the runoff of the loosened top soil layer into the lake.

A few years after we started living in the village, the authorities decided to build a college on the barren hill. The setting for any institution could not have been more idyllic. The hill was a peninsula surrounded by the clear, still waters of the lake. A famous temple was located at the entrance to the peninsula and thousands of devotees visited it every year. Other than the college building on the top of the hill, there were only a few small huts with roofs made of thatched coconut leaves scattered on the slopes of the hill, close to the waters of the lake.

On the far side of the hill, across the lake, was a small town. A ferry service operated from there to the foot of the college hill. The lake supplied drinking water to the town of Quilon some twenty miles away. Motorboats were banned in the lake to avoid polluting the waters. Whoever coined the phrase 'God's own country' to describe the state of Kerala must have seen our pretty little village.

The lake was unique. Its crystal-clear waters came solely from springs below it. A large building, the filter house, stood on another part of the shore of the lake, over a mile away. It purified and pumped over thirty-seven million litres of water from the lake daily to Quilon town.

Half a mile before the temple, by the side of the road, was a large marketplace. A few small shops selling basic everyday necessities lined one side of it. The open market, the size of two football fields, was desolate except on Wednesdays and Saturdays, which were the market days. On these days, the village came to life, bustling with activity. Farmers from the surrounding areas brought their produce to the market and set up temporary stalls. The cargo arrived by every mode of transport imaginable – bicycles, bullock carts, buses, vans and even on human heads. The buses, on market days, carried more goods atop them than passengers inside. The roof racks of the buses gave the impression that they were ready to burst at the seams, but it never happened.

The ferry boats were packed to the brim on market days with people and local produce. The cargo included seasonal fruits, vegetables and even chickens and goats. Two strong ferrymen, one at the front and one at the back, used ten-metre-long barge poles to reach the bottom of the lake and slowly push the boat forward. There were no health and safety rules as such. The experienced ferrymen decided when to declare the boat 'full' and set off. More cargo meant more money, and so they ensured that the boat was tightly packed.

It was a pleasure to watch the longboats move across the lake to the little town on the far side at sunset. They glided slowly and gracefully, becoming smaller and smaller as they approached the setting sun. The lake was so vast that the boats were just tiny dots as they reached the far end.

From time immemorial, monkeys were a part of our village. There were two groups of monkeys. The first was the marketplace monkeys. They thrived on morsels from the traders and petty theft. If the shopkeepers were not vigilant, a monkey would climb down the roof and with lightning speed snap off a bunch of ripe bananas displayed in front of the shop. Within seconds, it would be back on the rooftop, grinning at the irate shopkeeper like a naughty child. It was a joy to watch the mother monkey tending to and playing with her little ones, just like humans. We did not need Darwin to tell us who our ancestors were.

The second group was the temple monkeys. They were so called as they lived in and around the temple. After all, it was their birthright. According to Hindu mythology, the god Hanuman took the form of a monkey in the epic, *The Ramayana*. Inside the temple, monkeys commanded particular respect. After every offering made to the gods, they would get their share of food and therefore did not have to steal for a living. When the devotees walked into the temple, the descendants of God would lazily sit around, observing them. The woods surrounding the temple were their home. If a marketplace monkey strayed into the temple monkeys' territory, it would be attacked and chased back by the male temple monkeys, and vice versa.

A narrow road ran through the heart of the village, connecting it to the rest of the world. A limited number of buses went from there to the neighbouring towns. The air in the village was clean. There were no factories pouring out poisonous gases to pollute it. The village was a great place to live, but the only drawback was that there were no English medium schools in the area. The nearest reputable school was a boarding school in Quilon town. That is why my elder brother and I ended up there. My younger brother also joined the boarding school, but as he was too young and felt very homesick, he was taken out and enrolled in the local school in our village.

## *Chapter 10*

# BOARDING SCHOOL

Staying away from my parents and my little brother in the boarding school was a big shock in the beginning. At the school, we had to sleep in dormitories, and my brother and I had never seen a dormitory before. There were two large halls. Each had fifty beds, arranged in two straight rows of twenty-five each.

Having to wake up early every morning was torture, and it took a long time to get used to. Sharp at 5.30 a.m the Principal Father Elias, would come up to the dormitory and ring the bell. Most of the students would get up straight away, albeit grudgingly and cursing. Ten minutes later, the warden would be back with a jug of water for round two. He sprinkled it over the few who had chosen to ignore the bell and remained under the sheets. If round two of the wake-up call was ineffective, round three ensured everyone was up. This time, the sadistic warden came in stealthily with a cane in hand. Even the last man lying would shoot out of bed as the warden's cane made firm contact with his butt. The guy whose bed was closest to the door was at a disadvantage as he would get the cane first. On hearing the distinct sound of the cane, a couple of others in beds further down would fly out. Once out of bed, you were in the safe zone. However, I must give credit to the warden for his fairness and for introducing an element of surprise. The following day, he would quietly creep up to the far end of the dormitory and start the caning from there. Soon, the cane became redundant as getting up early became the common habit.

Breakfast was served in a large hall. Every boarder had a designated place. The tables were set out in three straight rows, and there was a reason behind that. The first row was for the common boarders, the next row was for the first-class boarders, and the third row was for the premium or so-called parlour boarders. The difference in the type of food served to each row was little, but the cost difference was out of proportion. If the common boarder was given a glass of water with the meal, the first-class boarder would get a glass of milk instead and the parlour boarder would be given a glass of milk with *Horlicks*. My brother and I started in the middle row. Later on, as my mother was convinced that her boys were wasting away, we were upgraded to parlour boarders.

Every child hated school as we had to wake up to the bell ringing in our ears. We had to get up, get ready and sit in the classrooms until 4 p.m. Then, it was tea, games for a couple of hours and back to homework for the following day. The bell, for some reason, sounded melodious on the weekends. We spent all of Saturday playing football or grass hockey. On Sundays, going to mass in the church was compulsory. After mass, we finished breakfast quickly and played until lunch. Then we carried on playing until teatime. After tea, we were at our desks for a couple of hours, doing homework for the coming week. This was our routine.

Other than normal subjects like English, science and mathematics, we had a special subject called moral science. I cannot remember anything from moral science lessons, except a question and answer session on day one. The teacher gave us a textbook each. It was a thin, colourful and beautifully-illustrated book of tales with moral messages. She asked us to read the first chapter carefully and said that she would ask us questions to see what we understood.

The opening chapter was titled 'God, the universal creator'.

The first question was to one of the naughty boys in the class: "Who made you?" He replied immediately without any hesitation, "Mummy and Daddy made me."

The teacher struggled to control her laughter, along with the rest of the class. She explained that it was God through Mummy and Daddy who creates us all.

The mathematics teacher was a short, plump young lady with a great sense of humour. She reminded us of a giant pumpkin, especially when she wore a deep-yellow-coloured saree. Her sense of humour made her popular. She made numbers enjoyable by making up sums relating to everyday life.

One day, she made up a sum in her head and began, "Suppose there are three pumpkins in one room (there were three plump boys in the class) and a truckload of fresh pumpkins are brought in a truck…"

No sooner had she finished the sentence than one of the fat boys in the class, who did not lack in humour, put up his hand.

"Yes, Tom. What is your question?"

"Sorry, Miss. There are four pumpkins in the room," he said with a smile. "You forgot to count yourself."

The teacher was slightly embarrassed but smiled, corrected herself and carried on, "Okay. Suppose there are four pumpkins in one room," and the entire class laughed.

My brother, who was twelve (two years older than me), felt homesick. He tried to persuade me to join him in running away from school to our home, twenty miles away. Initially, I disagreed as I could not understand how we could get home when we had never been out of the school gates on our own. He was unhappy when I did not agree, so he changed tactics and put psychological pressure on me to change my mind. On the way from our house to Quilon there was a long wooden bridge called Longshore Bridge. The bridge had been built over a big lake, close to the estuary, by the British years ago. From the bridge, one could see the sea on one side, two hundred metres away. My brother told me that if I did not go with him, he would go alone and jump off the bridge into the sea. As I loved my brother, I was left with no choice but to agree.

Whenever Dad came to school to take us home for the holidays, he would first take us to a hotel in town called Hotel Everest for a treat. It was located three miles away from school. The hotel owner (Everest Uncle) was a good friend of Dad's. We would be treated to the tastiest snacks while my father had a drink or two and caught up on matters with his friend. Right next to the entrance to the hotel was a corner shop. The owner of the corner shop (Corner Shop Uncle) was also Dad's friend. If the shop was not too busy, he would also join their company. He would give us a small bar of Cadbury chocolate each. It was a big treat in those days as Cadbury chocolate a foreign brand was expensive.

My brother's cunning plan was for us to walk to Hotel Everest and convince Everest Uncle there was an emergency at home and to take us home. At four in the afternoon, the main gate in front of the football field was usually left open for the delivery van to come into school. All the students were busy playing games in the main field as well as in all the other open spaces in the school campus. One day my brother and I quietly snuck out through the main gate, unnoticed. The road in front of the school was straight and about two hundred metres long before it turned left towards the town. We started walking up the road when at the far end we saw the figure of a priest coming in the opposite direction, towards the school. We swiftly did a U-turn and got back into the school through the small side gate. This little gate led to the courtyard in front of the church campus next to the school building.

Various games were played in the courtyard at different times. A badminton match was in progress at that time with many students watching. We joined the spectators, pretending to be interested in the game. After a few minutes, the headmaster, Father Gomes, entered through the small gate and walked past us into the church. Through the corners of our eyes we looked to see if he had noticed us. Fortunately, he had not. His long-distance vision was poor, and so we avoided being caught red-handed just as our attempt at running away had begun.

Ten minutes later, we went round to the main gate once again and quietly walked out. We walked fast up to the end of the road and then turned left towards town. Having travelled that route many times with Dad by car, we had an idea of which direction to take. We walked swiftly, and at one point, when not sure which way to turn, we asked a respectable-looking gentleman if we were on the right road to Hotel Everest. He said yes but became suspicious at seeing two kids alone and asking for directions to a hotel. He asked us why we were going to the Hotel Everest.

My brother confidently replied, "We are going to meet our dad, who will be coming there in twenty minutes."

The reply convinced him, and he did not ask any further questions. After this we decided not to ask for directions any more to avoid suspicion, and carried on walking. The three miles seemed like three hundred, but we finally reached Hotel Everest.

Everest Uncle was surprised to see us alone and welcomed us in. My brother confidently told him that we had got a telegram from home that father was ill and wanted to see us. There was no one else at home he could send to collect us. He asked us to go to the hotel and ask Everest Uncle to take us home. As he was a good friend of Dad's, Everest Uncle was convinced and agreed to take us home. As usual, he got us tea and snacks and said that as soon as we'd finished, he would get a taxi and take us home. The snacks seemed tasteless that day. We finished them quickly in our eagerness to get out.

As soon as the taxi arrived, Corner Shop Uncle walked into the hotel. He recognised us and asked Everest Uncle why the cab was there and where we were all off to. Everest Uncle explained the situation to him, but the devil was a shrewder man. He said he had finished for the day and would also come along for company. Everest Uncle sat in the front seat and

Corner Shop Uncle in the backseat. I was in the middle, with my brother to my right.

As the car started to move, Corner Shop Uncle told Everest Uncle, "Why don't we drop in at the school on our way and let the warden know we are taking the boys home so that they don't panic."

Everest Uncle replied that it was a good idea and asked the driver to go to the school first before driving us home.

As soon as my brother heard this, he had a panic attack and said, "No. No. I do not want to go to school. Take us straight home. I don't want to go back to school!"

The cat was out of the bag. My brother then tried opening the door to jump out from the moving car, but the child lock was on. We genuinely felt like we were lambs to the slaughter.

On reaching the school gate, we saw the commotion outside. The headmaster, Father Gomes, was standing outside, looking tense and worried. The school had sent search parties in all directions to look for us. They had noticed we were missing at dinner because of the two empty plates and had started the search immediately. Father Gomes thanked Everest Uncle for letting the school know and joined in escorting us home.

My mother was worried to see all of us arrive at 11 p.m. Dad was away on tour and due back in two days. Father Gomes explained what had happened and made it clear he was outraged. My mother stayed cool and listened patiently. Father Gomes told my mother, "The elder boy is the culprit and organiser of the runaway; the younger boy, who is innocent, was dragged into it." My mother told Father Gomes that Dad would come and see him at the school as soon as he was back.

After Father Gomes and the uncles left, we were expecting a thrashing. However, my mother gave my brother her trademark painful pinch on his shoulder, asked why he had done this and told us to wait until Dad was back. I escaped as the innocent younger sibling who simply followed his naughty brother.

My dad did not see the runaway incident as a big issue. He asked us not to worry but never to repeat it. The next day, he took us to school to meet with the headmaster. Father Gomes was adamant he would not take my brother back into the hostel, as he was a troublemaker and would be a bad influence on others. He agreed to take me back to the hostel and allowed my brother to continue in school as a day scholar. My brother was put up in one of Dad's friends' houses in town. His children were also studying in our school, and so my brother had good company.

## Mr Allen's Boarding

The following year, I too quit as a school boarder. My brother and I went into a private boarding school called Mr Allen's Boarding. There were forty boarders there, and it was considered a good school, judging by the exam results. Mr Allen was a tough taskmaster. Every evening, we had to study from six to eight thirty. On Saturdays, we played until teatime and then had to study for a couple of hours. Those who went to church for the first mass on Sunday morning, starting at six o'clock, could have breakfast at half-past seven and start playing by eight. They could play until lunch. Following lunch, we were back on the field, playing until tea at five o'clock. Afterwards, we had to get back to our books and do our homework. During exam season, we were not allowed into the playground and had to study throughout the day. Mr Allen would do periodic secret checks to make sure we were all studying and not fooling around.

Mrs Allen used to be a teacher in our school, but after arthritis crippled her, she stopped working. However, she would take private tuition in the English language for any of the boarders if their parents requested and paid for it.

Life at Allen's Boarding was fun. The number of boarders was just right, and the atmosphere in the boarding house friendly. The playground in front of the boarding house was a coconut plantation. The trees were planted wide apart, and through the middle of the plot ran the road into the bishop's mansion next door. This road was ideal for a cricket pitch. When we played football or hockey, two big stones marked the goal. There was very little traffic into the bishop's house, but the drivers of the occasional van and car that did go in our come out would honk to warn us to stop play. The game would resume once the vehicle had passed.

We started off playing cricket with a tennis ball and a small piece of wood, about the length of a real cricket bat. Sticks from trees on the campus became stumps. One day, a cricket-mad senior student had a brilliant idea: "Why don't we all pool our pocket money and buy a real cricket set?" It worked, and we soon had the proper kit. The feel of playing cricket with the real bat, ball and wickets was different and made us feel like professional cricket players. We did not mind a few bruises inflicted by the real stony-hard cricket ball.

Mr Allen was particular that every one of his boarders did well in their studies. He had his way of ensuring this. At the year-end, we had exams. They were followed by a month off for the Christmas holidays. Mr Allen insisted that all the rooms were cleared of everything, including mattresses, to deep-clean the rooms. Parents would start arriving one by one in cars and vans to collect their sons. Suitcases with belongings and books would fill the boot of each vehicle, and the rolled-up thin cotton mattress was usually placed on the roof carrier and secured firmly with ropes. The general mood on that day was very low, although we parted only for a month. The boarding school felt lonely and empty, even for a few hours, if your parents were the last to come to collect you.

## *Chapter 11*

# SCHOOL HOLIDAYS AT HOME

A month of holidays initially seems a long time away from school. At home, in our village, where the air was clean, water clear and with our little brother for company, time passed quickly. Mum fed us with the tastiest food to compensate for what she was certain was the appalling food provided in the boarding school. We enjoyed the luxury of a lie-in every morning until Mum woke us up with coffee in bed. The short lie-in after the coffee was sheer bliss. Dad was a morning person. He believed that one should jump out of bed in the morning, as it is the most productive time of the day. My brother would drink his coffee with eyes half-closed, rub his eyes lazily and go back to sleep until it was breakfast time. After breakfast, it was time to jump into the inviting blue waters of the lake. We swam, splashed each other with water and learnt to dive into the water from a small wall beside the lake, which served as a platform. Our playtime lasted until Mum shouted at us to get out of the water and go back into the house for lunch.

One morning, I started experiencing intense, throbbing pain in my left ear. Dad took me to Quilon to see an ear, nose and throat (ENT) specialist. I was diagnosed with a middle-ear infection. The specialist gave me drops for the ear, and we had to go to the hospital in town daily for a week for me to have penicillin injections. They were painful, and I dreaded every trip into town. After I was cured and let loose into the water again, we had strict instructions to stay in the water for only a couple of hours at a time, and Mum would make sure we were out after that.

Rainy days were fun too, in a different way. The grey and cloudy sky reflected on the waters of the lake, making it appear miserable and even slightly frightening. Tropical rains are heavy, and can beat any modern shower. It did not just rain, it poured and, at times, it went on for hours. We learnt to make good use of it. Running madly outside in the rain, thoroughly drenched, and singing and dancing was good fun. By the time we were tired, fresh, delicious snacks made by Mum would be waiting for us. After enjoying them to our heart's content, we played indoor games like Carrom Board, Snakes and Ladders or Monopoly.

Father had foresight. While our house was being built, he had been to the best plant nursery and purchased seedlings of the finest varieties of mangoes and planted them around the house. We had delicious mangoes of different types in abundance. Most of the trees were of the grafted dwarf variety and not very tall. We could climb up and pluck the fruits ourselves. Green mangoes, eaten raw with a pinch of salt, are mouth-watering. Ripe mangoes plucked straight from the tree and devoured sitting on the branches were a treat. A small, sweet juicy variety of mango was meant to be squeezed and massaged till it became soft and squidgy, and its sweet nectar sucked straight from it.

Jackfruit was my favourite fruit. The fruits are big and weigh a couple of kilos each. When ripe, their sweet fragrance could be smelt from a distance. Jackfruit jam is second to none in taste. Dad had also planted exotic fruits like sapota, mangosteen and custard apple. One season, he planted watermelons. They spread wildly and yielded the sweetest watermelons in abundance.

As our house was far from the main road and isolated, we always kept two big guard dogs in a kennel next to our home. At night they would be let loose, and in the morning sent back into the kennel.

About two hundred metres from the house, on one side of the rubber plantation, by the hedge, grew a wild cherry tree. One day I discovered it was full of purple-coloured ripe cherries. I had just managed to pluck a few from the lower branches when suddenly I heard a mighty, frightening hiss from the bushes under the tree. I could not see anything under the bushes, but instinctively shot back to the house with the few cherries I had collected as fast as I could. When I told my mother, she asked me not to go there again as it was possibly a snake. Poisonous snakes are known to hiss loudly as a warning before attacking. The cherries were bittersweet and extremely tasty and I had the urge to go and get some more, but was too scared.

A few days later, one morning, when we opened the front door of the house, our Alsatian dog, Lakshmi, was lying dead on the front steps of our house. It was strange as she had been in good health when we let her out of the kennel the previous evening. Her tongue was hanging out, and we could see three tiny red dots on it. The death of a healthy dog was a mystery. Later that day, the postman informed us that he had seen two dead snakes a hundred metres from our home, by the side of the road leading up to it. We went to the scene, which was not far from the cherry tree. The spectacle mark on the hoods of the snakes left no doubt they were cobras. One of them had teeth marks on its hood. The two cobras must have attacked the poor dog. Each snake was eight feet long, and the saying goes 'Eight-foot cobras are the deadliest snakes in the world.' I imagined the noisy battlefield that night, and the frightening hissing that had instinctively made me run to safety from under the cherry tree a few days ago echoed in my ears. The dog had killed both the snakes and just managed to get to her master's front door before dying.

Fish were in abundance in the lake. There was a unique fishing technique we called 'frightening fish.' Long, thin segments of coconut tree leaves, each about half a metre long, were tied to a twenty-five-metre-long rope at intervals of twenty centimetres. At one end, this rope was attached to a basket with a float, which allowed three-quarters of the basket to remain submerged in the water. The basket had a lid. A man in a paddleboat would take one end of this rope, row five metres off the shore and parallel to it away from the basket. He would row until the whole length of the rope was immersed in the water.

All the fish within five metres of the shore would spot this monstrous rope and freeze with fright, thinking it was some strange new predator, and stay still. The main man (diver), with the semi-submerged basket tied to his waist with a longish rope, would then go down under the water with eyes open. He would see the fish that remained still with fright and pick them up one by one with his thumb and index finger, avoiding their sharp fins. Then he would come up above the surface of water to fill his lungs and simultaneously lift the lid of the basket to put the live fish into it. The fish remained alive in the water inside the basket. By the time he reached the paddleboat, the basket behind him, on a good day, would be full of fish. The diver would then get to the shore, sit down, rest and have a fag. His eyes would be bloodshot from continuously remaining open underwater. The diver's companion would sell the fish to the people gathered around. The fish could not get any fresher as they would be alive when purchased.

A month's holiday flew by, and before we knew it, the car was waiting, packed with our belongings in the boot and the mattress on the roof rack, ready to take us back to school.

## Progress Reports

A week after classes started, we were handed our progress reports at school. They had to be signed by parents or guardians and returned to the class teacher in a week. Mr Allen, our local guardian, had to sign it for us. The signing of the progress report card was a ritual Mr Allen thoroughly enjoyed. He would collect the progress reports, and on Saturday, after tea at five o'clock, with glee in his eyes, he would gather all the boarders in the lounge. He would sit in his big chair in the middle of the room behind the desk. The progress report pile would be on his desk and a metre-long cane by his side. With a smirk on his face, he would pick up the reports and start calling us one by one.

The progress report recorded the marks you had secured in each subject, but what interested Mr Allen the most was your rank in the class. It would be written on the top right-hand corner of the report. He kept a record of each boarder's yearly rank from the previous year. If you went up in ranking, he would shake your hand and say, "Well done. Keep it up," and hand back your progress report. If your rank remained the same, he would just return the progress card without a handshake saying, "Try harder and do better next time." If your rank went down, your name would be called with a sadistic smile. The punishment depended upon how far down the ranking you had fallen. "Stretch out your hand," he would say in his stern voice. You had to extend your hand, palm facing up and the cane would come flying down onto your palm. Each hit was called a cut. The grimace on the face of the boarder on the receiving end was proof of how painful it was.

I received a cut once for sliding down the rankings by three. Believe me, it hurt, and I can imagine how it felt for someone who received five substantial meaty cuts. The natural reaction of anyone at the receiving end was to pull the hand away just before the cane touched it or to strangely contort his body, bend the knees and look away, hoping to cushion the impact of the cut. Some would beg for mercy: "Please, please, Uncle." But it made no difference. Mr Allen had a modification of the cut for anyone who repeatedly pulled away his hand before the cane touched it. He would hold the student's fingertips firmly with his left hand until the cane made full contact with the palm. The physical pain from the cuts was bad, but it was the pain from the shame of receiving it in front of all your mates that made it worse.

I had done poorly in one exam and was sure to get a few cuts on my return from my holidays. My brother had finished his final exams in school that year and joined the college in our village. I did not enjoy that holiday. My thoughts often drifted to the prospect of having to face Mr Allen and his cane. I was wondering how many cuts I had earned. However, I escaped. I was saved from the trauma by a tragic miracle.

A week before our holidays were over, Dad got a phone call from Mrs Allen. She informed him that sadly Mr Allen had passed away. He had become very unwell suddenly and was diagnosed with advanced cancer of the stomach. During the holidays he underwent major surgery and unfortunately did not recover. Allen's boarding was downsizing. My brother had finished school that year and dad decided to shift me to a different boarding. Although I felt happy I was spared the cane, deep down I felt sad – sad, thinking of the good things Mr Allen had taught us. He taught us discipline and made us work harder. The atmosphere in the boarding was friendly, and we felt we were all part of one big happy family.

*Chapter 12*

# BACK TO BOARDING SCHOOL

## Justin's Boarding

I had to find new accommodation elsewhere. I shifted to a smaller boarding facility with a friend, Sashi, from my class. It was a little place called Justin's Boarding, situated just fifty metres from the main gate of my school. There was room only for ten boarders. The boarders were smaller children from the fourth and fifth standards, and only the two of us were 'big boys' from the ninth standard.

Justin Uncle was a jolly character. During the day, he was quiet and spent most of his time reading. In the evenings, after a couple of drinks, he became unusually jovial. We liked him. He never once asked us to sit and study, as he did not think it was his job. In reality, it was Merlyn Aunty (Justin's wife), who was running the show. The year I joined, she was busy looking after her one-year-old daughter, Sharon.

The main reason for me joining Justin's Boarding was its proximity to the school. Lunch break at school was from 12.30 to 2 p.m. Sashi and I would rush back from school at the bell, have lunch quickly, and get back to the courtyard in front of the church by the school through the little gate. It was the same gate through which my brother and I got back into the school during our first attempt at running away. During lunch breaks this area was usually free. A group of friends organised tennis football (football using tennis balls) here. The main door of the church, which remained closed at this time, was the goal on one side. On the other side, two stones placed next to the wall made up the other goal. We regularly got fifty minutes to play and five minutes to wipe the sweat from our faces and necks with handkerchiefs and get dried up on our way back to the classrooms. Some friends from the group even managed to get to the school at eight in the morning and play for forty-five minutes before the school general assembly.

The church courtyard was ideal for five-a-side tennis football. The only negative part was the opening into the graveyard on the right side of the church that did not have a gate. If anybody kicked the ball hard to that side, it would go into the cemetery. It was the duty of the kicker to fetch the ball back.

Graveyards are spooky places, and I never enjoyed going in to retrieve the ball. However careful we were with our kicks, the ball would occasionally bounce into the graveyard. The walls of the cemetery were painted white. The gravestones were white. The inscriptions on the stones showing who rested beneath it were in black. If it were not for the rustle of wind through the leaves of the trees at the corners of the cemetery, one could hear a pin drop. It must have been the ghost stories we heard from friends that created an innate fear of cemeteries. In all those stories ghosts would take the form of beautiful women dressed in white sarees, with thick, flowing black hair. Legend has it that the ghosts don't walk; they float, defying all laws of worldly gravity. Their feet don't touch the ground. If you ever see a beautiful lady walking in a white saree, whose feet are not on the ground, you should be very worried!

Life in Justin's Boarding was hassle-free. There was freedom to do what you wanted when you wanted and if you wanted. The food was good, which was a bonus. Once in a while we even managed to pinch a few tablespoons of the delicious baby milk powder Merlyn Aunty bought for baby Sharon, if she forgot to lock up her special cupboard.

Outside the church gate, during school breaks, a little old woman called Kooni Mariam (Hunchback Mariam) sat in the shade of a tree by the side of the road selling homemade toffees. During breaks, students rushed to buy her toffees using their pocket money. They were the most delicious toffees I have ever tasted. Rumours were plenty about the unhygienic conditions in which they were made in Mariam's home (a small hut) just opposite to the school. All the same, if you were not quick to get there, the toffees would be sold out as she only made enough to fill the basket she carried from her hut to her trading spot under the tree.

One evening, after returning from the holidays, a classmate and I went to see a movie in town. Going to the cinema was the ultimate luxury. My classmate lived at the far end of the long, straight road in front of the school and the bus stop was right in front of his home. After the movie, we got off the bus at 9.30 p.m., he said, "Good Night!" and went into his house. The road was dark, except for the dim street lights, which were located a fair distance apart. There was total silence and not a soul on the street. I could hear my footsteps and walked as fast as I could to reach the boarding house quickly. Soon, I was near the church. It was eerily quiet. As I passed the church gate, instinctively my legs carried me faster, and I looked straight ahead. I dared not turn my head to the right to look towards the graveyard. However, something made me glance in that direction from the corner of my eye. I could swear I saw the figure of a lady in white in front of the graveyard. I did not look down to the ground to see if she was floating or had her feet planted on the ground. All I can remember was that I ran. I ran as fast as my legs could carry me until I reached the boarding house.

When I entered, Justin Uncle was sitting in the lounge reading a magazine. He looked up and asked me cheerfully, "How was the movie?"

"Very good," I replied.

"Why are you panting?" he asked

"Practising for the hundred metres sprint race. The school sports day is next week," I replied.

The following day, during the lunch break, our game of tennis football continued. The church and the graveyard looked the same. There was no white figure to be seen anywhere in the vicinity. Reflecting on my experience from the night before, I wondered whether it was a real ghost that I saw, or could it have been Father Gomes on a late evening walk? *But then, why would Father Gomes go out for a walk at 9.30 p.m. to the graveyard? Is he not frightened of ghosts? I guess not!*

It was at Justin's Boarding that I first learnt to ride a bicycle. I took a few tumbles before learning to balance on the small bicycle and then began enjoying it. My legs were not long enough to get me on the adult bike, unless there was a small platform to stand on to mount it.

It was during this time that I needed some new trousers, as I was beginning slowly to grow taller and my old ones were getting short. When Dad visited me one day, he took me to a shop in town, bought the cloth for three pairs of trousers and gave it to a tailor, whom he knew, to stitch them. In those days, readymade clothes were rare, and there were lots of tailors stitching 'made to measure' clothes. Nowadays, tailors are a dying breed, as everything comes machine-made and in all sizes and shapes. The tailor promised he would have them stitched and ready to collect in a week.

On the way back from town, about two miles before our school, the road bifurcated. The one to the left went to our school. The road to the right headed towards the highway in the direction of our village. Fifty metres before the road bifurcated, there was a bakery called Crown Bakery on the left-hand side. On many occasions, while going back home for the holidays or returning from holidays, when the weather was sweltering, Dad used to stop the car there to get freshly baked bread and a refreshing cold drink called ice cream soda.

The weekend following the shopping trip, my father could not come to town for some reason. I seized the opportunity to try my first outing into town on the bicycle to go to the tailor. I went to the cycle shop after breakfast to hire one. The small cycles had already been hired out. The shopkeeper offered me a normal bike. I took it, although I had never ridden a normal-sized bike before. I hired it for a couple of hours but dared not attempt to mount it in front of the cycle shop. I was sure that if the owner witnessed the spectacle of me clambering onto the bike, he would not let me have it. So, I walked with the cycle to the nearest milestone. It was one foot tall. I stood with one leg on the stone, climbed onto the bike with the other and started riding. Once I set off, it felt good. The ride to the shop was smooth, but I got off (tumbled off to be more precise) fifty metres before the tailor's shop so that he did not witness the scene. It all worked well.

The tailor had not finished the sewing and apologised for not completing the job on time. He promised he would finish it in the next two days. I said that it was okay and confidently walked away, holding the bike, towards the nearest milestone. With help from the milestone, I got back on it and happily rode back to school, feeling proud that my mission of riding into the busy town was accomplished.

As I approached the bifurcation on the road near Crown Bakery, I was surprised and shocked to see Dad's car overtake me. Dad was in the back seat. Luckily, he did not see me. I thanked the gods for my narrow escape and was riding on when our car suddenly overtook me again. My father put out his hand through the window and signalled me to stop, like a police officer. The driver had seen me in the rearview mirror and told my father. Dad asked him to make a U-turn and go back to find me. I explained that I had been to the tailor. Father was not a happy man and ordered me to go back to school carefully. He said he would collect the trousers and deliver them to me in two days and not to go for them again. Luckily, I had stopped close to a milestone and managed to get back on the bike and went straight back to school. I had got away lightly.

The main attraction of Justin's Boarding – tennis football – soon came to an end. One morning on his way to the assembly at nine o'clock, Father Gomes spotted a footballer walking to the assembly, dripping with sweat.

He had just finished the morning session of tennis football. At the general assembly, Father pulled him out from the line and made him stand in front of the school assembly on a chair, for everybody to see that he was drenched in sweat. There were light brown marks from the ball on the white shirt of his uniform as well. Unfortunately, he had been chewing Kooni Mariam's toffee when caught. Father Gomes made him hold a piece of cardboard with 'cud-chewing animal' (cow) written on it and he banned tennis football and eating Kooni Mariam's toffees on the school campuses from that day. I am not sure if Kooni Mariam's toffee sales went down after the incident, but I suspect not, as they were too tasty to give up.

In the year of my GCSE (General Certificate of Secondary Education) exams, I moved to another boarding school called Gonsalves Boarding. It had a reputation for getting good GCSE results. Mr Gonsalves was a giant of a man, over six feet tall, and appeared equally wide. He was strict. The final year students had to study all the time but had a perk: we got a single room each. It was more accurate to call it our own little space rather than a single room. It accommodated the smallest single bed and the tiniest of tables and chairs that were ever made by man. The box with the student's belongings went under the bed. Mr Gonsalves often made surprise walks around the blocks, peering through windows to check if we were studying or not.

Mr Gonsalves ran a small corner shop in town. His customers were mostly his boarders. You had to tell him what you wanted, and he would bring it in the evening on his way back from the shop, with a sizeable premium added to the price for home delivery. As the students taking their GCSEs had to work harder and needed more energy, they were given a glass of Horlicks in the evening and the parents were charged twice the price. In the end, it all paid off. I finished school with good grades and went back to my village to continue my studies at the local college on the hill, opposite our house.

## Chapter 13

# THE FORTUNE TELLER

I am not a believer in fortune tellers. However, a curious incident that occurred once made me question my belief. Our family owned rice paddy fields three miles away from the house. During harvest season, ten workers would be hired to harvest the paddy. They had to work for two days from dawn to dusk, cutting the mature paddy using razor-sharp sickles and then tying it up into large bundles. The majority of the workers were women, and it was backbreaking, hard labour. At the end of the day, the neatly tied-up paddy bundles would be loaded on to two bullock carts and transported back home. One member of the family had to accompany the load back to the house otherwise the paddy bundles would mysteriously decrease in number, and the bullock cart driver would get merrier and start singing by the time the carts reached home. On the way back from the fields, there were a couple of *arrack* (the local liquor) shops, and if no one from the house accompanied them, the bullock cart drivers would trade a few bundles of paddy for bottles of arrack, the poor man's whisky, and consume it on the way. The job of walking with the bullock carts fell to my brother and me, and we took turns.

On supervision duty one day, I was sitting in the shade of a tree next to the paddy fields, watching the workers cutting the paddy, when a little old woman approached me. She had sunken eyes, shrivelled skin hanging loosely over her tiny frame, a stooped gait and carried a small cage with a parrot in her left hand.

She said, "Son, please allow me to read your palm. I will precisely forecast your future."

I was bored to the core and tired of the monotonous job of supervising paddy harvesting for the second day on the trot, so I agreed. My brother had managed to wriggle out of his supervisory role this time as he had to go on an excursion with his class, and I was left with no choice.

"How much will you charge?"

"Anything will do," she replied in a soft, barely audible voice.

"Ok, go on then," I agreed.

The woman pulled out a pack of cards and arranged it neatly on an old newspaper, which was as wrinkled and dark as her skin. She opened the cage to let out her pet, the most beautiful little green parrot. The parrot hopped out of the cage. I thought it might make a quick dash to freedom, but to my surprise it looked at the pack of cards, hopped around a couple of times, leant forward and picked up the king of spades with its red beak, handed it over to its master and went back obediently into the cage.

The old lady studied the card carefully, looked at me without any change in expression and pointed her index finger up towards the sky. "What?" I asked eagerly.

"Look up," she said.

I looked up and saw a plane in the sky.

"Soon, you will be flying away to a far-off land."

Everyone likes good news, but then I had heard fortune tellers only predict good things. No one wants to hear bad news. I asked her, "Where to?" with a degree of sarcasm. I could not have dreamt of going abroad, as I had just finished my A-Levels and was hoping to get a place to study medicine in my home state. That was the sky for me, and even that was going to be difficult as there was fierce competition to get into medical school. Medicine was the most sought after and respected profession in those days.

She said, "I don't know," but added confidently, "Son, you mark my words. You may not see me again, but remember me when you get there."

I was planning to give her a bundle of paddy, but feeling good upon hearing the great news, unwittingly I gave her an extra bundle and a few rupees from my pocket money. A smile lit up her dark, sad wrinkly face and I saw a twinkle in her deep-set eyes as she collected the fee.

"God bless you, son," she said as she packed her means of livelihood – the pack of cards – and picked up the cage with her breadwinner and soulmate. The parrot also muttered something. It sounded like thanks. The little old woman just about managed to carry the bigger bundle of paddy in her left hand and the cage with her precious little possession and the smaller bundle of paddy in the other, and slowly trudged away. I forgot all about the incident until the moment when it flashed back into my memory. *Was it sheer luck, or had she really seen this coming? Was it just by chance that I came across the advertisement calling for scholarship applications to the Peoples' Friendship University, Moscow, USSR in a local newspaper?* I had good marks and applied. I did well at the interview and was successful.

I was still unsure about one thing. *Why was the USSR providing scholarships to students from all the developing countries of the world? Was it just a kind gesture to help the developing economies in these countries? There is no such thing as a free lunch!* The name of a popular play, performed by a famous travelling drama troupe in Kerala, *You Made Me a Communist*, came to mind. *Besides studying medicine, was I going to be brainwashed into becoming a die-hard communist, as one of my friends had suggested?*

## *Chapter 14*

# FIRST YEAR AT MEDICAL SCHOOL

Medical students were divided into groups of fifteen. Our group had students from several different continents. Besides me, there was one student each from Bolivia, Panama, Laos, Tanzania, Yemen and Jordan, two from Lebanon and six from the USSR. Everyone from the Soviet Union was called a Russian (as they all spoke Russian). One of them was from Belorussia and another from Ukraine. The international students in our group did not particularly like a Russian guy called Kostya. He happened to share a room with Mario, our classmate from Panama. Kostya was short and slim, with a long, sharp nose. On the bridge of his nose sat a big pair of thick-rimmed spectacles. He looked like an intellectual but asked the most irritating questions at lessons. Rumour had it that he was high up in the Communist Party rankings of the Russian students and a member of the KGB. When a group of students was discussing an international issue, one of the Russian students voiced his honest opinion on the matter. Kostya told him, "You keep quiet. You were not at the party meeting yesterday." It made us more apprehensive and suspicious, and we began to be extra careful when talking to him.

Lectures for the entire group of medics were held in the big hall. The practical classes were conducted separately for each group. As the medical faculty building had not yet been completed in the first year, we had to travel by metro to the centre of the city to the lecture theatre and anatomy dissection halls of another medical college, the First Medical Institute, Moscow. The arrangement was to share their dissection halls temporarily until ours were completed. The journey started with a ten-minute bus ride to the nearest metro, South-West Station, and then there was a forty-five-minute train ride to Moscow city centre. The journey by train was comfortable, as South-West Station was the starting point on our metro line, and a seat was guaranteed. Forty-five minutes on the metro was enough time to do some useful reading. It was the only regular reading we did up to the exams. If you were reading something seriously or pretending to do so with your head buried in your book, generally you could sit till your destination. However, on the odd occasion, a cunning and crafty older woman, who may have got in midway and could not find a seat, would come and stand in front of you. She would interrupt your reading and ask in a firm, loud voice so that others around could hear, "Young man, would you mind giving me your seat?" It was rude not to because as per the etiquette in public transport, you had to give up your seat to an elderly or disabled person. You invariably got up and gave her your seat, and although fed up, carried on reading, standing up. This was difficult as you had to hold the book in one hand and the vertical pole in the compartment with the other, to prevent falling if the train braked suddenly.

## Anatomy Lessons

Anatomy lessons were boring in the beginning. We started with lectures on the musculoskeletal system. There are two hundred and six bones in the human body. We had to know them all and the unique features of each one of them. One wondered why the good Lord had made the human body so complex. *Was it to make life difficult for medical students? Could he not have kept things simple?* Practical sessions with the human skeleton followed lectures in the anatomy lab. The lab was full of formalin-filled glass jars containing human organs. These jars were a reminder of what we had to learn in future.

A unique feature that distinguished medics from other specialities was that medical students had to wear long white coats. The white symbolised health and hygiene, and we had to wear the coat to every class and clinic. All the doctors and nurses also wore them. The term 'white coat syndrome', in relation to patients' reactions when seeing a doctor, had not been coined then.

Anatomy lessons became interesting once dissection classes began. The dissection hall had ten tables. Before lessons, the lab assistants would take out the cadavers (dead bodies preserved in formalin and refrigerated) from the large pull-out freezer cupboards and lay them on the table. It seemed a very strange place in the beginning. The room smelt strongly of formalin, which made the cadavers last long enough for groups of medical students to finish with them. They were not the pale colour of death but a dirty grey from the formalin. With time, we got used to the smell. Two students were given a cadaver to dissect between them. One had to dissect the left limb and the other the right. Parts of the body that did not come in pairs, like the liver, heart and spleen, had to be shared. My good friend Kimaro and I were dissection table mates.

Kimaro came from a town called Moshi in Tanzania. He was pleasant, gentle natured and always appeared calm and collected. A reserved person by nature, he replied to any question only after a long pause, as if he had to think carefully before replying. Usually his answer was right and everyone regarded him as the 'wise man' of the group.

Our group was lucky enough to get the best anatomy teacher, Dr Irina. She was a very likeable woman in her early sixties. The first thing she told us in a firm tone, after introducing herself, was to respect the cadavers: "Do not treat them as a piece of meat. These were living people like you and me until recently. They had a brain that could think, a heart that could love and pump blood to the whole body without pausing for a moment, and a pair of lungs to supply oxygen and remove carbon dioxide waste from a host of other organs to make one a living being. Cadavers are the bodies of people who volunteered to donate their bodies for science. After dissection, today and every day, I want you all to place back the structures you studied to their original position, and to leave the dissection table as clean as it was when you started."

The lessons started with Irina quickly demonstrating to the group, on a cadaver, what we were expected to do that day. Then we would go to our respective tables and perform the dissection. Irina would walk around the tables, observing us, giving us tips and helping out when someone was struggling. At the end of the dissection, she would gather us all around a table and sum up the day's work. She pointed out what we had done well and what we had not, but she made the lessons enjoyable by telling us practical stories about the parts of the body we had just dissected. As she knew anatomy like the back of her hand, one of my friends told her at the end of a class, "Dr Irina, you should have been a surgeon as you know anatomy by heart."

With a smile Irina replied, "I was a surgeon during the war. We were in the final year of medical school when the war broke out, and all of us had to go to the army hospitals near the war front to treat the wounded. Our generation became surgeons by necessity and not by choice. We learnt things the hard way. I remember operating continuously for seventy-two hours once. Towards the end, I was helped out of the operation theatre by colleagues to a side room to get some sleep, and another colleague took over. It was war, and we had no choice. The practical knowledge we gained by treating the war-wounded stood us in good stead. If you want to be a good doctor, irrespective of the branch of medicine you choose, you should know your anatomy well, and I will make sure you do!"

At first, dissection seemed difficult. We were all apprehensive and did not enjoy it but gradually got used to it. We had to dissect every muscle, track every major nerve and identify every artery and vein. Anatomy atlases lay open on a table nearby to guide us. It was gratifying to be able to unravel the secrets of nature. Once, while waiting for Dr Irina to come around and show us something we were struggling to find, a strange thought came into my mind: *Every religion in the world, be it Hinduism, Islam or Christianity, believes in the existence of the soul and that souls go to heaven or hell after leaving the body, so where could the souls of the cadavers, whose every body part we were dissecting, be at this moment in time? Were they watching their worldly bodies being taken apart from heaven above or hell below?* I felt like asking Irina this question, but my better judgement prevented me from doing so. After all, people in the USSR were atheists and probably did not believe in the existence of the soul.

My friend Carlos and I decided that on the way back from anatomy classes we would go swimming. The university had hired a section of the swimming pool near the metro station Krapotkinskaya. The pool was built on land where once a church called the Cathedral of Christ, the Saviour had stood. It was built in the nineteenth century, but was destroyed in 1931 on Stalin's orders. Large amounts of gold, present in the domes of the church, were used to pay for the industrialisation of the country. Stalin planned to build a colossal Palace of the Soviets (parliament house) in its place. Construction was started in 1937 but stopped in 1941 when Hitler invaded the Soviet Union. Marble from the walls and benches of the cathedral was used in the construction of nearby Moscow Metro stations.

1n 1958, during Khrushchev's rule, the site was transformed into the world's largest open-air heated swimming pool, the Moscow Swimming Pool. It was twice the size of a soccer field and made in the shape of a big circle. The pool was divided into many smaller pools by walls that stood up one foot above the water. Ours was pool number three, and it did not have a separate entrance. To get into pool three, we had to go through pools one and two. A swimming coach from the university was available in the pool during the allocated times to help, advise and, if necessary, teach us to swim. A dip in the pool after a hard day of anatomy was very refreshing.

For a few weeks, this routine swim in the pool after anatomy classes carried on. Then, winter came and things got tricky. On a day when the temperature dipped to ten degrees below zero, Carlos and I went for our regular swim. The water was heated to twenty degrees Celsius and the whole pool was so steamy and misty that you could barely see more than two feet ahead of you. We jumped into the first pool and walked across the shallow portion to the second pool. The pools were deserted but for the odd swimming enthusiast like Carlos and myself. We climbed onto the little partition wall to go into the second pool. From plus twenty degrees Celsius to minus ten degrees was a big drop. A momentary throbbing headache hit us both. We quickly jumped into pool two and stayed in the warm water for a couple of minutes until the headache went. The same thing happened when we crossed over into our pool. The intensity of the headache became more severe. We were glad to be back in the twenty-degree warmth of our pool, and in it we felt much better. The swimming teacher was present in the pool along with a friend. I heard her say to her friend, "Look at the dedication of these foreign kids. They come from hot countries and still come out to swim in this cold weather. Our boys are too lazy and cannot be bothered." It was flattering to hear this comment. We experienced the same throbbing headaches of slightly higher intensity while walking back to the changing room from our pool. That was our last trip to the swimming pool in winter, despite the encouraging remarks from the teacher.

One Monday morning, we noticed that our friend Mario from Panama was absent from class. When the teacher inquired, a Russian classmate replied, "He decided to discontinue his studies and went back to Panama yesterday." It all seemed a bit bizarre, as he had been perfectly happy on Friday, but had suddenly decided to stop his studies and fly back to Panama in South America on Sunday. We heard that before leaving he had poured black ink on all the clothes belonging to Kostya, his roommate. It was clear that the bad blood between the two had reached boiling point and led to Mario leaving. All the international students assumed Kostya had used his KGB connections to kick Mario out of the university. Understandably, after that day, all the foreigners kept a safe distance from Comrade Kostya.

Anatomy got harder as the days went by, and the temperature outside dropped. Soon, we were due to have our first class test in anatomy. The *zachyot* (class test) was different from real exams. The date for the test was announced a few weeks before the test, and if you took the test on that date it was considered good and a testimony to your systematic hard work and dedication. However, it was not mandatory to take the test on that date. If you did not take it on the first date, you had to fix another date and time with your class teacher. It would be inconvenient for the teacher, as she had to find the time to examine you separately and also difficult for you, as the class would have moved on to other more advanced topics. I could not see any advantage in this system, but I guess it was meant to reduce the pressure on the students. I met a medical student from Yugoslavia once. Yugoslavia, under President Tito, was also considered a socialist country but followed a different line of socialism to the Soviet Union and its allies. While discussing exams, he told me that in Yugoslavia you could move on to the next year even if you had not passed one of the subjects. The student just had to retake and pass that exam within the next six months.

Dr Irina informed the class that our test would be in one week and that we all needed to work harder as she felt a certain complacency. "Who will be taking the test next week?" I was the only one who foolishly put up my hand. Judging by the expression on her face, she was not pleased that only one hand went up. "Only one person is ready?" she asked in an angry tone. "What have the rest of you been doing all this time?" There was silence. "You guys better get your act together and do it soon!"

I had worked hard, but there was so much to learn. The test day arrived faster than expected. The way the test was conducted was very different from what I was used to. I assumed I would be taken to the room and would have the viva one to one and then would be taken to the cadaver to be tested alone, while the rest of the group were given other tasks to do. Unfortunately, that was not how things were done. Irina led me to the cadaver like a lamb to the slaughter. The rest of the group stood around, watching the fun, and got a free revision session. I felt it was very unfair and sincerely wished I had not volunteered.

The viva began. Irina started with the basics, and when she saw that I was managing to answer most questions, they got harder. There is a limit to how much anatomy a student's brain can retain. After a few questions I fumbled, and the look on Dr Irina's face became sterner. After forty-five minutes of questioning, she took up my progress report and wrote satisfactory (Grade 3), a mere pass, in front of the whole group. I was shocked and saw the worried look on the faces of my friends when they saw my mark. After the test, we had a ten-minute break, and the group moved on to the adjacent hall for the lectures. Classmates consoled me, saying that if satisfactory was what I got for that performance, they could not see themselves ever passing anatomy. I was glad the ordeal was over but sad that I did not get the grade I had expected for my hard work. I had been expecting at least the next level up, good (Grade 4), and not a mere pass. After the lectures, Dr Irina called me to her office and insisted I retake the test in two weeks along with the others. *Oh, not again!* I thought to myself. "You deserve a five, and I insist you come again in two weeks along with the others to retake the test," she said with an encouraging smile.

I felt like never opening my anatomy textbooks again. A couple of days later, however, I pulled myself together and decided to brush up on my anatomy while some of it was still left in my brain. Vanya, my classmate, happened to drop into the room. He was surprised to see me with my anatomy textbook open and asked me, "Why the hell are you reading anatomy again? You have passed the test. Are you mad or what?"

"Dr Irina insists I retake the test."

"Then the pair of you are bloody mad," he said as he left the room.

A friend who was studying Russian literature came to my room one day. I was revising with my anatomy atlas open and on the page describing the male sexual organs. He looked at it in surprise and asked me, "Are you studying pornography or what?"

I showed him the next pages with the cross-sections of these parts. He was shocked when I explained that the scrotum was made up of so many layers, pointing to the diagrams.

"What?" he said, and his eyes nearly popped out. "Who would have imagined that balls are so complicated. The female sexual organs must be simpler. At least there are no bits hanging."

He was more surprised when I told him it was equally complicated but in a different way. My friend was glad he had not taken up medicine and swore he would rather be reading Russian literature any day. "It is the language of literary giants like Pushkin, Tolstoy, Dostoyevsky, Chekhov and many more. It is a joy to read them in their language, and you don't have to memorise these bloody complicated body parts." I did not argue.

In two weeks, I went along with the rest of the group for my resit. Irina said she would test me at the end. The others were grilled harder this time in front of the cadaver and I was the happy spectator until the end. She passed a couple of students, and the rest had to come back to retake the test at a later date. When my turn came, a different, pleasant Irina asked me a few simple questions and with a smile wrote Grade 5 in my progress card. I was thrilled. My solo test ordeal two weeks ago had been more of a show to stimulate the rest of the group to get their act together. From that day, anatomy became one of my favourite subjects.

## *Chapter 15*

# HISTORY OF THE USSR AND LATIN

I was anxiously waiting for the brainwashing sessions. Surely, there had to be one. *History of the Soviet Union was one of the subjects in our curriculum.* C*ould this be the one?* I wondered. Why one had to learn the history of the Soviet Union to become a doctor was beyond me. However, history turned out to be an interesting subject. The teacher, Dimitry, spoke excellent English, as he had worked in Russian embassies in English-speaking countries as a diplomat until a few years earlier. He explained the theory of Marx and Engels, which formed the foundation of Soviet society in a simple way. According to them, the history of society is the history of class struggles. Society has to go through different stages in its evolution.

The first stage is Primitive Society. In it, there is no concept of ownership beyond individual possessions.

The second stage is Slave Society. The idea of classes in society begins here. There is the slave-owning ruling class and the slave class.

The third stage is Feudalism, when many classes like kings, lords and serfs emerge. The serfs have more rights than slaves.

The fourth stage is capitalism, where market forces take over and guide the entire economy. The bourgeoisie owns the means of production and ruthlessly exploits workers, to maximise production for their own profit.

This stage of society has the seeds of destruction within it as the working class sinks deeper into poverty and the capitalists owning the means of production get richer. The working class will eventually rise against exploitation and take power into their hands, leading to the next stage of development of society, called socialism.

Lenin advocated that for this to happen there should be a strong organisation to educate the working class and to organise and lead the people, as the working class has no experience in running the state. In his book *Shto Gelach* (*What Is To Be Done*), Lenin emphasises the need for a strong party that unifies the workers and peasants, overthrows the capitalists and takes over power. The military and the police made up of the common man will support this party. With this aim, Lenin founded the Communist Party.

When all this happens, society reaches the fifth stage – socialism.

During socialism, all the means of production are taken over by the state, and there will no longer be any form of exploitation. Workers govern themselves and become the ruling class, establishing the dictatorship of the proletariat. The worker's state takes over factories and farms to be run by the very people who generate the wealth – the workers and the peasants. Gradually, the distinction between classes ceases to exist.

The sixth stage is communism. Here, it becomes a little vague. The term came from the Latin word *communis* (common, universal). A simple difference between socialism and communism was that in socialism only the means of production would be socialised. In contrast, during communism, both the means of production and consumption would be socialised (in the form of free access to final goods). Everyone has to work. Each one gets as much as they need and works as much as they can. Social classes will be abolished altogether. There will be no rich or poor. Gradually, there will be no need for a state as such. But when this will happen was a moot point. Khrushchev once mentioned in a speech in the sixties that thanks to the fast pace of development of Soviet society, the country would reach the final stage of development – communism – in the 1980s. However, none of the ideologists of the party had a clear idea when exactly this would happen, so they conveniently added an intermediate stage between socialism and communism called Developed Socialism.

We were not given any homework on this subject. We only had to turn up and listen to the lectures, so nobody took it too seriously.

I noticed something common among Russian students. All of them carried identical briefcases. They were all of the same design – black or brown in colour and expandable. I asked a Russian classmate if there was a reason behind this. He replied that it was because it was the most practical briefcase. You could carry a lot of stuff in it when required. At other times, it served as a regular briefcase. On the day we received our stipend, I understood what he meant. The Russians would each buy fifteen bottles of beer at the buffet, sit around the table, chat and drink as many bottles as possible. At a guess, they would have five each. The rest, they would carry home in their expanded briefcases for later consumption.

The Russian girls also had the trademark briefcase although they seldom carried them. I remember an incident that occurred at a physiology class when we were studying the nervous system. Aseeza, a naughty girl from the class, slipped a frog we had done experiments on and that was still under anaesthetic into Tamara's briefcase. On her way home Tamara opened the briefcase in the packed bus, to get her season ticket out. The frog had by then recovered from the anaesthetic and jumped out of the bag, causing a commotion in the bus. It was an embarrassing moment. Poor Tamara had some explaining to do to the fellow passengers. She was such a sport that she did not take offence at the prank but made an appeal the following day to whoever did it not to repeat it, as it had been very embarrassing. Aseeza must have felt really bad.

Every student received a stipend of ninety roubles. It could take you a long way because we had no bills to pay. Electricity and water were free. There was no room rent and we had no books to buy as the library lent every student the required textbooks. Transport was cheap. Hence, this amount was enough to see us through the month comfortably. However, for students, as always, it was either feast or famine. During the first weekend of the month, we would all have lavish parties in our rooms with guests. Only on weekends were guests from outside the university allowed into our hostel. They could come in after 5 p.m. and had to leave by 11 p.m. Outsiders were required to leave their identification badges with the security at the door upon entry and collect them on their way out. The security guard was usually an older person, doing the job to supplement their meagre pension and avoid the loneliness of being on their own at home. The weekends were lively in most rooms, with loud music, wine and merrymaking. Towards the end of the month, the money ran out, and most survived until stipend day on bread, butter, milk and yoghurt, which only cost pennies.

## Latin – The Universal Language of Medicine

Latin is the universal language of medicine. Although no longer a spoken language, medical terminology all over the world is in Latin. We had one class of Latin every week. Compared to anatomy, physiology and biochemistry, Latin was a lifeless subject. *How can a language that is no longer spoken be made attractive and exciting?* Fortunately, we had no exams in Latin but only a test at the end of the year. The interesting part of Latin was the teacher himself. He was an elderly gentleman, Comrade Yuri, who reminded us of a 'daddy long legs' in a pair of trousers. He was bright as a button but frighteningly frail. When you saw him walk from the bus stop to the university building, you worried that a strong wind could topple him over or even simply blow him away. Yuri had a passion for difficult-sounding big words. He enjoyed taking the attendance register aloud and read out in full the long names of every student from the different countries, with perfect pronunciation. The student whose name was called had to raise his hand. Since our class had students from different continents, the full names of some students were a few lines long. After the very first attendance, he remembered every student's full name by heart. At the second lesson, he would call out each student's name with such ease, as if he had rehearsed it a hundred times. That time, he also asked the name of the town you were from and what your mother tongue was. In the next class, he would pronounce your full name, your hometown and the name of your mother tongue fluently and clearly. Imagine remembering over one hundred names and details like 'Parameswaran Nair Hari Kumar from Thiruvananthapuram, who speaks Malayalam' without jotting it down.

Between practical classes in physiology and Latin lessons, we had a gap of twenty minutes. Our group would go into the little café in the building for a cup of coffee. Yuri also turned up for coffee regularly. We gathered later that he came early not for the coffee, but to ensure no student disappeared during the interval between lessons.

One day, my friend Carlos told me after the physiology class that he was skipping the Latin lesson as it was too boring. He asked me to tell the teacher that he had to leave early to attend an urgent meeting of the Bolivian students' association in town. When the teacher called out Carlos's name during attendance, I stood up and conveyed the message. Yuri nodded and moved on. During the next class, while taking attendance, he called out Carlos's name. Carlos put his hand up. Yuri told him, "Carlos, I was extremely worried about you last week. I was finding it painful to imagine you sitting at the urgent Bolivian students' association meeting with severe diarrhoea." Carlos blushed and had no reply. He told me later that the previous week, when he had left early to skip Latin, he had bumped into the Latin teacher outside the building and been caught off-guard. Yuri had asked Carlos where he was going. Carlos had forgotten the excuse he had given me to pass on to the teacher and replied, "Comrade Yuri, I have a dodgy tummy! Severe diarrhoea." From then on, Carlos never missed a Latin lesson.

Yuri noticed that the attendance in his class was going down, so he came up with a new strategy if anyone was absent from class. The following week, Yuri would go into the hostel unannounced, ten minutes before the start of the lesson, and knock on that person's door. The unsuspecting student, who was planning to skip the Latin lesson again, was in for a shock when he opened the door. "How are you comrade [X]," Yuri would say, shaking his hand. "You look well! See you in class in ten minutes." Then, there was no escape.

One day, Kimaro was admitted to the hospital with very high blood pressure. When the Latin teacher heard that, he asked us who was going to the hospital to visit him. "I am going tomorrow," I replied. I wanted to save Kimaro the embarrassment of the Latin teacher turning up at the hospital and asking him when he would be coming back for Latin lessons. Yuri took out a five rouble note from his pocket and gave it to me, saying, "Buy Kimaro some fruit, ask him to get better, not to worry about Latin and wish him a speedy recovery from me."

I visited Kimaro in the hospital and gave him the fruit and the get well wishes from our Latin teacher. Kimaro was happy that Yuri was kind enough to think of him. He was bored in the hospital but had made good friends with a middle-aged gentleman called Ivan in the bed next to him. Ivan was a short, stocky, muscular man who had fought in the Second World War and had many tales to tell. He was a chain smoker, and as smoking was not allowed in the wards, he spent most of his time out of the ward having a fag. Ivan never talked of his family, although he once mentioned to Kimaro that he lost everyone and everything when the Germans bombed his village in the Moscow suburbs. The only visitor he had was a nephew who would bring him lots of goodies – fruit, pickled vegetables, nuts, dried meats and cigarettes. Ivan offered everything to Kimaro, except the cigarettes, and insisted he try everything. Kimaro introduced me to Ivan. He was a charming guy with a great sense of humour. However, Ivan's eyes reminded me of a description by the Russian poet, Mikhail Lermontov: '*In the first place, [his eyes] never laughed when he laughed. Have you ever noticed this peculiarity some people have? It is either the sign of an evil nature or of profound and lasting sorrow.*' In Ivan's case, it had to be the latter. Ivan offered me some of the goodies and insisted I try them. A week later, Kimaro was back in good health with his blood pressure under control and attending classes.

We had our final exams in anatomy three months later. On the Saturday before the exam, the dissection hall was kept open for our final revision on cadavers. Dr Irina insisted the whole group attend.

"However much you read from textbooks, practising on the cadaver is what will stick in your mind," she said.

She moved from one dissection table to another, giving us tips and pointing out the most common mistakes students made under pressure during exams. Irina called the whole group to a table. The group had just revised the anatomy of the spine, and the cadaver was lying on its tummy. Irina wanted to demonstrate something. The lab attendant, with our help, turned the cadaver on to its back. We were to revise the anatomy of the chest. Irina separated the chest wall, which had been opened previously, by splitting the breast bone, and picked up the left lung in her gloved hand.

"Notice any difference? Look at the colour. It is not grey like normal lungs, but black. Jet black. Black as night. Typical smoker's lung," she added.

As she said this, I noticed Kimaro go pale and almost faint. I held him up and helped him onto the chair in the corner of the room. As he sat down I heard him mutter, "It's him. It's definitely him. Ivan." I went back to the cadaver whose face was clearly visible after the body had been turned over. The formalin-soaked, dirty, brownish-grey and lifeless face with shrivelled skin could not hide the identity of its owner. I could tell it was Ivan without any doubt, although the eyes that never laughed remained permanently closed. I had a strange feeling in my stomach and thought I was going to be sick. Luckily, it was the end of the lesson. We were glad to get out of the room. The chilly wind blowing on our faces as we walked to the metro station made us feel better. On the metro journey back to the hostel, Kimaro and I didn't speak a word.

It is not my intension to bore you with the umpteen subjects we had to study, but I will briefly dwell on the more interesting ones and recall related incidents that stand out in my memory.

## Chapter 16

# POLITICAL ECONOMICS, PHILOSOPHY AND PHYSICAL EDUCATION

Political economics was a subject in the second year of our curriculum. I was almost certain these lessons must be the brainwashing sessions, but I was wrong. It turned out to be everyone's favourite subject, not that anyone understood it or had a burning desire to do so. The lecturer, Pavel, was a middle-aged, pleasant Pickwickian type of gentleman with a smiling face. Political economics was mostly a continuation of the history of the Soviet Union. He spoke about the importance of a 'centralised planned economy' for the development of the country. He explained that it helped the predictable evolution of society as a whole, as opposed to the chaotic progress of the unstable Western market economy. There would be no black holes, depressions or crashes of the economy. The planning of everything was for the next five years and was called *pichiletka* (five-year plan).

Russians, as usual, saw humour in everything and there were many jokes about the pichiletka too. Here is one that comes to mind. Comrade Brezhnev was delivering a speech to the Party Congress (the parliament). "By the end of this pichiletka," he said, "every Soviet citizen will own a car." The audience applauded. "By the end of the next pichiletka, every Soviet citizen will have his own helicopter." Everyone applauded except one man.

He put up his hand and asked, "Comrade, why does every Soviet citizen need a helicopter?" Brezhnev paused for a moment and replied, "Tomorrow morning, if you hear they are selling Levis or Wrangler jeans in Leningrad, how else can you get there before they are sold out?" Youngsters had a craze for jeans, which was the fashion in the West, but the USSR did not manufacture them or even import them. The reason why they did not remains unclear. Maybe the authorities did not want Western habits to corrupt the Soviet youth.

What made the political economy teacher endearing was his firm belief that the human mind is not designed for multitasking. His view was that you cannot concentrate on the lecture and take down notes at the same time. We had to put down our pens while he was lecturing. Pavel would explain a topic for fifteen minutes and then summarise it in two minutes. He insisted on everyone jotting down the summary. Before summarising, he would say aloud, "Start writing." It was the wake-up call. It was in his lectures that many of us perfected the art of 'sleeping with the eyes wide open'. Upon hearing the words "Start writing" you wake up, scribble the summary in two minutes and then go back to sleep. No wonder we felt refreshed after his lectures.

A student once asked Pavel, "Why is it that there is so much unrest, strikes, inequality and poverty in the wealthy Western countries and not in the Soviet Union?"

The teacher replied with a smile, "Because they never had a Lenin in the West."

## Philosophy

Philosophy was a subject in the curriculum in the third year.

"Why does a doctor need to study philosophy?" I asked the teacher Maria.

She calmly replied, "You will be surprised how many tricky problems you will encounter in your practice as a doctor to which you cannot find a straight answer and will need a philosophical approach."

The classes were interesting, like Maria herself. She was a brunette, under five feet tall and dressed very casually. Maria's shrivelled hair looked as if she had started doing it but gave up halfway or forgot to complete it in a rush before leaving home. Her picture would not be complete without a cigarette in her mouth. It was hardly surprising she had a chronic cough. Kimaro and I could see a pair of black lungs in her. Maria was a firm believer that philosophy was to be understood and not learnt by heart. She became our favourite teacher when she told us she had no objection to students bringing books into exams. Philosophy, according to her, was a way of thinking, and books could not do that for you. She spoke of philosophers of ancient Italy and Greece and made the subject exciting by narrating stories from their lives. Maria also explained the philosophy of Marx, Engels and Lenin and the philosophers who had influenced their thinking. To be honest, a lot of what she said went straight over our heads.

True to her word, Maria allowed books into the exam hall and proved she was right. They were of no use. The answers to her questions could not be found in any of the books as they were real-life situations. One just had to think and come up with a logical answer. However, with her probing questions, Maria could easily make out who had listened and understood at least some of what she had discussed during lessons.

## Physical Education

Physical education (PE) was a compulsory part of the syllabus in the first year. The Russians firmly believed that a healthy mind could only exist in a healthy body. Everyone had to go to the sports hall for PE lessons. The PE teacher would begin with stretching exercises and progress from there. In the beginning, we all thought it would be a walk in the park when we saw the teacher was a middle-aged lady, but she was a former gymnastics champion and proved us wrong. She was so supple and had such great stamina that keeping up with her was impossible and she put us all to shame.

During winter, when there was sufficient snow, we were taken out of the sports hall and shown how to do cross-country skiing. After putting on skis, we had to glide over the thick snow with special poles in each hand to propel ourselves forward. Invariably, we took a few tumbles but laughed it off. Once we learnt to balance on skis, it was easy, but unpleasant in the biting cold with the wind blowing against our faces.

The funny part of winter sports was ice-skating. Students needed to learn to skate and do three rounds in the skating rink to pass the test, which was compulsory. It was a joy to watch the experienced skaters swiftly and gracefully gliding on the ice, leaping up and doing all sorts of complicated twists and turns and still landing on both feet. Our first attempt at skating was comical. Kimaro and I picked up our skates and put them on seated on the bench next to the rink. Even by holding on to the wooden rail, it was a struggle to stand upright on the skates. Holding on to each other, we somehow managed to enter the rink. The teacher came over and showed us how it was done and left us to get on with it.

Our grand entry into the rink was hilarious. As per the teacher's instructions, I kept my centre of gravity low by bending my knees. I took my first step and then the second step, looking straight ahead, just as the teacher told us to. My plan was to go straight forward as the rink was rectangular and I could reach the other side sooner if I went that way. However, I found the skates leading me towards the right-hand corner of the rink. Before I knew it, I was on all fours and could not help laughing when I saw Kimaro on all fours in the opposite corner of the rink. The teacher came over, extended his hand, lifted me back on my feet, and said, "Relax; do not tighten your muscles." The easiest thing to say to someone who can barely stand up with both feet locked in skates is to relax. The teacher held my hand and helped me take a couple of steps. Soon I was back upright in the corner of the rink, holding onto the railings. Nervously, praying to all the gods, I took a couple more steps. The initial steps were like those of someone who had just finished off half a bottle of vodka, neat and on an empty stomach. I persevered, as there was no choice. Slowly, after a few more falls, I got the hang of it and was able to skate slowly without falling. By the end of the year, somehow, I managed to do the three rounds with all my bones intact and passed the test. To this day, I consider this the most significant achievement in my sporting life.

It is best to stay indoors in severely cold, windy weather. I learnt this from experience. One wintry Saturday afternoon, when the weather outside was not too cold by Moscow standards (only minus five degrees Celsius), I decided to visit my friend who was studying mining and geology. His hostel was in a place called Pavletskaya, about forty-five minutes away by metro from our hostel. The hostel was an old converted military barrack, and I had to walk for two hundred metres along the side of the building to its far end where the entrance was. I had dressed up warmly. Adjacent to the building was open land with no other buildings or trees. A strong wind was blowing in my direction. On that day, I realised that minus five with strong winds was equal to minus twenty-five degrees. The ushanka covered my head and ears, but my nose was exposed. It began stinging and then felt numb.

An old lady coming from the opposite direction shouted over the wind, "Son, look after your nose. It might drop off." I cupped my nose with my right hand and ran as fast as I could until I reached the entrance to the hostel. I went straight into the washroom to inspect my nose. It was pale as death. Had the old lady not warned me, I dread to think what could have happened. I rubbed it gently with both hands and repeatedly washed it with warm water to slowly bring it back to life and its original colour.

## *Chapter 17*

# GENERAL MEDICINE AND PHYSICS

I hoped the lectures on general medicine would be interesting and get us all excited, as that was when the clinical subjects dealing directly with patient care started. However, this did not happen. The reason was possibly the poor timing. The lectures were held in the small lecture hall of hospital number sixty-four at 2 p.m. The day started with practical classes in physiology in the medical faculty building opposite our hostels. After that, there was enough time for a sumptuous four-course meal in the canteen, including a delicious pudding for dessert. After the meal, a short bus trip, followed by a quick tram ride, got us to the hospital.

By the time we reached the hospital for Professor Kiriev's lecture, we were all tired. He was a thin, silver-haired gentleman in his late sixties, who wore a grey suit. His was the most monotonous voice I have ever heard. Professor Kiriev got fully immersed in medicine right from the beginning and walked up and down the middle of the hall slowly while lecturing. I usually took a corner seat. A colleague sitting next to me listened to the first ten minutes of the lecture with great difficulty and then nodded off. Unfortunately, he snored. Students from the front rows began turning back to see who was snoring. I had to elbow him to wake him up. He woke up looking dazed, orientated himself, listened to the lecture for a few minutes and again fell back into slumber and snored. I had to elbow him again. The snoring and elbowing cycle repeated a few times during the lecture.

We thought Professor Kiriev was hard of hearing, as he appeared not to notice.

During the lecture on the physiology of the gastrointestinal system, he asked if anyone had heard of a Russian saying: 'Eat your breakfast alone, share lunch with your friend and give away your dinner to your enemy.' Then he asked, "Do you all have a heavy meal before coming to the lectures?"

"Yes," we replied.

"Pudding and all?"

"Yes."

He went on to explain the physiology. "After a heavy meal, blood rushes to the stomach and intestines to help the body with the process of digestion. It reduces the relative amount of blood available to other organs, including the brain, causing hypoxia (lack of oxygen) to the brain. It makes one sleepy and causes some people to nod off and snore." He said it with a smile on his face, turning towards our corner. Professor Kiriev was definitely not hard of hearing.

The practical classes in medicine were conducted by one of Professor Kiriev's assistants, Dr Maks. He was a man with a diametrically opposite personality. Dr Maks was strict, demanding and seldom smiled. There was never any ambiguity in his thoughts. He disliked the words 'possibly' or 'just a little'. The pulse rate, according to him, was never seventy to eighty. It was either seventy or eighty. Dr Maks placed the utmost importance on history-taking and would get cross if anyone talked when the patient was narrating the history of his illness. He considered history-taking an art and insisted the patient was not giving the history but telling 'his-story'.

"Listening carefully to the patient alone is enough to make a provisional diagnosis," he used to say.

Dr Maks taught us how to use the stethoscope. If someone listened to the chest with a stethoscope and told him there was possibly a wheeze, he got cross and made them listen again and again until they confirmed whether or not there was a wheeze. Medicine, he insisted, is an exact science. Dr Maks made sure we regularly revised what he taught. Every lesson would start with questions on what we had been taught during the previous class. We had to read for his classes to survive and this 'perfectionist' helped us develop a good foundation in general medicine.

There was a senior nurse in the medical ward called Galina. She was known as the Vampire, as all she did was gain venous access (insert a needle into the vein), take blood and administer intravenous drugs. There were a lot of chronic patients on the ward who needed daily administration of intravenous medications. With repeated, regular injections, finding the veins would become more and more difficult. Galina had been doing this job for over twenty years. There was never a vein, however small and hidden, that she could not get into with a needle. Students had to shadow her in turns. The majority of us took her job lightly. Ignorance made us think then that it was purely a nursing job and most of us hated going around the wards with her. I felt it was a great skill to learn.

Galina once told me, "What is one of the first things you have to do when a very sick patient is brought into the hospital? Get venous access. Getting into the vein is an art. If you cannot see a vein, you should be able to feel one," she said. She let me try once and I failed miserably, although the vein appeared prominent. Galina showed me how it is done a few times, and then I got the hang of it. Whenever I had some free time on the ward, I would go around with her to hone this skill. One day, in the coffee room during a break, Galina announced loudly, "Do you know what a patient told me today? I have been doing this job for twenty years, and it is the first time I heard a patient say this: 'Galina! Why don't you let that coloured chap [pointing to me] do the injection? He does it quicker than you and it hurts less when he does it.'"

Galina said it like a heavyweight boxer who had lost his crown. Her voice, however, echoed the pride and joy of a teacher: a teacher who had succeeded in passing on a great skill to her apprentice. "*Mologets!*" ("Well done!") she added. It made my day.

## The Physics Nightmare

Physics was not my cup of tea. I don't think it was any medical student's cup of tea. However, it had to be learnt as it was a part of our curriculum. Fortunately, we had no practical classes in physics. There were regular lectures and an exam at the end of the year. Professor Petrov himself read the lectures. He was a renowned physicist who had won many accolades for his contributions to science. The lectures were held in the main hall of the university. For fear of failing from lack of attendance, the physics lectures were very well attended. I am not sure if any student understood the majority of what he lectured. Right from the start, the professor got engrossed in the topic. He did not notice, or probably did not mind, students walking in and out of the hall during the lecture. Usually, we could understand the introduction to the topic, but then, as he progressed to deriving complex formulas and writing big equations on the blackboard, he lost us.

One day, I was late for his lecture, and as I walked into the hall, I caught the tail end of a practical demonstration. Professor Petrov was explaining something about waves, assembling some small parts and explaining aloud as he did it. After a few minutes it all made sense when it worked. The topic was radio waves, and he had just assembled a transistor radio after explaining the principle on which it worked and its components. I felt bad that I had missed the beginning, although my friends assured me they had not understood much either, except that he had assembled a radio from scratch and made it work.

At the year-end, there was the biggest hurdle to cross – the physics examination. There was no fixed syllabus. All we got was a printout of the list of topics covered at the lectures and nothing more. We did not even recognise some of it. No one had a clue what to study and how to prepare for this exam. It was humanly impossible to learn enough physics by heart to pass. However, we had to get through the physics exam to carry on with medicine. Until we got to physics, I had done well, keeping a clean sheet and scoring Grade 5s in all the exams. I would consider myself lucky if I managed to scrape through physics.

The physics exam was a surprise. Professor Petrov was the only examiner and had an assistant seated next to him to verify the details of the candidate. He was quick with the questions and made up his mind straight away. If you knew something about the question he asked, or to be more precise, anything at all, you got a pass mark. If you were totally blank, you failed. Judging by the facial expressions of those who went before me, we gauged that he was in a good mood and passed almost everyone. It was not surprising that he was liberal with us, as he never wanted to see the faces of the same medical students again. The professor believed that medics were not cut out to study physics and I don't blame him.

Then it was my turn. I tried to look calm but was trembling inside. The professor asked a few basic questions. I answered most of them but fumbled on a few. He took up my progress card and was about to mark it. I was unsure if he was going to fail me by giving me Grade 2 or give me a passing Grade 3. In the spur of the moment, I decided to push my luck. I plucked up the courage from somewhere and told him, "Professor, please ask me some more." The professor's eyebrows arched up with a look of extreme surprise. Every student before me had been happy to see the back of him, but this one was one asking for more. Curiosity and boredom made him glance through my progress card, and seeing that I had a good record (all Grade 5s till then), he decided to ask me 'one simple question'. It did sound easy, but I was sure it must be tricky as I had asked for it. I realised that if I got it right, the professor would be happy, but getting it wrong guaranteed me a Grade 2 and a repeat meeting with the man.

The professor said, "Young man, keep both your arms straight on the table with your palms facing up." Pointing to my wrists, he said, "There is an artery in your left arm and one in your right arm. They both have the same diameter. Blood is flowing through one at seventy miles per hour and the other at forty miles per hour. In which artery will the pressure be higher? Think for a minute and give me your answer. Don't rush."

While I was supposedly thinking, I heard him say to his assistant, "When Comrade Brezhnev visited America last year, President Nixon presented him with a limousine. I wonder what present Comrade Brezhnev will give President Nixon when he visits Moscow next week?"

At that critical moment, it mattered little to me who gave what to whom, as I had to cough up the correct answer in the next thirty seconds or I was doomed. I probably would have passed, but I had a feeling that the professor was going to fail me for daring to ask for more physics.

"In the artery where the blood is flowing at forty miles per hour," I replied.

There was a look of great surprise on the professor's face as he looked at me with a frown.

"Why?" he asked. "Blood is flowing faster in the other arm."

The word that God put on the tip of my tongue at that crucial time was a name – a name that I had heard the professor say at one of his lectures when he had brought in a system of glass tubes, poured water into one end and talked about speeds, velocities and pressures. After that, he wrote a long formula on the blackboard. I remembered his concluding statement: "This principle was discovered by the Italian scientist Bernoulli."

"Bernoulli's principle," I replied.

It was a eureka moment. The professor's face lit up. As he picked up my progress report once again I heard him tell his assistant, "At least somebody was paying attention at my lecture to the medics," and he wrote in the progress report 'Grade 5 in Physics'. I thanked the professor and left the exam hall happy and with my progress card unblemished. My friends could not believe that any medical student could get a Grade 5 for physics. Neither could I, but miracles happen.

Surgery appealed more to me than medicine. Operations were thrilling. The atmosphere of the operation theatre, the surgery, blood and the concentration required to perform the procedures made one forget time. Quick recovery after surgery and grateful patients were particularly gratifying. A patient with appendicitis would be admitted with excruciating pain, have the surgery, be up and about the next day and go home. In medicine, recovery was slower and there were not too many hands-on procedures. It mostly involved talking. Surgery was mainly hands-on. To become a skilled surgeon, one had to work hard, have sound knowledge, a steady hand and get plenty of practice. It is probably an over-simplistic view, but that was my understanding of surgery then.

Where does one get the chance to practise? Of your own accord you had to go and spend sleepless nights in the hospital with the on-call surgeons as apprentices. Surgical emergencies happened more at night. The on-call surgeon was a resident at the hospital. As there would be no trainees at night, you could get the opportunity to assist the surgeons with all the operations and slowly gain their confidence. Eventually, they would let you start the operation and stitch up the wound at the end of the procedure. When the surgeon became confident in your knowledge and skills, he finally let you do the operation from start to finish.

Emergencies requiring operations are like buses. They do not come regularly and at a particular time. Sometimes, you may not see one for a couple of on-calls, and then you may get three in one night. You had to take your chances and do as many voluntary on-calls as possible to be able to get enough opportunities to learn the trade and hone your surgical skills.

## *Chapter 18*

# SURGERY ON THE SURGEON AND PAEDIATRICS (STUDY OF CHILDREN'S DISEASES)

Anwar, one of our colleagues from Nepal, knew from the start that he was born to become a surgeon. Every evening after class he would go back to the surgery department and stay on call the whole night. He practically lived in the hospital. The surgeons loved him. Even in the middle of the night, they had someone eager to learn the craft and an extra pair of good hands. Gradually, he did most of the emergency operations on his own, until one morning we heard the news that he himself had been operated upon in the middle of the previous night. He had developed a perforated ulcer and had emergency surgery. Often, while on call, you do not get time to have a regular meal. You survive on the biscuits and chocolates the patients shower the wards with for looking after them and seldom get the opportunity to have a hot meal. It was physically demanding and emotionally draining to do frequent and regular on-calls and attend classes the next day. Hence, at times, you pay the price.

Surgeons are different from physicians. The nature of the work must influence what you do. The physicians were a bunch of geeks who talked of nothing other than medicine – "I had an unusual case last week" or "I saw a fascinating case of tuberculosis yesterday", and the list went on. Their whole life revolved around medicine. The surgeons did a more physical job, and were generally sporty, more interesting, had other hobbies and saw more to life than just pills and ills. Having to socialise with physicians was painful, as medicine would be the only topic of discussion. The surgeons were fun. You could have a laugh with them. They never took life too seriously. It is wrong to stereotype doctors, but this was my view. Physicians might disagree. After completing postings in the different specialities of medicine, I noticed that the speciality had a tremendous influence on one's personality. Every paediatrician had a bit of a child in him or her. Psychiatrists were not all mad, but it helped if you were a little.

## Paediatrics – The Study of Children's Diseases

During our posting in paediatrics, I felt that it was probably the career for me. Our teacher, Vera, was a kind and affectionate middle-aged lady. The day started with each one of us seeing the allocated patient in the ward at nine o'clock. Half an hour later, we had to present the case to the teacher in front of the group, which was followed by bedside teaching. After that, we assembled in the small hall next to the children's ward for lectures. Vera read the daily lectures, but on Fridays the Professor of Paediatrics, Svetlana, delivered the lecture. She was a very matter-of-fact person and always had a stern expression on her face, unlike the typical paediatrician with a permanent smile. She reminded us of a school headmistress and thus earned the nickname 'Headmistress'.

Usually, when we took the history and examined a patient in paediatrics, a parent would be present. If not, a nurse would chaperone and help if necessary. I was given a pretty six-year-old blonde girl called Natasha. Her parents were not present, and so a nurse came with me. Natasha was a bright little kid with light-blue eyes and she took a liking to me. She was being treated for severe asthma. After the ward work, we moved next door. Natasha followed me with her doll in hand and sat next to me in the lecture theatre.

While taking attendance, the class teacher noticed her sitting next to me and asked aloud, "Who is that little girl sitting next to you?"

"Natasha. I am six years old," she replied shyly with a smile and carried on doing her doll's hair.

The teacher reciprocated with a smile and started her lecture. Little Natasha kept herself busy with the doll throughout the lecture. After the lecture, she walked out with us, holding my hand. When we reached the ward, she said, "*Do svidaniya, uvigimsa zaftra*" ("Goodbye. See you tomorrow").

My classmates asked, "Is she your daughter?"

I replied, "Not to the best of my knowledge."

Natasha was eagerly waiting for the student doctors to arrive the following day. Her face lit up as soon as she saw me. This ritual continued. Each day we were given a different patient to examine, but little Natasha would be watching and waiting for the class to end. After the ward sessions, when we moved to the lecture hall, she would come running with her doll and sit next to me. She almost became a part of our lecture group. On the Friday, the Headmistress walked into the lecture theatre and saw Natasha sitting next to me. She walked up to Natasha, took her by the hand, and loudly, in a stern voice, ordered, "Little girl! Come with me."

Natasha was frightened and started crying, as she was led back to her bed in the ward. I felt bad. That was our last practical class in paediatrics, and I never saw her again. I hated the professor that day. She could have been kinder to Natasha. After all, she was a little patient!

## *Chapter 19*

# ENT, PATHOLOGY, OPHTHALMOLOGY

### The Hardman of Ear, Nose and Throat (ENT)

We were warned by seniors, "Never miss ENT lectures. Otherwise, you pay the price!" The ENT professor, Peter, was a hard man. He was six-foot-three, strict, spoke little and no one had ever seen him smile. Like most doctors of his generation, the professor had served in the Soviet Army during the war. He had been left partially deaf in the right ear from a land mine that had gone off nearby. Luckily, he'd had a narrow escape and was left with only this slight handicap.

The professor insisted on reading the first three lectures in the anatomy of the ear, nose and throat personally and considered that his right. He made sure that besides the students, all the teachers from the department were also present at these lectures. "The anatomy of the ear, nose and throat is intricate and the foundation of our speciality," was his view. He used to say, "You need to have the anatomy of the ear, nose and throat at your fingertips to pass the exams."

The ENT exams were different from the others and in two parts. Every student had to go to the professor first to be examined. He would quiz you on his favourite subject – the anatomy of the ear, nose and throat. If you failed, you had to go back at a later date to clear that first and most difficult hurdle of the ENT exam referred to as 'Anatomy with Professor Peter'. Only after passing it could you move on to one of his assistants for the rest of your ENT knowledge to be tested.

There was only one occasion when we saw the professor burst out laughing. It was during the ENT exams. A friend of mine, who was a good student, was being examined. Although bright, he was overconfident and had no fear of any exams, let alone the ENT one. He started the exam with Professor Peter and answered most of the questions.

Towards the end, the professor asked him, "How will you treat a patient with a middle-ear infection?"

"Give him a course of antibiotics," replied my friend without any hesitation.

"And what else besides antibiotics?"

The answer he was looking for was ways to keep the middle-ear clean and dry to prevent skin irritation from the secretions of ear infections. In Russian, the term for it was 'toileting' of the ear. My friend lost it and went totally blank. The technical assistant standing behind the professor wanted to help. He cupped his hand around the mouth and whispered the word 'toilet' for the student to read his lips without the professor noticing. My friend read the lip movements correctly but misunderstood 'toilet'. Under pressure, sometimes the brain behaves weirdly.

"Enema!" he replied, "I will give the patient an enema."

That is when the professor burst out laughing and said, "An enema will make the patient sit on the loo, but how is sitting on the toilet going to help the patient's ear infection?"

My embarrassed friend got away with a pass mark.

## The Distinguished Professors of Pathology

The subject of pathology (the science of the causes and effects of diseases) was divided into two – pathologic anatomy and pathologic physiology.

Our group was lucky to have the most distinguished and senior professor in pathologic anatomy in the country – Professor Esipova. She was the Deputy Chief Pathologist of the Soviet Army during the war. The professor took practical classes for only one group, just to keep in touch with the practical side of things. However, she continued reading pathology lectures for the year group once every fortnight. The professor was a big lady and could only move slowly. She had the most piercing eyes, the sharpest of memories and the most sublime observation skills. Her voice was soft, low and monotonous. It hypnotised you, and a few students did occasionally nod off at her lectures.

I liked her lectures as she would often spice them up with fascinating stories of her experiences during the war. The majority of our batch hated the lectures but came to make up the attendance. During one of her lectures, a couple of our classmates decided to break the boredom with a game of chess. They brought a small chessboard, sat in the back row and started the game. The lecture theatre was a modern one with steep rows of seats. Even those in the back row could see and hear the lecturer well. The player who was to make the next move looked down at the board, covering his eyes with the palm of his left hand planted on his forehead. The player who had moved his piece looked down at the professor and pretended to listen. Fifteen minutes into the lecture, the professor abruptly stopped, looked up at the back row, raised her voice and asked, "Is it checkmate in the last row yet?" The entire hall turned round to look at the chess players, whose faces were red with embarrassment. That was their last game of chess in the lectures.

On another occasion, a student Aseeza limped into the professor's lecture fifteen minutes after it had started. She apologised to the professor for being late, saying she had had a fall in the snow on the way and hurt her leg. The professor allowed her to join the lecture. After the lecture, when Aseeza was just about to leave the lecture hall, the professor called her back. Aseeza limped back to the professor. With a sarcastic smile, the professor said, "The next time you have a fall, make sure your story is consistent to make it believable. You limped in on your left leg, but limped out on your right leg." Aseeza was left speechless.

The pathology lectures ended every time with a short question relating to the lecture. We had a couple of minutes to scribble a one word or one-line answer on a piece of paper, put our name and date on it and give it to the professor. The professor would collect the papers, take them away and file them. No one was sure why this was done. We guessed it was feedback to see how well we understood the lectures, or for the department to know who had attended them.

After the final lecture in pathology, Professor Esipova made a surprise announcement: "We have an unwritten rule in the department. The students who attend every lecture and answer the question at the end correctly each time get a pass with distinction automatically. They do not have to sit the pathology exam."

The hall went quiet. "This year, we have one student." There was complete silence. *Who could it be?* Then she announced my name. A thrill went down my spine. It was unbelievable. I would be spared the agony of sitting pathology, one of the most challenging exams in the semester. Everyone congratulated me. Getting a distinction in pathology from Professor Esipova without sitting the exam was one of my greatest achievements in medical school.

Professor Frolov, the Professor of Pathologic Physiology, was a unique person. He was the most liked and admired professor. Professor Frolov was a completely bald, pleasantly plump, vivacious character. His lectures were so interesting and informative that they were always fully attended. They started bang on time and ended on the dot. We could set our watches by the start and finish times of his lectures. We wondered how he managed to do this consistently. One evening, after a late class in biology, we passed the lecture theatre. We could faintly hear the lecturer from outside.

Usually, there were no lectures after five o'clock, so out of curiosity I put my head through the door to see who was lecturing at seven o'clock. It was Professor Frolov, rehearsing his lecture for the following day in front of an empty lecture theatre. I had discovered his secret. '*Poftoreniye Mach Ycheniye*' (repetition is the mother of learning) was his favourite saying.

## Diseases of the Eye – Ophthalmology

Ophthalmology is an exciting speciality. What could be better in life than being able to return eyesight to somebody who has lost it? However, it was too delicate a speciality for me. We had our classes in the premises of the First Medical Institute in the centre of Moscow. Professor Bilyaev, a softly spoken, immaculately dressed gentleman who wore thin-rimmed, high-powered spectacles, was the head of the department. The professor told us we should be proud to work in such a historic building. The French army had occupied Moscow briefly during the war in 1812, when the building was a urology hospital. Napoleon secretly went there every evening to have a bladder wash as he suffered from a parasitic disease called schistosomiasis, which had affected his urinary bladder.

Professor Bilyaev had invented an unusual procedure to treat chronically dry eyes, which can be a very distressing problem. The operation involved diverting one of the salivary glands (the glands that produce saliva in the mouth) to the lacrimal glands (glands of the eye that produce tears). It was an effective procedure but he told us of the tragedy of the first man on whom he had performed this operation.

The young patient, who was delighted with the results of surgery, took his beautiful new girlfriend out on her birthday to a restaurant. The waiter handed a copy of the menu to each of them.

His girlfriend studied the menu and said, "Since it is my birthday, I will start with caviar [an expensive exotic dish made from the eggs of fish] and champagne."

She raised her eyes from the menu and looked at her boyfriend. He had tears in his eyes.

She thought the tears were because it was too expensive for him so she took another look at the menu, thought for a moment and said, "I have changed my mind. I will not have caviar and champagne. I will have some Stolichnaya salad [a popular salad made from potatoes and mayonnaise] and a glass of sparkling white wine."

She looked up and saw tears rolling down her boyfriend's cheeks. She got up and stormed out, saying, "You stingy bugger, I don't want to have anything to do with you ever again."

## *Chapter 20*

# THE EXAMINATION SEASON

The term examination period lasted twenty days. We would have four full days of study leave before each exam. It was enough to revise the whole subject if you had paid attention in class and attended the lectures. My friend Shyam and I stuck to a strict routine of studying during this period, as we rarely did any reading during the term. We read throughout the day, taking short breaks for cups of tea. Our third roommate, Fis, was from the part of Ethiopia that later became the separate country of Eritrea. He was lazy, never touched his books and frequently missed lectures under the pretext of being busy with the Eritrean students' association work, but Shyam and I made sure he read for the exams during the study leave. We often locked the door from inside and hid the key to prevent him from going out for a walk and disappearing for the rest of the day. Like a naughty child in detention, he obeyed and never once protested. He knew we were playing this game for his own good.

At midday, we would all take a break together and go to the canteen for a hot meal. By then, our heads felt heavy from the continuous study. The canteen was half a mile away. The refreshing walk in the snow cleared our heads. Hot soup with a freshly cooked meal re-energised us. On returning to the room, we listened to music for a short while before getting back to our books. In the evenings, we cooked a meal and each of us took it in turns. Thanks to the little fridge we had acquired, a cooked meal would last us two evenings. With each one of us cooking once a week, we had homemade meals for almost the entire week. Moreover, we could avoid going to the canteen in the evening when it was dark and cold.

Our menu was limited. It was mostly chicken or fish curry with rice, as we did not know much else. There was no set recipe. We simply added some spice, tomatoes and onions to the meat to make the gravy. Fis had a signature dish – spaghetti with minced meat. Ethiopia was once an Italian colony, and that is how spaghetti came to Ethiopia. With practice, our dishes got tastier. We learnt the minor details of when and how many spices to add and the right amounts. We had to keep an eye on the days when Fis was the chef as he overindulged in chillies. The popular belief was that only Asians enjoyed hot food, but Fis proved us wrong. He added so many chillies that even we found it too difficult to eat.

When Shyam and I went to India on holiday, we would bring back spices and bottled mango and lime pickle. This delicacy was not available in Moscow, and so we used it sparingly. Russian food is rather bland and does not have any hot, spicy dishes. One day, while we were having dinner, Romaan, a Russian friend, walked into our room. He got greedy, seeing the pickle bottle with the picture of ripe yellow mango fruit on the label. Little did he realise how hot and fiery it was and insisted on trying it. Romaan had heard that mango was a sweet and tasty fruit, but he had never seen one in his life. We warned him this was pickled mango and very hot, but he insisted, saying, "If you all can eat it, it should be fine for me too."

Fis purposely gave him a large spoonful. Romaan bravely put all of it into his mouth. For someone who had only known bland food since birth, it was so hot that his eyes nearly popped out and started watering. He swallowed the pickle and ran to the washroom and kept on rinsing his mouth for the next ten minutes. After that, he went back to his room and swallowed a few sugar cubes, and gulped a few glasses of water to calm everything down. That was the last time Romaan came into our room while we were having dinner.

Although lazy, I was certain Fis would become a good doctor. He was kind and caring and started practising medicine early. In fact, too early. He had Ethiopian friends on other courses at the university who visited him frequently. They addressed him as Dr Fis. He enjoyed that and felt proud.

One Sunday morning, Fis appeared unusually busy. I saw him take a packet to our neighbouring room. I did not think much of it and guessed there must be a meeting of Ethiopian students going on there. Ten minutes later, he came rushing back to our room, panicking, and said he needed urgent help. Shyam and I followed him into the neighbouring room, not knowing what was going on. On the bed lay one of Fis's Ethiopian pals. He was all sweaty and shivering, but fully conscious.

"What happened?" I asked Fis.

"My friend has a little problem, so I gave him a penicillin injection," replied a worried Fis.

"Why did you give him the injection?"

"He was complaining of pain when passing urine and told me a few drops of thick yellowish pus was coming out of his penis before the pee. I was certain he had gonorrhoea [a sexually transmitted disease] and gave him an injection of penicillin."

Fis knew penicillin was the treatment for gonorrhoea, as his group had just finished their posting in the Department of Skin and Venereal Diseases. I went back to my room and fetched a paracetamol and an antihistamine tablet, which I kept with me for allergies. I gave it to his friend to swallow and reassured him that all would be fine. I knew it would not do any harm but would, at least, help psychologically.

A few minutes after taking the tablet, the guy told me, "Thank you, brother. I am feeling very much better now," and sat up in bed.

Later, he got up and walked around, and when he felt fine, went back to his hostel. When back in our room, we told Fis off.

"Don't you ever do this again, you f***ing idiot! Your f***ing friend could have died from anaphylactic shock, and you would have had a dead body on your hands. You could have ended up in jail for murder. Do you realise that? Never bring any of your bloody naughty friends into our room," I told him.

"That is why I did not bring him into our room for the injection," replied a guilty Fis, trying to apologise and defend his foolish action, like a little child.

Ignorance is bliss. Looking back today, Fis had some balls to administer a treatment of which he knew very little himself. I did not bother to ask him from where he had got the penicillin, needle and syringe, but told him to make sure his friend went to the STD (sexually transmitted disease) clinic the next day for proper treatment.

# Chapter 21

# BACK HOME ON HOLIDAY

During the summer break in the second year, I decided to go back home on holiday for two reasons. Firstly, I missed my family and secondly, my mother was worried, as in many of the photographs I had sent home she had noticed a lady with long hair standing next to me. She thought I had found myself a girlfriend. I had to reassure her that this was not my girlfriend but my good friend and classmate from Bolivia, Carlos. He had straight, long black hair, but no beard or moustache. She probably believed me when she saw me too with long hair in subsequent photographs. Having long hair and wearing bell-bottom trousers was the fashion at that time, although the older generation did not approve of this trend. I remember one of my friends with long hair and goatee beard arriving late to the biology lecture. The professor stopped the lecture for a moment and said to him in an irritated tone, "Come in. You are late. Are you a boy or a girl?" My friend just smiled and mumbled, "Being the Professor of Biology, I guess you would know the difference." Luckily, the professor did not hear him.

The air tickets to India were not expensive, as we could buy them in Russian roubles. However, the trip would hit my pocket hard as it was customary to get presents for my family and close relatives. Since there were a lot of children among my relatives, I went to the famous toy superstore Detskiye Mir (Children's World) to shop. The store was situated next to the metro station Dzerzhinsky Square. The notorious KGB building was also located on the square. The statue of the first head of the secret police of the USSR, Felix Dzerzhinsky, stood in front of it. This dull, yellow-coloured, ordinary-looking building had only five floors, but there were so many stories about it.

Once, a Russian and an American were arguing about which country had the tallest building. The American said, "The Empire State Building in the USA is the tallest building in the world."

"How many floors does it have?" asked the Russian.

"One hundred and two floors," replied the American.

The Russian smiled and said, "We have a taller building in Moscow in Dzerzhinsky Square."

"How many floors does it have?" asked the American.

"One hundred and five," replied the Russian, "Five floors above the ground and one hundred floors below the ground."

The Detskiye Mir toy superstore had a variety of toys at reasonable prices, and I found something for everyone. The toy that I liked the most was a gun. It was a replica of an AK-47 made in plastic. When you pulled the trigger, it made the sound of a real gun too. I bought it for my nephews, not realising it would fill up most of my suitcase. I had to carry it in my hand luggage. During the security check, I was told I could not carry it in my hand luggage, and the officer put it aside. I was certain that would be the last I saw of the toy gun and was bitterly disappointed, not knowing what to now give to my favourite nephews.

There were no direct flights to the capital of Kerala. I had to fly from Moscow to Delhi. The following morning, I caught another flight to Madras, where there was a wait of two hours. While waiting in the airport lounge, I saw one of the most recognisable faces in the state of Kerala: the veteran communist leader EMS Namboodiripad (known to everyone as EMS). EMS was the chief minister of the first ever democratically elected communist ministry in the world, in Kerala in 1957. I went up to him and introduced myself. He knew my father and started talking to me like a friend he had known for years. I was lucky to sit next to him on the flight.

EMS was accepted by friends and enemies alike as an eminent and entertaining public speaker in spite of a little handicap. He had a slight stammer.

A journalist once asked him, "Comrade EMS, do you always stammer?"

He smiled and replied, "No, only when I speak."

The fifty-minute flight sitting next to Comrade EMS was the most unforgettable one in my life. The warmth, genuineness and sincerity in the man shone through. He was born into a wealthy, upper-caste Brahmin family but donated all his inherited wealth to the Communist Party of India. I made use of the chance to ask him questions about political and social issues in India. EMS's encyclopaedic knowledge and clarity of thought amazed me. He answered every question and enlightened me.

EMS had visited Moscow ten years ago. At that time, he met my friend and newsreader at Moscow Radio, Chandran. Chandran was married to a pretty Russian lady, Ella, and had a beautiful daughter, Karina. During our conversation, EMS asked me how they were all keeping. He thought for a second and said that Karina must be thirteen and a half years old now. He was right. He remembered that she was three and a half years old when he visited Moscow. Ella's mother, Babushka Sasha, lived with them. EMS fondly remembered her and even the names of the traditional Russian dishes she cooked for him.

"Do they still use *'banki'* to treat chest infections in Russia?" EMS asked me. "Not frequently, although I have seen it used," I replied. 'Banki' or fire cupping is an age-old treatment using tiny glass cups shaped like bulbs. Using a flame the cold air in the cups is heated up. The cups are then attached by suction to the back of the patient who is lying on their tummy with cream applied over their back. The hot suction draws blood to the skin, creating a bruise. Simultaneously it is supposed to increase the blood supply to the lungs and help fight the chest infection. Apparently it was a popular treatment during the war when there was a shortage of antibiotics. Today it is considered the grandmothers' effective remedy. "How did you know about banki?" I asked out of curiosity. "I remember Babushka Sasha explaining it to me and I was fascinated." What a memory! While talking to the great man, I never noticed the time go by and suddenly we were landing at Trivandrum.

A little surprise awaited me at the airport. The captain stood outside the cockpit with the toy gun slung over his shoulders. With a smile, he handed it to me saying, "Nice toy, sir. I wouldn't mind getting one myself."

It was great to see my family after two years. A courtesy call to all the relatives is customary in India and I was glad to meet up with everyone, but it was hectic. All Indian families have countless uncles, aunties and cousins. I had to repeat stories about my life in Moscow to everyone, and by the end I was exhausted.

One of my friends expressed a concern, which I will never forget. I told him about the incident of the bottle of milk next to the windowsill freezing when the temperature outside fell below zero degrees. "If that happened, how can one wee when the temperature falls to minus twenty degrees and the heating has broken down in the bathroom from power failure?" He wondered if the stream of urine froze in mid-air so that it had to be broken off like icicles and put it into the toilet. I could not help laughing as I explained that that never happens.

The holiday at home went by quickly. Mum was sure I was wasting away in the cold Moscow weather and over the holiday had prepared all her signature delicacies. Travelling abroad had made me realise how picturesque and beautiful our village of Sasthamkottah was. The sun rising over the lake and its reflection in the blue waters were breathtaking. At night, when there was a gentle breeze, the reflection of the moon in the little ripples of water painted a pretty silver picture. A swim in the lake felt more refreshing now than ever before.

*Chapter 22*

# PROTEST DEMONSTRATION AND A BIRTHDAY CELEBRATION

## Protest Demonstration in Moscow

Before I knew it, I was back to my routine in Moscow. Yusuf from Ethiopia was a good friend who lived next door. He was the coolest guy with a charming personality. Nothing worried him, and he was never in a rush. He was extremely popular with his countrymen as he was affectionate, forever helpful and had a permanent smile on his face. He was the President of the Ethiopian Students' Association in Moscow, and most of the time he would have Ethiopian students from other universities in the USSR coming to see him for advice. One evening, there was a party going on in Yusuf's room when I accidentally dropped in. Many Ethiopians were seated around a fully-laden table and had just started a traditional meal. Yusuf invited me to join them, but I tried to decline politely.

One of Yusuf's friends, a pretty Ethiopian girl, Miss Indale, whom I knew well, pointed to a dish and said, "Hari brother, I bet you have never tried this before. It is a famous Ethiopian dish and very, very yummy. You must try it." I could not resist. Indale took a spoonful and put it into my mouth. It was tasty, but the taste was different from anything I had ever tried before. After I ate it, she explained it was the best quality raw dressed beef. I nearly threw up, but somehow managed to hold back and left the room.

Three weeks after I had tried raw meat for the first and possibly last time, the ruler of Ethiopia, Mengistu Haile Mariam, visited Moscow. He was a friend and ally of the Soviet Union. I asked Yusuf if he was going to meet their leader. Yusuf, a man of a few words, replied with his characteristic innocent broad smile, "Maybe."

On Saturday, Mengistu visited Moscow. I heard in the evening that a group of masked students blocked the main road near our hostel in protest when Mengistu's motorcade was passing by. They were protesting against human rights violations in Ethiopia and demanded freedom for Eritrea. The police cleared the protestors almost immediately, and the motorcade carried on towards the Kremlin. I was shocked to hear in the evening that the leader of the demonstrators, Yusuf, had been arrested, questioned and subsequently let free. There was no mention of the incident in the Moscow television or radio news. When I met Yusuf in the evening and asked him if it was true, he smiled as usual and replied, "Yes," but did not go into the details.

Our posting in general surgery was an hour's drive away from the hostel. A minibus took us to and from the hospital. The next day, a few minutes before we were due to leave the hostel, I looked through my window to see if the minibus had arrived. It had not come, but there was a black Volga car with tinted windows parked outside. I did not think much of it. Ten minutes later, our group was in the minibus. Yusuf was sitting in the back row as usual. A few minutes into our journey, he looked through the rear window and noticed the black car was right behind the minibus, like its shadow. With a smile, he told us, pointing to the rear window, "Look. We are being escorted."

He was right. Midway through our journey, the minibus stopped to pick up a member of staff. Yusuf decided to verify if we were really being followed.

He went to the front of the minibus and told the driver, "Comrade, please stop for a minute. I am feeling sick. I might throw up and I need some fresh air."

He stepped out of the bus. The Volga stopped behind us. As Yusuf got out of the bus, a man got out of the Volga and looked away disinterestedly. When Yusuf got into the bus, his shadow got back into the car. The same car escorted us to the hostel on our way back from the hospital in the evening. On Saturday, Yusuf told us that he was going to have some fun. Fis and he decided to go to Red Square for a stroll. They took the bus to the metro station. The black Volga car was again spotted following the bus. Yusuf and Fis got onto the metro. The two men got into the same compartment and sat about seven metres away. One of them was pretending to read a magazine. When Yusuf and Fis got out in the city centre, the men got out too. On reaching Red Square, Yusuf and Fis started walking up and down the square at a slow pace a couple of times. The men followed. To irritate their followers, Yusuf and Fis walked at a faster pace, and then started slowly jogging up and down the square. At this stage, one of the men lost his patience and stopped them.

He showed them his KGB badge and told Yusuf, "I suggest you stop playing games and go home. If not, you will have to come with us."

Yusuf, with his usual innocent and childlike smile, calmly replied, "Yes, officer," and decided to go back to the hostel.

They were escorted back to the hostel.

The following morning, Yusuf told us he was leaving for Sweden and said his goodbyes. He packed his bags and left the hostel, clutching an airline ticket to Sweden in his hand. The black Volga escorted his taxi to the airport. If Yusuf was sent back to Ethiopia, it meant certain death. We gathered that Amnesty International had intervened and made arrangements for him to be given political asylum in Sweden.

Yusuf sent us a letter from Stockholm, saying that he had been given a large house to stay in and felt lost in it. He preferred his tiny hostel room to the mansion any day and missed us all. Arrangements had been made for him to learn Swedish. Once he mastered the language, he was planning to continue his medical studies in Sweden. That was the last I heard from my good friend Yusuf.

Talking about this incident, I must stress that Moscow was a very safe place. I had travelled alone many times on the last metro train from Moscow city centre to our hostel on the outskirts of Moscow. It was common knowledge that punishment for crimes was harsh and Big Brother was omnipresent, although not obvious. It was this fact that probably made Moscow one of the safest cities in the world at that time. A friend and his wife from New York once visited me. By 8 p.m., he was looking at his watch, saying they would like to go back, as they were staying in a hotel an hour away by metro. He was surprised when I told him to stay as long as they wanted and I could put them back on the metro or get them a taxi to take them to their hotel.

"Is it safe?" he enquired and was surprised to hear me say, "Absolutely."

They said that they would never dare to travel by metro after 9 p.m. in Manhattan.

"Is racism not a problem in the USSR?" my friend inquired. "Not really" I replied. We had students from all over the world, including many countries in Africa. All of us travelled late and often on our own by public transport. I could not remember anybody mentioning that they were ever subject to racist abuse.

"What do you think is the reason for this?" asked my friend.

"Because the state does not tolerate it. Even children are taught that racism is a crime. Angela Davies, the US civil rights campaigner who fought for racial equality, was a well-known figure in the Soviet Union.

News about her struggles was frequently broadcast by the media. When she was imprisoned, the 'free Angela' campaign gained momentum all over the world, and especially in the USSR. Making children and adults understand the evil of racism and making it clear that racism will not be tolerated is probably the reason for it," I replied.

However, I would be lying if I said that racism was non-existent in the USSR. In any society, you are bound to find the good, the bad and the ugly. I remember a conversation at a gathering of the orthopaedic department one Friday evening after work. We'd had a couple of drinks and the discussion drifted to South Africa and their policy of apartheid. The struggle against white supremacy was gaining ground in that country. One of my colleagues, Shenya, a young orthopaedic surgeon who I thought was slightly odd, made a shocking statement. He said, "I will be more than happy to go to South Africa to fight the blacks. I hate black people." I told him he was pathetic and how could he even think that way, let alone say such a thing. He realised that I was offended and told me, "Hari, I did not mean you. You are not black. You are an Indian. I like Indians. You guys are honest, hardworking nice people." I did not speak to him for a long time after that incident as I knew what was in his head.

## Guest at a Birthday Celebration

One evening, a friend and I went to see a movie at the cinema near the hostel. The gentleman sitting next to me was with his wife and started talking to me before the film began. He spoke a few words of English, and told me, "My wife is curious to know whether you two guys are from India."

"Yes," I replied.

He extended his hand and said, "Namaste."

His breath smelt of vodka, but he was not drunk. I shook his hand and hoped the film would begin soon and it would shut him up.

However, he carried on, "My name is Paul, and this is my wife, Tanya. Today is Tanya's birthday. If you don't mind, we would like to invite you home for dinner after the movie."

To avoid further questions and to shut him up, I replied, "Okay."

As the movie started, I noticed Paul and his wife get up and leave. *Good riddance*, I thought to myself and imagined he had gone to finish off his vodka. The movie was disappointing. Italian movies are usually classy, but this was an art film and didn't meet our expectations. It finished at 8.30 p.m., and as we came out of the cinema, Paul was waiting for us at the exit.

"My wife is eagerly waiting for the guests," he said, "Our flat is only a three-minute walk from here."

We had no choice but I felt uneasy about going at night to the house of a person we had just spoken to for a few minutes before the movie and knew nothing about.

Three minutes later we were in front of Paul's flat. Tanya opened the door. Paul and Tanya turned out to be one of the loveliest couples I had ever met. He was a physics professor at the Moscow State University and she a history teacher in a school nearby.

It was a tiny, two-bedroom flat. The table was immaculately laid. Every delicacy one sees typically at the Russian dinner table – Stolichnaya salad, pickled gherkins and onions, smoked fish, pickled mushrooms, cold meats like ham and sausages, sliced ox's tongue and different types of bread and butter – covered the table. Ox tongue slices were a Russian delicacy I had never seen before. There was a choice of baked fish or steak for the main course. A delicious cake baked by Tanya was the dessert.

Judging by the decor of the flat, they were not affluent, but the true warmth in the house made it feel like a home. There is a saying in Russian that goes something like this: 'When you go to a Russian's house, the table is full and the fridge empty, and when you go to an American's house, the fridge is full and the table empty.'

Paul opened a bottle of French champagne to toast the new friends and celebrate Tanya's birthday. Tanya was interested in Indian history and could not believe she had guests from India in her home on her birthday. We discussed everything from India and life in the USSR to world politics, and did not notice how quickly the time went by. Paul presented us with a book he had published on molecular physics. After a great evening, they put us in a taxi and made sure we got home safely.

*Chapter 23*

# SPORTS AND PUBLIC HOLIDAYS IN THE USSR

The Soviet Union prided itself on its sporting achievements. A lot of resources were spent on developing every kind of sport. The increasing medal tally at subsequent Olympic Games was sufficient proof of this.

Although a leading sporting nation, there was no big money to be made in Soviet sports. All their sportsmen and sportswomen were amateurs. One of the orthopaedic surgeons with whom I worked and later became good friends with, Vasili, told me about his son. The boy, a talented swimmer, was in year eight in a special sports school. Vasili and his wife hoped that their son would represent the country in the next Olympics for the 50-metres breaststroke. The school was a boarding school and the kid got only two days off every month to come home. When he came back, he was moody and unusually demanding.

"Why is it so?" I asked.

"Because of the pressure," replied Vasili.

Only the top three in the country for each of the events were chosen for this school. They had to get up at five thirty, and by six they were in the pool. Practice sessions went on until eight. From eight to eight thirty was breakfast time. Then, an hour of lessons, and at ten o'clock the kids were back in the pool for the next training session until noon. Lunch was from twelve to twelve forty-five. From one until two o'clock they had another hour of study, and then at two o'clock the kids were back in the pool until four. After tea, at five o'clock, they had a session of targeted exercises in the gym, followed by games like basketball to increase general fitness. After dinner, at seven o'clock, they had an hour to relax (watching TV or playing board games). This cycle carried on every day, including weekends, and the only days their kid was off the rigid hamster-wheel lifestyle was when he came home.

"What happens if he does not come top of the three in his event, as only one person can represent the country?"

"That is our main worry" Vasili replied. "Then, he will have to go back to regular school and be a normal kid once again. Since he has not had many hours of study, he is bound to lag behind other kids and will have a mountain to climb."

"Your son is training like a professional," I said.

He agreed with a smile and said, "Only we don't call them professionals."

Talent is spotted at a very young age in the USSR and then the state looks after the child. The parents don't have to pay a single kopek. All the child has to do is to stay on top of the game (easier said than done). I felt sorry for the kid. To lighten the mood, my friend shared a joke, which I will never forget.

A delegation of foreign communists visited a Moscow kindergarten. Before they came, the kids were coached by the teachers to answer every question by the visitors in just one sentence, "In the USSR, everything is the best in the world."

The visitors came, inspected the facilities and asked questions.

"Children, do you like your kindergarten?"

"In the USSR, everything is the best in the world!" the kids shouted.

"And what about the food?"

"In the USSR, everything is the best in the world!"

"Do you have nice toys?"

"In the USSR, everything is the best in the world!"

At this point, the smallest boy in the group started crying.

"Misha, why are you crying? What happened?" asked one of the delegates.

"I want to go to the USSR!"

Chess is a sport that requires a sharp mind and an extraordinary memory. It was a popular sport in the USSR and requires special mention. Russians were excellent in chess, with many world champions to their credit. Every institution held regular chess competitions. Sometimes, a champion (grandmaster) would visit our university and play with twenty talented players at the same time. The players would be seated in a row behind small tables with the chessboards. The grandmaster would move from table to table, take a quick look, make his move on the board and go to the next table. I found this amazing. What an exceptional memory and incredible intelligence a grandmaster had to have to play simultaneously with twenty chess players of high standard!

The famous world chess championship final between Anatoly Karpov and Viktor Korchnoi in 1978 was an epic battle that will remain forever in the minds of all chess lovers. The Soviets considered it a battle between two political systems, socialism and capitalism. The young Soviet chess master, Karpov, was the world champion and carried the hopes of the whole nation on his shoulders. His opponent, Korchnoi, was a middle-aged Soviet dissident who had migrated to Switzerland. The match took place in the Philippines and was filled with drama and tension from the start. It was a battle of nerves and many bizarre incidents. The match was closely followed in the whole of the USSR. In the beginning, Karpov led at 5–2. Korchnoi then staged a dramatic comeback, winning the next three games in a row, making it five all. At this stage, the entire Soviet Union was on tenterhooks. The youthful Karpov won the next game, putting a whole nation out of its misery. The Soviet Union saw Karpov's victory as a victory for socialism over capitalism.

## Public Holidays in the USSR

Public holidays in the Soviet Union were different from the rest of the world. The anniversary of the October Revolution was the most important public holiday in the USSR calendar. Although the revolution took place in October, October Revolution Day, funnily enough, is celebrated on 7th November. This was because the new Soviet Government wanted a break from everything old. They changed the old-style Julian calendar to the modern Gregorian calendar and that altered the date of the revolution as well.

On 7th November, thousands of people paraded through Red Square, holding Soviet flags with slogans commemorating Soviet achievements. November was an extremely cold month, but so great was the enthusiasm that people came out onto the streets, braving the weather. The sea of red flowing through Red Square was a feast for the eye. Large posters of Lenin, the architect of the nation, and Marx and Engels, who conceived the communist philosophy, were widely displayed. One face, conspicuous by its absence, was that of Joseph Stalin. Brezhnev and other leaders of the Soviet Communist Party, as well as leaders from different European socialist countries who had come to attend the celebrations, stood on top of the Lenin Mausoleum, waving to the passing crowds. The people's parade was followed by the parade of the Soviet Armed Forces. The latest weaponry of the Soviet Army, including intercontinental missiles, was paraded for the world to see the military might of the USSR.

The most memorable and patriotic celebrations took place in Red Square in 1941. German troops were only twelve miles from Moscow. Their soldiers could faintly see the top of Moscow's buildings through binoculars. Even when the German army was only a stone's throw away, Stalin remained in Moscow and boosted the morale of the soldiers. The marching Soviet troops went directly from Red Square to battle against the advancing German army. With shouts of "For our motherland; for Stalin" the most significant counter-attack in the history of wars began. Hitler's Wehrmacht was not only driven out of the Soviet territory but also pushed back all the way to Berlin, where they finally capitulated.

Victory over Hitler's forces (Victory Day) is celebrated on 9th May. This day is dear to the hearts of all the Soviet people. Over twenty million Soviet lives were lost defending the motherland. There is hardly a family in the Soviet Union who did not lose a loved one in the war. On this day, the younger generation pays tribute to the veterans and all those who lost their lives for the motherland. Movies about the war are shown on television. Exclusive parties and concerts are organised for veterans. The day ends with spectacular fireworks. This day is also a stark reminder to the younger generation of the damage and destruction wars inflict on people's lives.

There were many veterans of the war working in different departments of our university. I remember a little incident that happened at a function organised by the university in May. A celebrated army general was the chief guest of the function. I was seated next to an elderly gentleman who had a lot of medals displayed on his coat. He was a professor in the Department of Nuclear Physics. To my right were two students from the Middle East who were chatting away in Arabic throughout the function.

When the chief guest was about to finish his emotional speech, the student sitting to my right leant over me and asked the professor, "Comrade! Could you tell me who fought whom in this war the major is talking about?"

I replied, "Germany and the USSR."

I saw the most unusual expression on the professor's face. It was a mixture of anger and pity at their ignorance. He did not reply and carried on listening to the speaker, but I noticed his eyes fill up, although he tried hard to suppress his emotion.

Anyone who has been in the USSR during the Victory Day celebrations would have heard the melodious, symbolic Russian song 'Katusha'. Katusha is the Russian pet name for Ekaterina (Kathryn). One of the key weapons the Soviet Union invented and effectively used during the war was a multiple rocket launcher fired from the back of a truck. It could fire four dozen rockets in quick succession, like fireworks. The terrifying whining sound the rockets made before hitting the targets and causing significant damage frightened the enemy. They were nicknamed Stalin's Organ by the German soldiers.

Katusha symbolises a young girl as well as this deadly weapon. The message of the song is Katusha sending greetings to her man fighting on the front line. She asks him to remember her and save the motherland and she would save her love for him.

Christmas was an ordinary day in the USSR. The founder of the nation, Lenin, believed in Karl Marx's saying that 'Religion is the opium of the masses'. There were no functioning churches in the USSR. National holidays were celebrated by youngsters getting together and partying in one another's homes and making merry. Birthdays were family celebrations. Club culture was not prevalent in the USSR.

Vodka was the prefered drink for men and wine for women. The Russians have an inherent stamina for vodka and only drink it neat, as shots. The famous Russian phrase for drinking vodka is '*do dna*' (straight to the bottom). When an American trade delegation visited Russia, they were treated to the original Russian vodka – Stolichnaya. After sampling it, they were asked what they thought about Russia's favourite drink.

The American replied, "It is good, but I don't like the packaging. There is no cork, only a thin metallic cap, which once opened can't be closed again."

The Russian delegate's reply was, "Once opened, why the f*** should you close it again? It should be finished straight away."

There is no denying that alcoholism was a problem in the USSR. There was a funny saying among the Soviets: *Tretyem boogish?* (Will you be the third one?) A bottle of vodka was normally shared between three people. It only cost two roubles and sixty-two kopeks, which was dirt cheap. If three people shared the cost by contributing a rouble each, they could not only buy a bottle but with the remaining thirty-eight kopeks could even get some snacks to go with it.

'Tretyem boogish' was the alcoholics' code to find a third person if there were only two of them. One man would stand outside the supermarket holding the left lapel of his coat with his right hand. The thumb and the little finger went under the lapel and the middle three fingers over it. He would lift and drop his index finger three times when he saw a passer-by. This was the sign language invitation to join as the third party in sharing the bottle. If the passer-by fancied a drink, he could join the company.

It was customary to say a toast before every drink, and most Russians, by repeated toasting, developed it into an art form. I remember an interesting toast proposed by a lady.

She stood up in front of the guests with a glass of wine in her hand and said, "Like all men, my husband likes to have a vodka or two with his friends. One evening, he returned late after meeting up with some old pals and rang the doorbell. I opened the door, and there he was, standing in his birthday suit with only his hat on. The hat was not on his head."

Lifting her glass, she carried on, "Let us drink to the force that held the hat."

The whole room burst into laughter.

The famous Russian writer Sholokhov in his novel *The Fate of a Man* describes the scene when the German army captured Stalingrad and its officers began partying. They ask the guards to fetch one of the captured Russian soldiers. The hero of the novel is brought into the room. The table is sumptuously laid for victory celebrations.

The officer teases the emaciated soldier by handing over a glass of vodka and ordering, "Drink to the German victory."

The soldier refuses.

The officer carries on, "Then drink to your death."

"That I will," says the soldier and drinks the whole glass of vodka.

They offer him some food, and the soldier replies, "Russians never snack after the first glass." He is given a second glass of vodka. The soldier empties it and calmly nibbles a slice of black bread. The German officers are amazed at his alcohol tolerance and courage and decide to spare his life.

In 1977, the Soviet Union celebrated the sixtieth anniversary of the October Revolution. Big celebrations were planned in the cradle of the revolution, Leningrad (today's St Petersburg). I had Russian friends who lived there, and they invited me to Leningrad to celebrate the anniversary with them. Since it was a last-minute decision, I did not have time to apply for a permit to go to Leningrad and decided to go without one. Usually, a visitor was not asked to show the permit unless they got into trouble with the law.

I took the overnight train from Moscow. Friends met me at the station. It was a sunny day, and we walked around the beautiful city that is steeped in history. Peter the Great, who built the city, intended to make it Russia's window into Europe. We visited the Hermitage Museum. It was the old Winter Palace, the former residence of the tsars and now one of the biggest museums in the world, housing collections of beautiful paintings and sculptures by famous Russian and European artists. We spent the afternoon admiring sublime art by the masters and did not realise how quickly the time had passed. It was minus ten degrees Celsius when we went outside. We walked past the Palace Bridge and Peter and Paul Fortress. The fortress was originally built to prevent foreign invaders from entering Leningrad and later it was converted into a prison. This prison once housed famous prisoners like Lenin and writers Dostoyevsky and Gorky.

We walked to the hostel where my friends lived. There was a security guard at the entrance. Since I did not have a permit for Leningrad, I had to find a different route of entry into the hostel. A friend took my bag in with him. He lived on the ground floor and opened the window for me. I got in through that. Luckily, it was dark by then, and nobody noticed me climbing in. My friends had organised a party in the room with music, drinking and dancing, and it went on late into the night.

The following morning, we got up late, had breakfast with a glass of vodka for the road and went out on the streets. As we went out of the hostel, I noticed the elderly doorman looking bewildered and wondering whether he was imagining things, as he had not seen me go into the hostel. He did not stop to ask me how and when I got in as I was deep in conversation with my friend whom the guard knew well.

There was a sea of people walking to the main square of the city. Many carried banners with slogans like 'Forward to Communism' and 'Lenin lives and will live forever'. Others held placards with the faces of past leaders of the communist movement and some of Comrade Brezhnev. Everybody was in a cheerful mood despite the cold. It was minus six degrees outside. I had been warned about the November weather in Leningrad and hence had wrapped myself up in multiple layers of warm clothing and made sure I had my ushanka cap on to protect my ears.

We walked the streets of Leningrad, the cradle of the October Revolution. It was here that the first regiments of the Red Army were formed to defend the gains of the revolution and ensure the old order did not attempt to turn back the wheels of time. Before the revolution the city was called Petrograd, named after Peter the Great, and later renamed Leningrad.

We strolled along the banks of the Neva River, around which the city is built. Stalls were selling hot coffee, tea and snacks by the wayside. We stopped to warm up and then carried on. The historic cruise ship *Aurora* was permanently moored in the Neva River. The gunshot from this ship was the signal that started the October Revolution. The attack on the Winter Palace followed.

The day went by quickly. It was time for me to catch the train back to Moscow. My friends invited me to come back during the White Nights (from late May to early July, when it doesn't get dark at night and twilight merges with daybreak). They told me that the bridge on the Neva River rising and separating in the middle to let the ships pass by during White Nights was a sight worth watching. People are up all night, strolling around the beautifully paved streets and enjoying themselves. I was tempted to go back someday to see the white nights and see more of this beautiful, historic city and its brave people.

Hitler had been confident of capturing the city, to which the Germans laid siege for 900 days, cutting it off from the rest of the USSR. So sure was the Fuhrer of German victory that he planned a victory ball in Hotel Astoria in the city centre and even printed invitation cards for the function. In the end, the grit, steely determination, resilience, will power and patriotism of the people of this great city prevailed. The Soviet Army finally broke the blockade and the Germans were defeated.

Anna Akhmatova, the Russian poet who has been called the greatest female poet in the history of Western culture, was a witness to the siege of Leningrad and wrote her famous poem 'Courage'. Here is my translation.

## 'Courage'

*We know what is at stake,*

*What should be accomplished!*

*The hour for courage has come.*

*If all else fails, with courage we are not unfurnished.*

*What though the dead be crowded, each to each,*

*what though our houses be destroyed? –*

*We will save you, Russian spirit,*

*from servitude in foreign chains.*

*We will keep you alive, great Russia,*

*and pass you on to our sons and heirs*

*free and clean*

*and they in turn to theirs*

*And so forever.*

## *Chapter 24*

# MUSIC AND KARATE

A mutual friend introduced me to Sergei and his wife and they invited me to a New Year's Eve party at their flat. Sergei was an architect and a talented painter. The walls of the flat were decorated with his beautiful paintings and resembled an art gallery. The pair were ardent fans of English rock music. They had a massive collection of music on tapes. English music was not sold in the USSR, but Sergei had connections and managed to get copies of the latest English rock, pop and country music records on bootleg tapes. Their favourite groups were Deep Purple, Led Zeppelin and Pink Floyd. After listening to pop and rock music regularly, I got hooked on it. I was a regular invitee to parties at their house and I got to meet many ordinary Russians of my age from different walks of life and made many good friends. It helped me gain a better understanding of the lives, dreams, frustrations and aspirations of ordinary Russian people. They were simple people who appreciated what they had and believed in a bright future for their country. I always felt at home in the company of my Soviet friends. They were the most welcoming, genuine and sincere people. To the outside world, behind the Iron Curtain was a land full of unhappy, morose people, shops with empty shelves, miles of queues and the complete absence of luxury items.

True, there were shortages of luxury items and occasional queues. Still, instead of being miserable and moaning about it, they learnt to be happy, looking at the positive things in life such as having zero unemployment, free healthcare, housing, education, subsidised holidays and a low crime rate. They were proud people who were happy to be living in one of the superpowers of the world.

An interesting person I met at Sergei's was Kolya. He was a Jew and took great pride in announcing it. Kolya was a smart, knowledgeable, witty man and an interesting conversationalist. While chatting, he tended to invariably drift off into his favourite topic – emigrating from the Soviet Union. One day, he invited me to his flat. We sat down for a drink and were talking when the phone rang. Kolya picked it up, and there was silence at the other end. He said loudly into the phone, "If you are wondering who this is, it is my friend Hari. He is from India, and he is not a Jew," and put down the receiver.

Kolya told me a joke about a pet parrot escaping from its cage. Its owner went straight to the KGB office and said, "I have come to report a missing parrot."

The KGB officer told him, "You could have reported it to the local police station. Why did you have to come to us?"

The guy replied, "I wish to declare in advance that it is an opinionated parrot, and I disagree with all its views."

Although many from the Jewish community occupied top positions in various institutions of the Soviet Union, the majority of them dreamt of emigrating to Israel, USA or Canada. A large number had already emigrated. There was a saying then in the Soviet Union that 'Israel was a fortunate nation. America supplied it with weapons and the Soviet Union with soldiers.'

## Karate Days

Bruce Lee made karate famous through his movie *Enter the Dragon*. Like many young men of my generation, I was keen to learn martial arts. One day, I mentioned this to Sergei.

He said, "Hari, I will put you in touch with the best teacher."

He introduced me to Michail (Misha). Misha was Sergei's colleague at work and taught taekwondo (a form of karate). Taekwondo was his hobby, passion and religion. He was a man of few words, and an air of calmness always surrounded him. I was apprehensive at first, as I didn't know anyone in the class. Misha conducted classes once a week in a hall near the city centre. The journey to the class took an hour by metro and another hour to get back home. However, my desire to learn karate was strong, and I decided it was worth the effort. The initial classes were hard, and I will never forget the first class. We had to work in pairs. As I was new, Misha delegated his assistant Alexei to work with me. He was a big, tall guy. After the stretching exercises, we had to carry our partner on our back while running to the far end of the hall and back. First, Alexei carried me, the lightweight. Then we had to reverse roles. Alexei was way heavier than me. I tried to avoid it for fear of breaking my back and pointed out to him that he was at least thirty kilograms heavier than me. His reply was, "Hari, nobody will ask you how much you weigh on the street. Don't be a sissy and just get on with it." I did it and just about survived. Gradually I got used to the hard training and started enjoying it.

Misha, the gentleman, was a tough taskmaster with rigorous discipline. Once you entered the dojo (training hall) you spoke only when absolutely necessary. It helped to keep you focussed. If you arrived late, the punishment was twenty-five push-ups the first time, and it doubled the next time you were late. Under Misha's watchful eye, I made good progress. Before long, I passed my first grading and got my green belt. Taekwondo made me physically fitter, mentally sharper and gave me a sense of wellbeing. One of my doctor friends, Oleg, also joined Misha's classes and we used to go together for lessons. While doing on-calls in orthopaedics, Oleg and I would use any spare time we got to practise stretching exercises in the duty doctors' room. The half-sized fridge in the room was just the right height to put our legs over and stretch till the muscles ached.

With the onset of summer, Misha moved his classes from the hall into the open air. He found a great space in the woods to have lessons closer to nature and his classes were different each time. After one tiring practice session, he introduced five minutes of meditation, which was unheard of then. It made us feel great and appreciate the effects of meditation on the mind and body. Misha told us that, after years of rigorous training and concentration, one reaches a stage when taekwondo becomes the martial art of the mind more than the body.

His next question surprised me. "Hari, do you believe in reincarnation?"

"I don't particularly, although Hindu religion believes in it," was my reply.

"I do," replied Misha seriously. "The suffering one has to endure in this life is the payback for misdeeds in one's previous life," he said with conviction.

After this enlightening spiritual conversation, I asked him a doubt I had about martial arts. "Taekwondo consists mainly of kicks, punches and blocks. I wondered what a taekwondo expert could do if a judo expert grabbed him, as taekwondo does not teach throws."

Misha replied with a smile, "Come, let me show you."

He invited me to the mat and asked me to grab his taekwondo uniform around the neck. I did it, and in no time I found myself flat on my back. As soon as I got up and stood straight, another effortless throw sent me flying, on to my face this time. I spent most of the next ten minutes in the horizontal position on the mat. Each throw was different, and he executed it so swiftly, but without hurting me. I got the answer to my question. Misha promised that once we perfected taekwondo techniques, he would teach us throws in which we would use our opponent's energy to bring him down. *How clever would that be?* I was wondering how Misha managed to master so many different techniques. A colleague told me that Misha practised many forms of martial arts and took classes in self-defence for the police and the army.

*Chapter 25*

# SHORTAGE OF CONSUMER ITEMS

Soviet citizens dreamt of travelling abroad to see the outside world with their own eyes. The majority of them only saw the outside world through a TV programme called *Travellers' Club*, filmed by a travel correspondent. It was a well-presented programme but certainly no substitute for seeing things with one's own eyes.

In the planned Soviet economy, unfortunately, choice was limited. All the resources of this massive nation were concentrated on developing heavy industry, building the strongest army and becoming the world leader in the space race. As a result, the small-scale industries producing luxury items were neglected, and any luxury items that were made in the USSR (like cosmetics and cognac) were not of the best quality. It is human nature to want what is denied. The youngsters in the country had a craving for Wrangler and Levi jeans, which were not available in the USSR, and considered it 'cool' to wear them. They would pay good money to get such items from people who could obtain them from abroad. The authorities were aware of this. One wonders why the first nation to put a man in space denied such simple pleasures in life for their people. In a world where 'might is right' they were busy building tanks and missiles, but the country could have at least imported the other items if they were not planning to manufacture them. It would have satisfied not only the needs but also the wants of the people and made a big difference to their lives and aspirations.

The shortage of quality luxury goods led to the evolution of a system of trade in society called *blat*. It was based on connections. If someone had access to a shortage item, they would secretly sell it to friends or acquaintances. The favour was to be returned by the other party who had access to something else. It was a kind of 'You scratch my back, and I'll scratch yours' exchange system. As an example, the manager of a canteen would sell through the canteen a proportion of a rare item like caviar that he had received. The rest would be exchanged with someone who worked in a shoe shop that had access to top-class imported women's shoes, which therefore rarely made it to the shop shelf. One can understand why the average citizen had the urge to go to the West, the magical land of milk and honey, where everything was available all the time.

A Russian friend told me a joke that a Western correspondent once asked the Soviet leader Brezhnev: "Comrade, what would you do if you suddenly got the urge and decided to open the borders of the USSR?"

He smiled and replied, "I would climb a tall tree."

"Why," asked the surprised correspondent.

"To avoid the stampede of people rushing out of the USSR."

Patience is a virtue that Russians did have in abundance. Essential items like bread, milk, butter, sugar, flour and meat were cheap and always available in the shops. Sometimes, a batch of shortage items would appear in a nearby store. As soon as it was displayed in the shop windows, an *ocherid* (queue) would form to snap it up. The quantity one could buy was limited, and as soon as the stock sold out, the sale ended. I remember joining a small queue while returning from classes one day and buying a case containing twelve one-litre bottles of Chivas Regal whisky. It was sold at the same price as vodka, which was a real bargain. Russian friends with whom I shared it did not enjoy it as they drank it neat and could never get used to diluting drinks.

They say 'Jokes mirror the realities of society'. Russians made up jokes and passed them around. These jokes highlighted the Russian sense of humour and at the same time showed their cynicism about the negatives in their country. I guess it was also a way to let off some steam over the dining table and have a laugh. American President Ronald Reagan had a hobby of collecting jokes that were commonly told among the Russian people. Here is a favourite.

There was a ten-year delay in the Soviet Union to buy cars, and only one out of seven families in the USSR owned a car. A man put down a deposit for a car on a Tuesday. The dealer registered the deposit and gave him a date to come back in ten years to pay the balance and collect his car.

"In the morning or afternoon?" the man asked.

The surprised dealer asked him, "Ten years from now, will it make any difference?"

"Well, it will for me," the man replied. "The plumber is coming that morning."

During July and August, when the citizens of Scandinavia went abroad on holiday, short-term job opportunities became available in those countries. Many international students from the USSR travelled to Sweden to fill the vacancies, make some money and buy fashionable clothes, vinyl records, cassette recorders and cassettes to bring back with them. The jobs they had to do could be anything. One friend got a job in an ice cream factory. He loved it. Another guy worked in a sausage factory. He was so put off sausages after two weeks of seeing the manufacturing process that he swore never to look at sausages again.

Human relationships change as societies develop. Another friend of mine went to Sweden and got a 'mum' for life. He found a job in a department store in the centre of Stockholm but accommodation in town was prohibitively expensive. His entire earnings would not get him a room near his place of work. He found a place to stay some forty-five minutes away by bus. A nice old lady who reminded him of his mum rented the room. The lady had two grown-up boys who had done well in life. One was a successful banker in America and the other a guitarist in a popular rock band in Canada.

"Do your sons visit you regularly?" he asked the landlady.

"No," she replied. "Every birthday, I get a phone call from my sons, wishing me Happy Birthday and telling me how much they love me. At Christmas, I get a card from them, wishing me a Merry Christmas, with a promise to meet up and spend the next Christmas together. Many Christmases have come and gone, but it never happened," she said, her voice almost choking. "They have their own lives and problems. Where do they have the time for their old mother?"

My friend had to get up early to travel to work. On the first day, he asked the lady if she would mind waking him up at 6 a.m. in case he overslept. She said sure and promptly knocked on his door the next morning at six o'clock. My friend remembered how his mother used to do the same back home to make sure he did not miss college. That evening, on his way back from work, he bought her a bunch of flowers. She was very moved. The following evening, when he returned from work, there was a new alarm clock by his bed and dinner laid out for two. If he were late returning from work, she would eagerly wait for him and only had dinner after he returned. He started calling her Mum, and she called him her son.

Mum bought him a lot of useful presents before he left, as she had worked out by then what he needed most back in Moscow. After returning, he kept in touch with her regularly through letters and telephone. Mum even came over to Moscow to visit him. Genuine human relationships mean a lot more than phone calls, postcards or promises.

## *Chapter 26*

# A TRIP TO GEORGIA AND AZERBAIJAN

The university regularly arranged excursions during the summer holidays to different parts of the Soviet Union. One summer, it was to the republics of Georgia, in the Caucasus, and Azerbaijan, by the sea. It was an excursion by road called 'road train'. I had heard that Georgia was a beautiful part of the country and signed up for it. There were three coaches full of students who were studying in Moscow. The majority were from Poland and other socialist countries. A Polish rock band was part of the group and they brought their instruments with them on the trip. It was a merry crowd, singing songs all along all the way.

The first stop was a small town in Georgia. We were put up in a primary school. A Russian-speaking female guide joined us, along with a smartly dressed young man in a brown suit. The guide explained that every morning we would be going to a different town. The young man spoke good Russian but was a man of few words. When we reached our destination – be it a school, college, factory or museum – he would be the first one getting out of the front coach. He would speak to the people waiting to receive us. Once he had spoken, we would be received like royalty and shown around. Someone mentioned that the young man was the head of the KGB in Tbilisi.

Tbilisi, the capital of Georgia, was a very green and beautiful town. It was blessed with good weather for most of the year and fruits and vegetables grew in abundance. The Georgian people looked different from the Russians. They resembled Asians more, with dark hair and brown skin. Most of the ground floor windows of houses in Tbilisi had iron grilles over them.

"Why do you have iron grilles covering the ground-floor windows?" someone asked the interpreter.

With a smile, she replied, "Because Georgian women are gorgeous and men do not want their women to be stolen."

When we visited a school, crowds of curious children surrounded us. They had only seen foreigners in films. I was with an African friend and an inquisitive little boy asked my friend if he could touch him. "Sure," he replied. The child touched his forearm and then looked at his. fingertip to see if any of the dark colour had stained it.

Another boy asked him, "Are you Pele?" Football was popular in Georgia. They were good at it and were known as the Brazilians of the USSR.

My friend replied, "No, he is my brother."

A little girl who was studying me carefully from a distance came up to me and asked innocently, "Are you Raj Kapoor?"

"No," I replied. "I wish I were! I am his friend."

Our accommodation was in the primary schools as it was school holidays. We were looked after well and treated to delicious local cuisine, which was different from Russian food. They had lots of salads made from locally grown fresh vegetables on their menu. In Moscow, pickled vegetables were more common as weather fit to grow vegetables lasted only a few months. The only thing I disliked about our stay was the toilets. There were ten toilets in the hall in a row with no partitions between them. As it was a school for little children, I guess privacy did not matter much, and it was easy for the teachers to keep an eye on the children. I found answering nature's second call in a group extremely difficult, and my bowels protested.

On the first day, I struggled. The Polish drummer and the guitarist from the band were seated on the toilets further down. They were happily chatting away and farting in between as if it was second nature to them. During the rest of our stay in Tbilisi, I woke up at 5 a.m. to do my business alone while everyone else enjoyed the lie-in up to breakfast.

We had an excursion to the tea factory one day. Georgia was the only place in the Soviet Union where the weather permitted tea to be grown. It was common knowledge that Georgian tea was not of the best quality. We had tea tasting with homemade biscuits. Before leaving, the pleasant, elderly manager of the factory gave us the visitors' book to write our comments. A Ceylonese friend asked her if he could write in English as his Russian was not very good.

"*Koneshno!*" ("Of course!") she replied, and he wrote, 'Ceylonese tea – first-class tea. Indian tea – excellent tea. Georgian tea – also tea.'

Luckily, the manager did not understand a word of English and thanked him for his comments.

The last two days of our stay in Georgia were spent in the capital, Tbilisi. On the first day, we had a city tour starting at Liberty Square in the city centre. We visited a couple of places of historical interest. In the evening, we attended a cultural programme in the town hall. A local group performed Georgian folk dances. A singer from our group sang some popular Russian songs and the concert ended with the Polish band playing for an hour.

While they performed, a pretty young girl approached me and asked, "Speak English?"

"Yes, I do!" I replied.

She introduced herself as Lana. She was sixteen years old and learning English. We talked in a mixture of English and Russian, and before leaving, she asked me if I'd like to meet her again the next afternoon.

"Sure," I replied and told her where I was staying.

She said that she would meet me at the bus stop outside the hostel at 2.30 p.m. Our group had plans to visit some more places of historical interest at two o'clock so I pretended to have a bad headache and excused myself from the trip. At two thirty I walked out of the hostel to the bus stop. Lana was waiting. She told me we could go to Liberty Square, which is a beautiful place. We had to go by bus. Lana told me not to speak and to pretend I was dumb while on the bus, as Georgian men are very possessive and become jealous if they see a Georgian girl with a foreigner. If anyone asked, she would tell them I was her brother and was dumb. That was a perfectly believable explanation going by the looks. Both of us had black hair, and my complexion was only a shade or two darker. We got onto the bus. There was a ticket machine by the driver's cab, but I saw that she paid for two tickets straight to the driver and did not collect the tickets. Some others did the same, although a few put money into the machine. I could not understand this, but a dumb man should not ask why they did that. It was a silent ten-minute bus ride to the square.

After getting off the bus, I asked Lana why she gave the money to the driver and had not put it into the machine.

She replied, "In Tbilisi, we do that to let the driver get rich and be happy."

We walked around the square. Lana was pretty and intelligent too. She was learning English in her spare time and wanted to become a diplomat and travel the world. I learnt a lot about the life and customs in Georgia from her. They reminded me of our traditions and values back in India. A couple of hours went by quickly. We walked towards an ice cream stall. She ordered two softees. The lady gave her one with a chocolate stick in the middle and asked me in Georgian whether I would like one with a chocolate stick too.

Lana answered for me. "Yes, please. My brother is dumb."

There was a look of pity in the lady's eyes as if she meant, "Poor boy."

She put an extra chocolate stick into my softee for my disability. After finishing off the softees, we took the next bus back to the hostel. We got off at my stop and she walked a few steps alongside me. Lana then stopped for a moment, looked around and, when she was sure there was nobody else around, kissed me on my cheek and softly whispered, "I love you. Come back to Georgia."

She also gave me a scrap of paper with her telephone number and told me that when I rang I should talk only if I recognised her voice. If not, I was to hang up. She turned and walked to the bus stop without looking back.

The following day, our road train moved to Baku, the capital of Azerbaijan. We were only there for three days. Baku was hotter and drier than Tbilisi, despite being near the sea. My Syrian pal, Mustafa, and I became friendly with the teacher in charge of our group. Her name was Miss Anna Ahmedova. She was in her late forties and spoke excellent Russian. It is always a pleasure to meet a happy-go-lucky person with a bubbly personality as it rubs off on you. Anna was one such. She adored children and loved her job as a teacher. She spent most of her time in school.

After lunch, we were served watermelon slices that looked pale and lacked any flavour or sweetness. "Can you tell without cutting it if the watermelon is red and sweet inside?" I asked Anna.

"With experience, you can," she replied confidently with a smile and added, "I will show you tomorrow."

The following day, we had some free time in the evening, and she asked my friend and me to go with her to the market, which was just up the road from the hostel. At the market, she went straight to a stall that had a mountain of watermelons in front of it. The little old man behind the mountain greeted her in Azerbaijani, and she reciprocated. Anna tapped on a few watermelons, one after the other, with the middle finger of her right hand while looking away but keeping one ear close to the fruit. It reminded me of Dr Maks attentively listening to a patient's chest while percussing (tapping) it with his finger in the clinic. She finally decided on one and told us that it was the best of the lot. "You get a slightly different tone when you tap one that is red and sweet inside. It must be from the higher sugar content in them," she said with a smile. Upon hearing her, the old vendor frowned and told Anna off in a loud voice in Azerbaijani. She answered softly in their language and it calmed him down. Anna told us, "Uncle was angry that I spoke to you in Russian. He is very particular that Azerbaijanis should only speak to each other in our mother tongue. I explained to him that both of you are foreigners and don't know a word of Azerbaijani, although you look like us."

The old man was happy. Before we left Uncle gave us a complimentary watermelon, with a broad smile that revealed his missing teeth.

Anna lived in a ground-floor apartment around the corner from the market and invited us there to try the watermelon. It was the tiniest one-bedroom flat one could imagine. The room was just big enough for a sofa-bed and a little folding table with three folding chairs. If the chairs were opened, you needed to know how to fly to move around the room. The kitchen was minuscule and the bathroom so small that an obese person could never get in. It was spotlessly clean. There was a little black and white TV on the wall in the corner.

"Welcome to my palace," she said as she sat us down. Anna fetched a cutting board and with a sharp knife cut into the redder-than- red heart of the watermelon. It was the sweetest watermelon I had ever eaten in my life. After that, she served us tea. "Have you heard the Radio Yerevan jokes?" Anna asked us. "No," we replied. Yerevan is the capital of the Republic of Armenia. Questions were put to its radio station and it broadcast funny replies. She entertained us with a number of them, but there was one which I will not forget. A listener asked Radio Yerevan, "Tell me the shortest joke ever." Radio Yerevan replied, "Communism." We chatted for some time and returned to the hostel.

As we walked back to the hostel, Mustafa and I only talked about Anna. What a humble, nice person she was. Anna was not ashamed and had had no hesitation in inviting us to her tiny pad to treat us to sweet watermelon and show us how she lived. Material possessions alone do not bring happiness. She liked children and had been doing the job she loved for years as a teacher. She gave it her all. That was what made Anna happy. Azerbaijan should have been a prosperous state with so much oil and gas in its territory. Yet, here was its honest, hardworking citizen living happily in the tiniest of spaces without complaining or feeling claustrophobic. We thought that she certainly deserved better and could not but help admire her.

## *Chapter 27*

# PART-TIME NEWS READER AT MOSCOW RADIO

One of my senior colleagues had a part-time job at Moscow Radio. The radio station had departments broadcasting news in many languages including my native language, Malayalam. He finished his medical degree and when he left the USSR he offered me the job. I gladly accepted.

A gentleman called Chandran was the chief newsreader for Malayalam. My job was to read the news on Saturdays and Sundays when he was off. Chandran was a gem of a person as well as a very mysterious being. No one knew of his past, and he never spoke of it. He had left India many years before, married in Moscow and settled down there. A friend told me that Chandran was unique, as when people were leaving the Soviet Union, he moved against the tide into the Soviet Union and settled there. Even after I got to know him well, he never spoke of his past. Chandran was the guardian of every Indian student in Moscow and a helper and guide to any visitor from India.

The main advantage of my part-time job at the radio, besides the money, was that there was enough free time to finish my homework and even do some reading. I had to get to the radio station by 8 a.m., translate the news into Malayalam, go to the recording studio at eight thirty and record it. At nine o'clock the recorded news bulletin would be broadcast, and it lasted fifteen minutes. After that, I was free until 3 p.m. but had to remain on site in case there was breaking news requiring immediate broadcasting. There was another useful perk with this job: Moscow Radio had a good café and an excellent restaurant.

One day, while having a cup of coffee with Chandran in the café, I spotted a tall gentleman in the queue for the till. He looked like someone important and had an aura about him. Every passing person greeted him, and he reciprocated with a smile. I wondered who he was. It was unlikely that he was a departmental head at the radio station, as big bosses never came down and queued for coffee. They had it delivered to their offices. Chandran asked me if I recognised the man.

"No," I replied.

"That is Yuri Levitan, the famous Russian newsreader."

On 22$^{nd}$ June 1941, when Nazi Germany launched its attack on the Soviet Union, it was Levitan who addressed the nation: "Attention. Attention. Moscow speaking! Here is an announcement from the Soviet Government. Today, at four o'clock in the morning, without any reason or warning, and without declaring war, the German forces have invaded our country."

His rare and expressive timbre of voice and uplifting manner of presentation caught everyone's attention. As one woman working at the radio station remembers clearly, "In those days, we couldn't afford a radio, but there were loudspeakers mounted on certain streets, and people would flock there at news time to listen to news from the war front read by Levitan."

Levitan's clear and velvety voice irritated Hitler so much that he deemed him 'public enemy number one' and promised that the first thing he would do upon entering Moscow would be to 'hang Levitan by his tongue'. Hitler also put a bounty of a million dollars on Levitan's head. It was a large amount back then. However, history proved that it was not to be. It was humbling to see this great man queueing up for a cup of coffee, just like anyone else, while the current generation of bosses had theirs delivered to their offices.

The news I read in Malayalam was aimed at the audience back home. It was also not particularly exciting. Once again, it was 'A lot about him, a little about the weather and a bit more about the developing countries like India.'

Newspapers in the Soviet Union, like the radio, were fully owned by the state. The two leading papers were *Pravda* (*The Truth*) and *Izvestia* (*The News*). There was not a lot of difference between the two as they both voiced only the views of the state. The Soviets used to sarcastically say about their leading papers, "There is no news in *The Truth* and no truth in *The News*."

During the summer holidays, groups of students went to faraway construction sites to help out and earn some pocket money. It was a working holiday and the wages were good enough to encourage young people to go. The thinking promoted in the USSR was that manual labour is in no way inferior to mental labour. Physical work was paid handsomely to encourage this idea. Certain workers, such as miners, were paid more than the white-collar office workers. Working in construction sites would make young people realise that manual labour is hard but fun too. As I earned my pocket money working at the radio station, I never needed to go to one of these sites, but my friends Carlos and Shyam went with a group to Siberia to help out with the construction of the longest railway track in the world – the Baikal–Amur railway line. The group was put up in tents by the side of the railway track. Every morning, at eight o'clock, a railway wagon would pick up the group and drop them off further down the track where they were needed. The work they had to do could be anything from filling pits with sand to fixing and painting poles. They worked alongside experienced workers who supervised them. It was hard work but fun when done together in the company of friends. At 2.30 p.m., the wagon returned with the 'temporary student workforce'. A cup of hot soup with the Russian favourite 'black bread' would be waiting as starters in the canteen tent. Black rye bread had a peculiar taste. Either you loved it or you hated it. Gradually, the hungry foreign students who hated black bread started appreciating the taste and enjoying it. The evenings at the construction sites were similar to the ones at the Black Sea coast, with plenty of fun and entertainment.

One Saturday in Moscow we had to participate in *subbotnik.* The word *subotha* in Russian means Saturday and subbotnik was voluntary work done on a Saturday. Lenin also used to participate in it. April was the beginning of summer, and it was a good excuse to get out into the fresh air. We were given brooms to sweep away the fallen leaves from the footpath. Others had to fill in holes in the football field next to our hostel with sand, using spades, and make the ground even. It was not a demanding job, but the idea was to participate and take pride in any kind of work, be it physical or mental. Students saw it as a fun morning out in the fresh air with friends, and it usually ended up with beers back in our rooms to celebrate the 'hard work'.

## *Chapter 28*

# ALL ARE EQUAL, BUT SOME ARE MORE EQUAL

It would be wrong to say that everyone was equal in the USSR, even though the ultimate aim of communism was to make everyone in the society equal. I realised this when I went to meet a friend who happened to be visiting the Soviet Union with his father. His father was a senior Communist Party politician from Kerala. I met them at a top hotel where they were being put up. The Russian hosts planned to take him shopping to the superstore, GUM, next to Red Square. He had a Russian limousine, a *Chaika*, which was provided only to VPs, and an official guide at his disposal. I went along with them in the Chaika. The guide took us to the superstore, but the Chaika entered GUM through a small inconspicuous entrance at the back of the building. We were met by a tall, athletic gentleman in a black suit and tie. He greeted us and led us down some steps into a clothes store in the cellar of GUM. There was only one salesman in the shop and no other customers. He showed us a wide variety of clothes of the latest designs and fashion never seen on GUM's shelves. Many of the items were foreign-made. My friend picked up some items. When he asked how much they cost, he was told not to worry, as they would be billed to the room. The bill never arrived.

On another occasion, I got the chance to visit a 'secret' hotel. A senior editor of a popular journal, published in my native language Malayalam, visited the Soviet Union at the invitation of the journalists' association of the USSR. He was a communist and had devoted all his life to the Communist Party of India. He knew my father well, and Dad had asked him to meet me while in Moscow. The editor telephoned me from his hotel, and I agreed to meet up with him.

"Where are you staying?" I enquired.

He said, "The Party Hotel," and handed the phone over to his interpreter to give me directions.

I had not heard of a hotel by that name before. The interpreter told me there are no signs outside the building and gave me the directions. He said it was right next door to the grocery store opposite Taganskaya metro station, and gave me the name of the grocery store.

"Ring the doorbell when you get here, and we will let you in."

The grocery store was easy to locate, but there was no building even vaguely resembling a hotel next to it. I rang the doorbell of the building next to the store, which was an old residential block. The door opened, and a gentleman in a three-piece suit and tie ushered me in. The entrance hall was big, with high ceilings, and elaborately decorated with beautiful chandeliers. There was no reception desk. A couple of other smartly dressed young men in black suits stood there. The look on their faces suggested they were also waiting for somebody.

The man showed me the stairs and said, "Up the stairs and to the fourth room on the left. Mr [X] is expecting you."

He never asked me my name or for any proof of identity. I went up the stairs and walked past the first three rooms. The doors to these rooms were left open. I met Dad's friend in the fourth room. It was a large, tastefully decorated suite with beautiful paintings on the walls. I told him that the hotel looked empty as the doors of the first three rooms were open.

He said, "This is a special hotel where only senior members of the communist parties from around the world are put up when they visit the USSR. You will not find this hotel in any directory. The guests are looked after as VIPs and all their wishes catered to. The custom here is to leave the room open when the resident is out. It is one hundred per cent safe as admission is only by appointment."

Moscow had a group of exclusive shops called *Beryozkas.* These shops sold foreign goods and Soviet goods not found in regular shops. They sold anything from jewellery, watches, chocolates, food items and alcoholic drinks to expensive mink coats. They even had a small section of books. Beryozkas were in discrete locations, had blacked-out windows and did not have a name board. The burly guards standing outside knew whom to let in. These shops were for use by foreign diplomats, news correspondents and others who had hard currency (dollars, pounds or marks). The Soviet currency, the rouble, was not accepted in these shops.

One New Year's Day, I was stuck for ideas about a good present to get for a very dear person – a close friend's grandmother (Babushka). I went into a Beryozka to buy her a tin of black caviar, which was a rare delicacy. It was expensive and never appeared in the ordinary shops. From the moment we were introduced, Babushka took a liking to me and treated me like her grandson. She was just over four feet tall with a twisted spine. The many wrinkles could not hide the graceful face behind them. There was always a smile on her face and a twinkle in her eye when she saw me. However, the sadness deep down in her eyes could not be hidden. A couple of old photographs on the wall that had faded over time revealed what a beautiful woman she had been in her youth. The hard life she'd had after losing her husband, living through the war and bringing up three children in difficult times, was reflected in her eyes. Babushka was from a Jewish family and told me stories from her youth. She used to work in a fish-processing factory near Moscow. They had to work long hours and extremely hard to provide processed fish, which was the primary source of protein for the soldiers.

As the Germans were approaching Moscow, the entire factory was evacuated by ship to the eastern regions of the Soviet Union, where it was safe. The factory workers spent a week on board the vessel.

The daily ration on the ship for each person was two hundred grams of bread and a knob of butter. The only thing they could eat to their hearts' content was caviar. There are two varieties of caviar – black caviar is the roe from the wild sturgeon in the Caspian Sea and the Black Sea, and red caviar is the roe of salmon, trout or cod. Caviar was one of the main items the factory processed. It was expensive and worth its weight in gold. As there were not enough freezers in the ship to store all the caviar, it was free for all. After day three, even looking at caviar made her sick. Since that trip, she told me, she could not stand caviar. However, she appreciated my thought and was grateful for it, and was very pleased I went to see her on New Year's Day.

The following year, I wanted to get Babushka a present she would remember forever. She was an avid reader and once I heard her talk about her favourite Russian poet, Marina Tsvetaeva. I had not heard the name before as Tsvetaeva's poems were not published and sold in the Soviet Union as she disagreed with the political system in the country and voiced it through her poetry. Babushka once told me that Marina Tsvetaeva was worth ten Pushkins. Pushkin is regarded as the greatest Russian poet that ever lived, and many compare him to Shakespeare. I bought a copy of Tsvetaeva's collected works from a Beryozka to present to Babushka when I visited her on New Year's Day.

In winter, it was impossible to find flowers in Moscow. However, there was a place where one could find fresh flowers all year round. It was a private market called Cheryomushkin Market. I went there with my classmate Jima to buy flowers for Babushka, to present them with Tsvetaeva's book for the New Year. Cheryomushkin Market was one of the few private enterprises allowed in the USSR. Only small commodities produced by individuals could be sold there. You could buy many different varieties of homemade cheese, sausages, pickles, fruit and flowers. All the goods sold in the market had to be produced in the USSR. This vast country had seven time zones and different climates. When it was minus twenty degrees Celsius in Moscow, it would be plus twenty-five degrees Celsius in Kazakhstan in the Asian part of the USSR.

In the market, I found the most beautiful bunch of roses I had ever seen – grey roses. It was the first time I had seen a grey rose. The price was ten times more than you would pay for a similar bunch of roses in summer. I decided to buy it when Jima recognised the vendor, and they exchanged greetings. The seller, Vova, was from Tbilisi. They had served together in the Soviet Army. Vova was an engineer by profession but chose to sell flowers for a living instead, as he was able to earn more money than working as an engineer. He had a plot of land in Tbilisi. There was a limit to the area of land one could own so he rented a couple of other plots from friends and cultivated flowers all year round. It was hard work but stress-free, and he could spend time in the fresh air of his garden. Once a week, he would pack two big suitcases with flowers and catch the early morning flight to Moscow. Air travel in the USSR was cheap, and the fares were nearly the same as for trains. Vova would sell the flowers at Cheryomushkin Market. By evening, he would have sold out and taken the return flight to Tbilisi. This grey rose was one he had developed by grafting roses. In summer, he switched to exotic fruit. Vova knew the market well and told me that he never had to take anything back on the return flight. The little bit of private enterprise permitted in the socialist system was keeping an engineer and his family happy by selling flowers.

As I handed over the grey roses together with Tsvetaeva's book, Babushka's face lit up.

"This is the best present I have received in my whole life," she said, and I saw a tear of joy in her eye that then rolled down her cheek. "You have made an old woman very happy," she added with a smile and kissed me, saying, "I will treasure it as long as I live!"

## *Chapter 29*

# LONDON AND PARIS

After saving money, international students from the USSR travelled to Europe on holiday to see the West. My friend Kamal and I saved all our allowance of ninety British pounds given by the Indian Embassy yearly for three years to make a trip to London. Train travel from Moscow to London was cheap as we could buy the ticket in roubles. The journey would take two days. Two hundred and seventy pounds was a tight budget. It was all we had for the week's stay, sightseeing and whatever little shopping we could afford. In Moscow we purchased a lot of tinned fish, meat and buns with a long shelf life to last us for a few days and delay spending the precious English pounds.

The first leg of the train journey was enjoyable, watching the changing scenery as we passed through the countryside of Russia, Byelorussia, Poland and then East Germany. At the East German border, all passengers had to get out of the trains. The compartments were thoroughly searched. We had to walk through a tunnel into West Berlin to continue our journey. It was at the height of the Cold War, and the atmosphere in the station was intimidating. Stiff-faced soldiers with guns were everywhere. They were even positioned on the rooftop. Everyone and everything was being watched, and it was an eerie feeling. After the thorough search, we were let into the tunnel connecting East Berlin to West Berlin. Life seemed normal again once we crossed through the tunnel. We boarded the train on the

West Berlin side and travelled to Amsterdam from where we had to catch another train. After two days of travel by train and having had nothing but tinned food, the sight of tinned sardines made us nauseous. We were hungry and went into a cheap-looking café and ordered a bowl of tomato soup and toast each. It was all we could afford from the menu. After two days of dried tin food, the bowl of soup and toast was a feast.

In London, we stayed at the Indian YMCA. The YMCA provided rooms at discounted rates for students with breakfast and dinner included, which was helpful. From the top of the hop-on buses we saw most places of interest. Unlike Moscow, there was so much variety in the shops and people of all nationalities, faiths and colours. However, life seemed to go on at a much faster pace. Everyone was in a rush. Time was money. By comparison, life in Moscow moved at a very relaxed and leisurely pace.

I was eager to visit Paris and booked myself on a one-day coach trip to Paris. I purchased sandwiches and Coke in London to see me through the day, as I was warned that food was dearer in Paris than London. I needed to save the pennies. On the seat next to me was a retired English professor from Calcutta, India. Indians, in those days, were permitted to carry only a small number of dollars when travelling abroad as the country needed hard currency for vital foreign trade. It was the professor's life ambition to visit the romantic city of Paris. The coach went to Dover and then onto the cross-channel ferry to Calais.

We arrived at Calais early in the morning. The coach stopped at a service station and the driver announced that everyone could get out, stretch their legs and have breakfast but had to be back in the coach in an hour. More than breakfast, what we wanted was the washroom. As the restaurant in the service station looked expensive, we decided to walk a little to see if there were any public toilets nearby. After walking for five minutes, we did not find any and asked an African gentleman who was passing by if there were any public toilets. He pointed to the left and said there was one about a five-minute walk from there. Then he thought for a moment and added, "If

I were you I would not go there. It is in a run-down area where only black people live. If you go there with your bags, you are sure to get mugged."

We were left with no choice other than to walk back to the restaurant, order a cup of coffee and use the restroom there. The coffee was awful, but the bathroom was a blessing. From Calais, we continued on our onward journey. The bus dropped us near the Eiffel Tower. We went up to the second level of the tower and took lots of photographs on my Russian *Zenit* camera. Like all Russian products, it was not the best of cameras, but was very robust, built to last and took reasonably good pictures. In the afternoon, we visited the Palace of Versailles. It was a great place with a large collection of the most beautiful paintings and sculptures. I wished I had more time to spend there. Versailles reminded me of the Winter Palace in Leningrad.

On our return journey, the security officer at Calais looked very surprised when he saw the Moscow seal on my passport. He was curious to find out how I'd ended up in Moscow and what the hell I was doing there, and asked me a lot of questions. I kept the coach waiting for fifteen minutes. On getting back into the coach, the Indian professor asked me why I had been delayed. I told him that the security officer was surprised to see that I had come from Moscow and asked me many questions.

On overhearing this, the elderly American gentleman on the seat to my left looked extremely surprised and asked, "Did you say you live in Moscow?"

"Yes," I replied.

His eyes nearly popped out. He would have been less surprised if I told him I lived on Mars. He turned to his wife and said, "Did you hear that, Jane? This young man lives in Moscow."

"What!" she exclaimed, "In Moscow? I don't believe it!"

They were retired teachers from Washington, travelling around the world.

"Of all the places in the world, why did you go to Moscow?" was his next question. For the next ten minutes, I was quizzed on Moscow. With a smile, the gentleman asked me if wild bears roamed the streets. I replied, "No, only human bears." I heard him tell his wife, "Jane, we must visit Moscow next year. It sounds like an interesting place."

Kamal and I enjoyed the sights of London and shopped with our few remaining pounds. I picked up a few vinyl records by famous rock bands, bought a couple of fashionable shirts on sale, a pair of jeans, a cassette player and a pack of empty cassettes before returning to Moscow. A 'sale' was something unheard of in the USSR. How can you have a sale when only the necessary number of goods are produced? Portable cassette recorders and cassettes had just come out and were getting popular in Moscow. Returning to the carefree, relaxed lifestyle in Moscow after the hectic European trip truly felt like coming home.

## *Chapter 30*

# THE GREAT VYSOTSKY

One evening at Sergei's house, I made a great musical discovery. One of the guests played a bootleg cassette with Russian songs. There was complete silence, and everyone listened attentively. The singer with a gruff voice accompanied himself on acoustic guitar. At first, it sounded strange and I did not like it, but a smile gradually lit up the faces of all the listeners.

"Who is that?" I asked.

"It is Vladimir Vysotsky."

As friends explained the meaning of the songs in detail, they grew on me. After hearing Vysotsky many times, I realised what a genius he was. He was not only an amazing poet but also a brilliant singer-songwriter. Vysotsky was an actor at the Taganka Theatre in Moscow, but writing and singing satirical folk songs was what he was more famous for. He had a very distinct, sweet voice when he spoke, but sang in the characteristic raspy voice, the voice of the proletariat (working class). As many of his songs were anti-establishment, they were not officially released in Russia. Gorbachev, in his autobiography years later, mentioned that his mentor, the KGB chief Andropov, was also a big fan of Vysotsky. He had played Vysotsky's songs when he first invited the young Gorbachev to his house. People crave what is forbidden, and Vysotsky's music was very popular with the younger generation. Although his songs were not officially recorded in the USSR, bootleg tapes of his songs circulated widely, and he had millions of admirers.

Some of the words Vysotsky used in his songs would not be found in any Russian dictionary but would convey a deep meaning, which the listener understood. There is a funny song about the inmates of a psychiatric hospital discussing the Bermuda Triangle while they were watching a documentary about it on TV. The Bermuda Triangle is an area in the Atlantic Ocean where a number of aircraft and ships have disappeared under mysterious circumstances. He describes the feelings of one of the inmates with the words 'Bermuda state of mind'. Vysotsky's sharp observation skills and enormous talent allowed him to write poems about every aspect of life – from alcoholism to animals, from sports to simple pleasures like visiting the circus or simply watching television. Vysotsky and his contemporary Okudzhava were not only gifted poets but talented musicians too. They wrote poetry that touched the soul and, accompanied by acoustic guitar, they recited it to small private audiences. This new genre of music became widely known as 'guitar poetry'.

Vysotsky has been compared by many to Bob Dylan. I am a fan of Dylan, but after listening to a lot of Vysotsky's songs and understanding his music, I was convinced Dylan was no comparison. A Russian friend once told me that if you can appreciate Vysotsky, you understand not only the Russian language but also the Russian spirit. He wrote about the ordinary people in Russian society, their simple joys in life, their dreams and aspirations, as well as writing numerous songs about the war. It is almost impossible to translate his songs without losing a lot of their poetic beauty. Even to this day, while driving back home after a tiring day at work, I sometimes listen to Vysotsky's songs. They still make me laugh, lift up my spirits and make me feel good. I was unable to find English translations of Vysotsky's songs that did them justice. As I knew Russian well and understood the Russian spirit, I could not resist the temptation to translate one of my favourite Vysotsky songs into English.

Many members of Vysotsky's family, like others of that generation, had fought in the Great Patriotic War. It was only natural that war was one of his favourite themes.

This song is dedicated to those who never returned from battle and to those who wait for them. Here is my translation of the lyrics.

## 'He never returned from the battle'

*Why is everything not the same?*

*Nothing has changed.*

*The same blue sky,*

*the same woods, and*

*the same waters;*

*only, he never returned from battle.*

*He was generally quiet,*

*and, at times, sang out of tune.*

*He went on talking about something or the other, and*

*did not let me sleep.*

*He was usually up at the crack of dawn,*

*but yesterday, he never returned from battle.*

*That only emptiness remains is irrelevant;*

*suddenly, I realised there were two of us.*

*For me, the wind put out the fire,*

*when he never returned from battle.*

*Feels like autumn has come out of turn;*

*unknowingly, I shouted out to him,*

*"Hey, pal, chuck us a fag,"*
*And there was no reply.*
*Yesterday, he never returned from battle.*

*Our dead will not forsake us in times of trouble,*
*our fallen will stand guard.*
*The sky reflects in the woods, as in the water,*
*and all the trees are blue.*
*There is enough room for us in the trenches,*
*It is time for me to go back to battle.*
*Now I realise I will have to go it all alone;*
*I feel it is me who did not return from battle.*[1]

([1] 'As long as we remember them, they are alive!')

*Chapter 31*

# DRIVING, PSYCHIATRY AND SKIN AND VENEREAL DISEASES

## Driving Lessons

During the final year of medicine, I decided to take some driving lessons. The agricultural department of the university had two drivers to teach students to drive tractors and other heavy agricultural machinery. Students from other departments could go and learn to drive cars after passing the theory test if the drivers were not busy. The lessons were free. I passed the theory test and registered for the practical classes. A stocky driving instructor with a thick moustache gave me a quick tutorial, and before I knew it, I was behind the wheel. I was apprehensive, as this was my very first time attempt at driving. Luckily, the car was the driving instructor's car, so it had a brake pedal on the passenger's side as well. As I was driving past a stationary bus, the instructor jammed the brakes on suddenly. A lady had got out and walked in front of the bus to cross the road. I had not noticed her.

Lowering the window, he shouted, "You bitch, are you hell-bent on dying under my car?" and without waiting for a reply, asked me to drive on.

The tip the instructor gave me after this incident stuck in my head. He said, "Whenever you pass a stationary vehicle, whether it is a bus or car, always cast your eye under it as well, as you might spot a pair of legs, and the head and body will suddenly appear out of nowhere. It could be a woman or a child." It was very true. At the end of the lesson, he told me that I did very well and asked me to come back in a week for the next lesson.

I eagerly turned up for the second lesson. The driver said, "Sorry, I cannot go on the road today. There is not enough diesel in the tank."

I returned to my room, disappointed. The following week, the same thing happened again, and again I was very disappointed. I asked a friend of mine from the agricultural department why their department did not provide diesel. He smiled and told me that there was enough diesel for the car, but one needed to periodically top up the driver's tank with diesel (vodka) for the vehicle to move. The next time, I took the driver a bottle of 'driver's diesel'. Miraculously, the car started moving and I had a few more lessons.

## Psychiatry Posting

I was worried about my posting in psychiatry. The only psychiatric patient I had heard of (but not seen) until that day was the man who lived across the lake from my house at the foot of the college hill, back home. Stories went around that he used to be chained to his bed if he became violent, or shut in a room if he became abusive. Some days, he would wake up in the middle of the still night and sing aloud and out of tune. We could faintly hear him. At times he was silent for days on end and at other times he would shout, but the words were incoherent. His was the image in my mind of a mentally unsound patient.

Psychiatry classes were held in a hospital in town. The teacher was a pleasant enough man, although the general impression of psychiatrists was that they were all a little odd. He explained that most of the psychiatric illnesses are a state of mind, and society should try and understand patients with mental health issues, just like patients with physical ailments. In olden times, patients used to be tied down when they became violent, but nowadays it was not required, as we had better medicines to control them. A few patients were sitting in the lounge and watching television. The teacher delivered the lecture in the small room adjacent to the ward. After the lecture, we went out of the room and walked towards the exit. A patient was coming in the opposite direction. After passing us, he suddenly turned back, knelt, kissed a male student's bottom and said, "Tasty butt."

We were all shocked. He got up and calmly walked away. The student was embarrassed and later was given the nickname 'Tasty butt'. From that day onwards, we all entered the wards with apprehension and in groups. We also ensured a three hundred and sixty-degree field of vision around us. The teacher explained that mental problems sometimes affect exceptionally talented people. At that time, a brilliant painter was an inpatient in one of the rooms. The teacher, with the painter's permission, took us to the room. The painter took out a stack of charcoal sketches he had completed and showed them to us. After seeing the sketches, we were convinced that a gifted painter sees things in a different light to other people. There was a girl in our class from the group that had finished their posting in psychiatry before us. She was a nice girl, but I suspect nobody would have called her exceptionally beautiful. The painter was smitten by her and made a couple of drawings of her from memory. Not only did we recognise the girl in the drawings, but she also looked much more beautiful than in real life. It was unbelievable. The patient told us that he sees the inner beauty of a person and copies it onto the canvas.

There were a few drawings of landscapes and some of the fellow patients he had come to know in the hospital. Posting in the psychiatry unit was a good experience, but I could not imagine spending my life treating patients with mental health problems.

## Skin and Venereal Diseases (Dermatology and Sexually Transmitted Diseases)

Dermatology was considered an easy speciality. It was coupled with an unusual speciality called venereal diseases (VD), or sexually transmitted diseases (STDs) as it is called today. Besides having lectures and tutorials, we were allowed to sit in on clinics with the specialists. I cannot forget an angry female Skin and VD doctor whose clinic I sat in on. She was nice to me, but I could see she hated the men. When a young male patient came in complaining of yellowish discharge from his private parts, she told him in a stern voice to go into the examination room and undress.

In the examination room, her first question, in an even sterner voice, was, "When were you with the woman?"

"Five days ago," he replied in a hushed and embarrassed voice.

"Pull back the foreskin of your penis," she ordered.

The patient obediently did so. There was some whitish cheesy debris there.

"When did you last wash your dick?" she asked in an angry tone.

The embarrassed patient did not reply. Back in the consultation room, she told me the diagnosis was obvious – STD, gonorrhoea. The doctor ordered some tests and wrote out an antibiotic prescription.

As the patient left the room, I heard her mumble, "These men, they don't have any sense of hygiene and always blame the woman. I am certain nature will punish humanity severely for loose morals someday."

I failed to understand why the doctor was venting her anger on the poor man. Perhaps she had seen too many women who were infected due to contact with careless men who had contracted STDs. However, I felt that was no excuse to take it out on a poor patient. Years later, sadly, the angry lady doctor's prediction and curse came true. A new disease called AIDS arrived on the scene.

We had an interesting visit to a leprosarium (leper colony) in the suburbs of Moscow called Zagorsk. All of us were under the impression that leprosy was a disease found only in Asia and Africa. There was a stigma attached to the condition back home due to the deformities it produced, often disfiguring patients significantly. People used to avoid lepers, although prolonged close contact with someone with untreated leprosy is required for transmission, and it is a treatable disease. However, nobody would employ lepers and they had had no option other than to beg for a living. It was the picture of the disease that I had in my mind. What we saw here was completely different. There was a housing colony built especially for patients with leprosy. The teacher took us to the houses of a couple of patients. They were clean, well maintained and had all the amenities, like TVs and fridges. Some of the patients were taught how to make handicrafts, and they made interesting little souvenirs. There were a few talented painters among them too. Their paintings, along with the souvenirs, were sold to institutions. The money raised was used for the upkeep of the commune. We were introduced to a delightful couple that met in the commune and got married. It was impressive.

"If they are not infectious, why do the lepers have to live in a commune away from normal people?" someone asked the teacher.

He said, "There is still a degree of stigma towards lepers, although it has decreased significantly. Hopefully, leprosy will be considered just another treatable disease soon."

After the visit to the leprosarium, we had a barbecue in the woods nearby. Our teacher had brought all the stuff required for the barbeque on the coach with us. It was a glorious day. While enjoying the barbeque, someone mentioned this was the place where the inmates of the leprosarium came to relax. For a moment, it hit everyone. *Should we carry on with the barbeque here or move away to some distant place?* Clearly we too needed to cleanse our minds of the stigma against the lepers whom we had just seen and appreciated so much. In the end, after reassurance and guarantee from the teacher that no one would contract leprosy, we carried on and enjoyed a great barbeque.

## *Chapter 32*

# OBSTETRICS AND GYNAECOLOGY AND THE RUSSIAN LANGUAGE

### Obstetrics and Gynaecology

I must be honest here. The speciality I disliked the most was obstetrics and gynaecology (OBG). I could never imagine myself spending my entire life working in a ward surrounded by 'women with large tummies'. Most male students disliked this speciality. However, a couple of nurses and lady doctors told me that if they had a problem in this area, they would prefer to see a male gynaecologist. The reason they gave was that male gynaecologists understand women better and would be more sympathetic and kinder to them.

We had the most beautiful teacher called Larissa. Although in her early forties, she had not lost any of the beauty, charm or curves of her teens. I remember one of the girls in our class admiring her and telling us that Larissa was one of the most beautiful women she had ever seen and she wondered how any male could take his eyes off her. No one disagreed.

One Sunday evening, I was at a birthday party of a close friend in town. Everyone had a good time. I had one too many drinks and got very little sleep as we partied late into the night. Larissa had told us that Monday's class was a crucial one and to make sure no one missed it. Despite the hangover, I had to go. The topic that day was abortion. We were taken to an abortion clinic, where the procedure was to be carried out in a small operating theatre.

With fifteen of us in the theatre watching the procedure, it felt very stuffy. The anaesthetised woman was placed on the operation table with her legs apart and fixed to stirrups high up. When the gynaecologist started curetting (scraping) and removing the soft material mixed with blood from inside her, I felt dizzy. I was desperate to leave the room for some fresh air. Larissa, who was explaining the operation to the group, noticed me going pale. She wrapped her arms around me, and helped by Carlos led me out of the operating theatre into the next room.

All the while I was trying to protest, saying, "I am okay. I am okay. I will be fine."

Larissa kept consoling me, "Not to worry! It happens when you see an abortion for the first time!"

How could I tell her I had been up all night, drinking and partying, and that it was possibly from the hangover rather than the sight of the abortion! It was a truly embarrassing moment. They put me on the couch and got me a cold drink and I gradually felt better. I made a firm resolution that day to never stay up too late or drink away the night before an important class or surgery!

## The Russian Language All Over Again

In the final year of medicine, we once again had Russian classes. It was because the exams were mostly vivas, and the authorities did not want anyone to fail because of poor communication skills in Russian. We were not sure what new Russian could be taught to students who had been studying medicine in Russian for five years. The Russian teacher, Irina, was a very experienced, mature, charming lady who understood our problems well and was more like a friend than a teacher to us. She made the classes enjoyable by giving us Russian short stories or an article from a newspaper for homework and said that she would question us on it at the next lesson in two weeks. Nobody ever read it before the next class but Irina never got cross.

One day Irina asked a student who said he had read the homework article what he understood from it. He replied instinctively, "I was reading and reading yesterday evening but not understanding what the f*** it is all about." In conversations with friends, the F word was used frequently, but here it slipped out accidentally. The student blushed with embarrassment. The teacher pretended not to hear and asked him which part of the article he did not understand, and told him the gist of it without any change in her facial expression. We enjoyed Russian classes more this time around as the teacher realised giving us homework was futile. She stopped giving it and made us read short stories by Russian writers like Chekhov and Tolstoy during class and then discussed them at the end of the lessons.

One day, Irina managed to get tickets for our group for a play by Maxim Gorky called *At the Lowest Depths*. It was being performed in the Little Theatre situated next to the Bolshoi Theatre. The average Russian was well-read and Russian literature was of a very high standard, with many world-class writers. Plays by Soviet playwrights were popular in the USSR and tickets to the theatres were sold out many months in advance. Irina somehow managed to buy tickets for the whole group, and we went to see it together. It was an excellent play and we thoroughly enjoyed it, as she had explained the story in a nutshell before it began.

During the interval, Irina told us that the same play was being staged in the Sovremennik (Modern) Theatre, but with a modern twist. The tickets, however, were impossible to get as it was booked at least a year in advance. The Tanzanian ambassador was a friend of Kimaro's. Theatres had a special quota reserved for diplomats and Kimaro got us tickets through the embassy. Irina was thrilled and we went for the same play in the Sovremennik theatre two weeks later. The play presented in a contemporary manner was also brilliant, and it was difficult to decide which version was better.

On Women's Day, 8th March, we decided to give Irina a surprise present. It was a photo album with a few photographs included. One of Irina's favourite plays she made us read was Tolstoy's *After the Ball.* It was a complex play, and we realised how she had put her heart and soul into making us understand it. Carlos, Kimaro and I decided to reward her for that, and we had a photography session in our room. One of us was sitting and attentively reading *After the Ball* under the table lamp. Next to him, on the table, was a mug marked 'coffee'. The clock on the wall was set at midnight. The next photograph was another one of us doing the same but standing up and reading the same book with full concentration. The following picture was the third person reading the same lying down with the clock on the wall showing midnight again and the mug of coffee by the bedside. Then, we changed roles and took more photos of the same but showing emotions of frustration, anger and laughter. When we presented it, Irina thought it was an empty photo album, thanked us and put it aside. We insisted she open it and look inside. She opened the album, saw the photos and burst out laughing. Irina was delighted and told us it was the most thoughtful, imaginative, lovely present and she would remember our group forever.

Time flies when you are having fun. Before we realised it, we had reached the end of a challenging but most exciting course. Although it had started slowly it picked up pace, and here we were on the threshold of our final exams. Passing the exams would give us the right to add two letters after our names and the licence to treat patients. We would have to make life and death decisions, and there would be no margin for error. The more we thought about it, the more frightening it seemed. How could we remember all that we had crammed into our heads over the past six years?

## *Chapter 33*

# THE FINAL EXAMS

But youth has a future. The closer he came to graduation, the more his heart beat. He said to himself: "This is still not life, this is only the preparation for life."

– Nikolai Gogol, *Dead Souls*

We had a lecture from an old student of our university who came back on holiday to Moscow. He had graduated from the medical faculty five years before and was practising as a gynaecologist in a remote part of Ghana in Africa. He told us an exciting story about how he had started with his practice. When he went back to work in Ghana, there were no other specialists, let alone obstetricians and gynaecologists, in the area or for miles around. Quacks delivered babies with the approval of the village chief. When a young, qualified doctor appeared on the scene, there was a lot of apprehension and resistance. A pregnant woman who urgently needed a caesarean to save her and her baby was brought to him. The chief was made aware of the situation. As there was no other option, the chief reluctantly allowed the doctor to go ahead and do the operation, but on one condition. He insisted the doctor first wash his hands in holy water (water from the well blessed by the chief). The young doctor had no choice other than to forget all the asepsis he had learnt, obey and proceed with the operation. He did so with a prayer. As soon as he started the procedure, the electricity went off. The chief provided a kerosene lamp, and the doctor had to do the caesarean in the light from the lamp. The doctor told us he realised that day that there is a God above, as both the mother and child survived. From that day, the chief trusted him and became his admirer and friend. The population began believing he was the new incarnation of God.

The doctor's advice to us was not to worry about the exams. He told us, "Teachers are human beings and were students once too. It is impossible to remember everything written in books. There is only so much the human brain can retain. You can only be asked about the principles and relevant practical questions, which require only common sense to answer. However, the real test will be when you go out into the wide world. Respect and keep your books, and treasure them as they will be your teachers and companions in the future. Never hesitate to look up anything if necessary."

To a medical student or junior doctor today, it would sound absurd and primitive, as all knowledge is at their fingertips. Unfortunately, Google was not available then, and this was the stark reality.

The final exams were no different from our regular yearly exams. It was a strange feeling once they were over – a feeling of immense relief mixed with sadness. Relief because we were all 'doctors' now, and could hold our heads up high. Sadness, as in a few days it would be time to leave our alma mater and disperse in different directions to various corners of the world. There was also a feeling of joy and trepidation: the joy of having realised our dreams and trepidation at having to make critical life and death decisions without the slightest margin for error. That whole week we partied late into the night, and there was hardly anyone without a sore head in the mornings. I remember a conversation with friends when we said we should agree to meet up after ten years. Carlos told me he had a friend in Bolivia who was from the first batch of medical students from our university. When they qualified, the students of his group had made a solemn pledge to meet up in Moscow ten years later and they fixed a date. Guess what happened?

His friend was the only one from the group who turned up for the reunion. Even after hearing this story, our group firmly decided we should meet up someday, but never agreed on a date.

At the weekend, we had the convocation ceremony at the main university building. It was a grand function attended by the teachers and staff members from every department. I received the diploma with distinction, called *Krasnaya diploma*. It was awarded to students who scored Grade 5s in over seventy-five percent of subjects. An interesting fact ought to be mentioned here. All degrees confirmed by universities in the USSR were called diplomas. They never used the term degree. No one knew why. I guess it was just tradition.

That evening, we had a sumptuous banquet. It was wonderful to see all the teachers and staff who helped us get to the finishing line under one roof. They were forever willing to stay back after working hours to help if someone needed it without any reward or extra remuneration. Their kindness will be remembered forever. It was a fitting finale to the most enjoyable degree course 'behind the Iron Curtain'.

The majority of the graduates went back to their own countries. Kimaro went back to do his internship in Tanzania. I had a couple of letters from him. He mentioned how busy the internship programme was in their capital city of Dar es Salaam, but he was enjoying it and learning a lot. Then the letters stopped. All of us tried hard to contact him many times through different sources, but failed. We were worried and feared the worst.

Some of us decided to stay back and do our internship year in Moscow. The internship included four months in medicine, four months in surgery and four months in obstetrics and gynaecology. As fully qualified doctors, we had more responsibilities and hands-on training. The time had come for us to decide which speciality to take up as a career. We could become general practitioners or specialise in a particular branch of medicine. Becoming a specialist was considered cool and glamorous. I enjoyed my posting in orthopaedics, which was a part of surgery. Orthopaedics had the right blend of medicine and surgery. I found fixing broken bones more fun than operating on smelly bowels as a general surgeon. The orthopaedic surgeons, as a group, were a friendlier bunch and taught me to perform all the routine operations. I felt more confident as days went by, and towards the end of this posting, I had made up my mind: orthopaedics was the career for me.

The Olympics was due to be held in Moscow the following year. Staying on in Moscow for one year would give me the chance to study the basics of orthopaedics as well as see the Olympics. I decided to stay on and pursue a Diploma in Orthopaedics.

During this period, an important international development had taken place. The Soviet Union sent its forces into Afghanistan 'at the request of the government in Kabul' to help maintain peace and stability in that country. There was widespread opposition to this in the world. The Soviet media highlighted the good work done by their army in Afghanistan. However, there was no mention of Soviet casualties.

I happened to bump into an old friend, Sasha, who was an engineer. I had not seen him for months. Sasha told me he had been in Afghanistan for six months as a military engineer. What he described surprised me. The time he spent in Afghanistan had been a nightmare. It was extremely dangerous. The mountainous terrain was difficult, and it was practically impossible to differentiate between friend and foe. "All men in Afghanistan have beards, wear turbans and look alike," Sasha said. "They are very polite and friendly people. If you are walking by a field and see an Afghan shepherd with his herd, he smiles and greets you: 'As-salaam Alaikum.' You reciprocate with 'Va-alaikum As-salaam' and carry on, but if you do not watch closely over your shoulder, he could be the one who, at any moment, pulls out an AK-47 rifle from under the bushes and shoots you from behind."

"Does that happen often?" I asked, as I had not heard of casualties in the Moscow papers or news.

Sasha smiled and replied, "You will not believe this, but trust me, planeloads of Soviet soldiers are going to maintain law and order in Afghanistan, and many are returning in coffins. No foreign country, however big and powerful and whatever sophisticated weapons they possess, can ever win against the Afghans in their land."

No wonder they call Afghanistan the Graveyard of Empires. People who have known nothing other than warlords, gang warfare, opium trade and fighting foreign invaders from birth can never be defeated on their own soil. Looking back over the years, I realised how true Sasha's prediction was.

Many years later, I met an Iranian doctor who worked in Kabul during the times the Soviet forces were in Afghanistan. He told me the Soviet forces helped create an atmosphere in Kabul where hospitals and schools could function normally. Most important of all, they encouraged women to play a creative role in society. Women were able to work freely in hospitals and schools. Unfortunately, the conservative forces that came to power in Afghanistan after the Soviet forces left turned back the wheels of time, and the rest is history.

## *Chapter 34*

# ORTHOPAEDIC TRAINING AND MOSCOW OLYMPICS

I started my orthopaedic training at University Hospital 64, but the part I enjoyed most was the six months I spent at the Institute of Orthopaedics (CITO) in Moscow. It was the largest orthopaedic institute in Europe and had separate departments for each sub-speciality. I had the privilege of working with Professor Volkov, the director of the institute, in the Paediatric Orthopaedic Department.

Like most renowned professors, he travelled around the world frequently, attending meetings and lecturing. Dr Ludmila was the second-in-command of the unit and an influential person. She was an excellent surgeon, kind, and she taught me a lot. The list of elective operations in all sub-departments in the institute was finalised and circulated two weeks in advance. Dr Ludmila asked me to look at the lists and let her know if there was any operation in any department that I wanted to participate in. She would ring the head of that department and get permission for me to attend. If Dr Ludmila asked, nobody refused. I remember her ringing Professor Sivash, the pioneer of hip replacements in USSR and Europe, and telling him that she was sending him a guest surgeon who wanted to watch him perform and learn hip replacement surgery.

"Look after him," she added.

"Does he speak any Russian?" the professor asked.

"Yes, better than you," she replied, laughing.

I attended a few of Professor Sivash's life-changing operations. That is where I developed an interest in joint replacement surgery.

During lunch breaks, Dr Ludmila treated us with delicious homemade snacks and cakes. Every lunch break was a treat.

The Moscow Olympics went ahead in July and August 1980, although boycotted by the USA and some other countries. The boycott was a protest against the Soviet intervention in Afghanistan. The Olympics was well organised. I saw a few events live at the Lenin Stadium. Soaking up the Olympic atmosphere and watching events live in the stadium was a good experience. However, I found watching it on the television from the comfort of my room better. When watching fast sports like sprint races and boxing from a distance at the venue, you cannot see the action clearly or from different angles. So you miss a lot of it. Besides, the experts' commentary on TV helps you appreciate it better at home.

I passed the Diploma in Orthopaedics and flew back home from Sheremetyevo International Airport. It was with deep sadness that I left Moscow. Winston Churchill once said, "Russia is a riddle, wrapped in a mystery inside an enigma." To me, Russia was no longer a riddle or mystery or an enigma. I had come to know Russia well, had made so many good friends and had had a fantastic time in Moscow. The Russians appear tough and hard on the outside, but once you come to know them, they are the most simple, affectionate, genuine, helpful and hospitable people.

I took the evening flight to Delhi. I struggled to get a wink of sleep. More than what awaited me the following morning, it was what I was leaving behind that filled my mind. I remembered my interview for admission to Lumumba University held in Delhi all those years ago. I interviewed well, but the last question by a senior member of the panel caught me by surprise: "What will you do if you lose your heart in Moscow?"

As I flew home, I realised I had indeed lost a big piece of my heart in Moscow. A popular soothing Russian song written by Michail Matusovsky called 'Suburban Moscow Nights' softly echoed in my ears.

*Not a rustle in the garden;*
*all has frozen till dawn.*
*If you only you knew how I treasure*
*these beautiful suburban Moscow nights.*

*The stream flows gently,*
*its smooth ripples*
*reflecting the silvery moon,*
*a love song faintly audible from afar,*
*in these quiet Moscow nights.*

*You look at me my dear*
*head bowed and tilted;*
*it is hard to say, but I must say*
*of the feelings that fill my heart.*

*Promise me my dear*
*as dawn approaches*
*and darkness yields to light*
*that you will cherish forever*
*these beautiful suburban Moscow nights*

I remembered what some friends had told me before I set off for the USSR, that I would be brainwashed into becoming a die-hard communist. Brainwashing, in my experience, was a myth. If you ask me whether the years I spent in Moscow made me a communist, the answer is a definite no. However, having lived in the USSR for many years, I can say with conviction that in spite of all the shortcomings and imperfections, if one considers the social set-up in the USSR as a whole without any bias, it was undoubtedly a fairer social system for the majority of the population.

I wondered if I would ever go back to Moscow, the city I had fallen in love with and where I realised my dream of becoming a doctor. *If I do, when will it be? What would Moscow be like then? Would it be a 'communist Moscow' that had made Lenin's dream come true?*

A joke on the subject made me smile. An incident happened during the time of socialism. A vendor brings barrels of the popular Russian soft drink *Kwas* to the pavement and is getting ready to sell it in glasses.

He is approached by an elderly gentleman who asks, "How much does a glass of Kwas cost?"

"Sixty kopeks."

"How much does the Kwas in all the barrels together cost?"

The vendor replies, "One hundred and twenty roubles."

The gentleman buys the whole lot from him, puts up a sign 'Free Kwas' and starts giving it out in glasses for free.

First, the passers-by are surprised. Soon, a long queue forms. Crowds gather. People start swearing and shouting. Some of them try to bypass the queue and make their way to the front. Others object. There is pushing and shoving, and a fight starts. The police arrive and use force to disperse the crowd.

They take the gentleman selling Kwas into custody and start questioning him. "Why did you cause the fights?"

"I swear I did not," he replies.

"You are trading illegally?"

"No, I was giving out the Kwas for free. There are witnesses."

"Then the Kwas must have been stolen."

"No. I bought it all, I have the receipt."

"Okay! We will let you go if you tell us honestly why you did this."

"All right, I will tell you the truth. I am getting old. I will not live to see the dawn of communism. I was eager to find out for myself what life would be like during communism when everything would be free. That is why I conducted this little experiment."

This was believed to be the favourite joke of one of the kingmakers of the Soviet Communist Party and the most influential member of the Politbureau during Brezhnev's time, Mikhail Suslov.

**Brotherly Love**

Sunrise at our village

**Russian roommate Alex in Uniform**

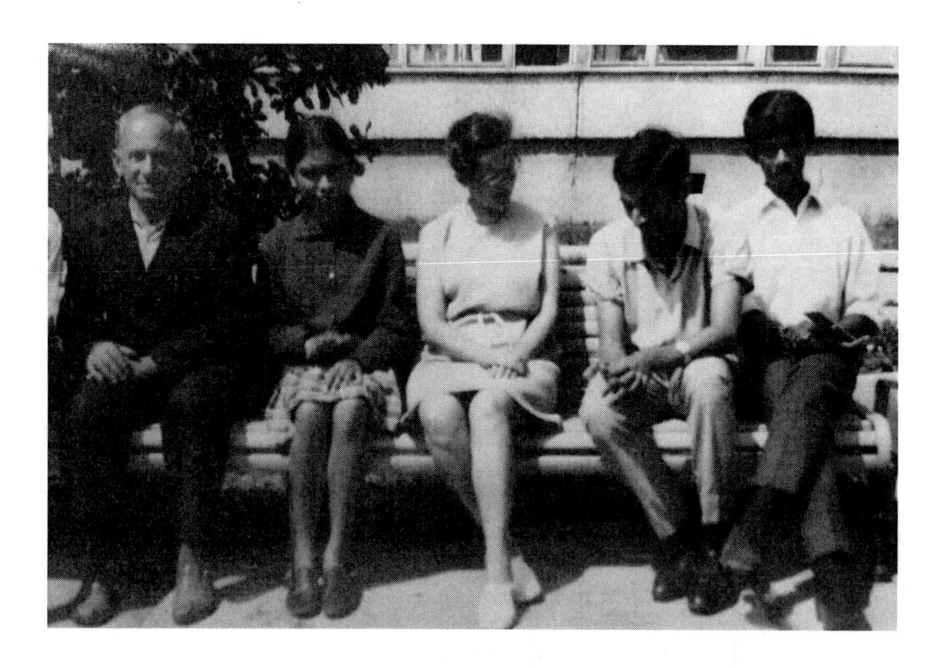

**With Russian Language teachers. Vladimir to the left. Natalya seated next to me**

**Blonde Russian language teacher Victoria**

**First winter holidays. With friend Thomas**

**Our class group outside the hospital in winter**

**Having a good time. Carlos with guitar**
**Hari kneeling to his right. Raga squatting on the left**

**On Subbotnik outside our hostel. Yusuf is holding the broom**

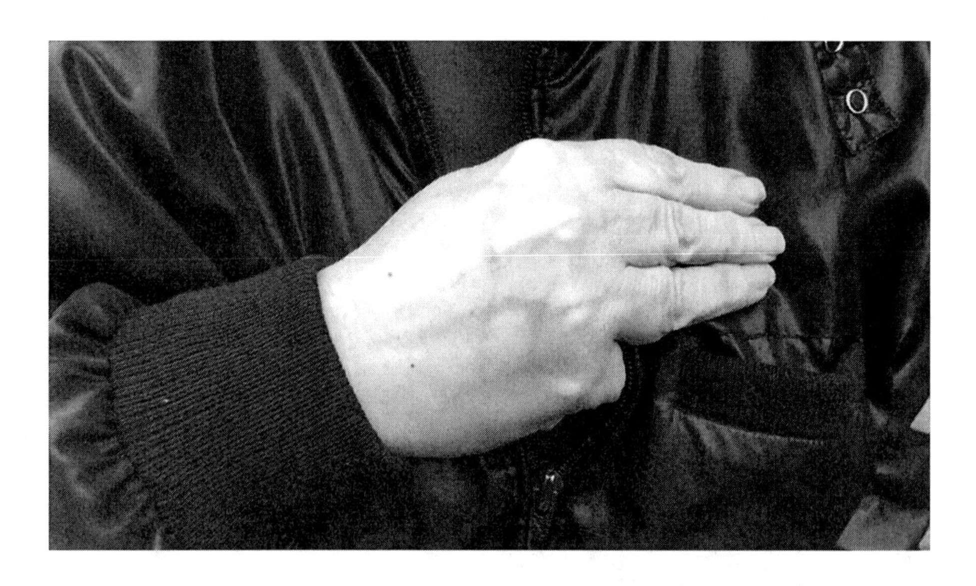

**Will you be the third one?**

**After visiting the Leprasorium. Hari kneeling on the left. Kimaro squatting in the middle**

**After the convocation. Hari to the left. Shyam is next to him**

# *Chapter 35*

# FAREWELL TO MOSCOW

Moscow. How many strains are fusing in that one sound,

for Russian hearts!

What store of riches it imparts.

–*Alexander Pushkin*

I was glad to be reunited with my loving parents and affectionate brothers. After completing further training in orthopaedics in Kerala, I got my first job was as a lecturer in a teaching hospital. Then, I met the most beautiful lady, got married and had two lovely daughters. A few years later, I travelled to the United Kingdom for further training and became a Consultant Orthopaedic Surgeon in Doncaster in South Yorkshire.

People promise to keep in touch when they go their separate ways after university. These promises are broken more often than not, as life is full of surprises, and none of us knows what is in store around the corner for each of us. Thirty-five years after leaving Moscow, I received a worn-out, wrinkled envelope with foreign stamps on it. Judging by the colour of the paper and creases, it had travelled a long way. The letter was addressed to Dr Kumar, Born Surgeon, Doncaster, UK. It looked like it was from a non-English speaker. I have been a 'bone' surgeon for many years, but humility does not allow me to label myself a 'born' surgeon. There are a few Dr Kumars working in different branches of surgery in our hospital. The envelope went to some of them before reaching me. I got a shock when I opened it. It was in Russian and came from Bolivia.

My friend Carlos had heard from someone that a bone specialist who had trained in Moscow was working in Doncaster. He wrote the letter to find out if it was me. I got in touch with him straight away. Carlos had been in contact with our classmate Jima in Moscow. Jima in turn was in touch with many of our group mates. We decided to fulfil the promise made when we finished medical school – to meet up once again. Jima took on the huge task of organising the reunion in Moscow.

The world had changed a lot since our university days. The Soviet Empire had disintegrated and disappeared from the face of the earth. To put things in perspective, it would be worthwhile remembering the events that led to these changes.

The seventies have gone down in the history of the Soviet Union as the 'period of stagnation'. This term stemmed from Khrushchev's prediction in 1961 of reaching communism in twenty years' time. Gorbachev coined the term Era of Stagnation to describe the economic difficulties that developed when Brezhnev ruled the Soviet Union from 1964 to 1982. Looking more closely at the history of the Soviet Union from 1985 to 1991, when it was dissolved, will help us understand the changes that took place. Martin Sixsmith, in his extensively researched book *Russia: A 1,000-year Chronicle of the Wild East*, describes events during this period in great detail. Here I give a summary of political developments in the country after I left Moscow.

In 1979, Gorbachev was appointed as Secretary of the Central Committee of the Communist Party of the Soviet Union. At forty-seven years of age, he was young in comparison to the rest of the Central Committee of the party. Many of the members were well into their seventies. Gorbachev was an energetic and dynamic leader, different from all his predecessors. He was intelligent, knowledgeable and spoke without notes. Like all the

Western leaders, he took his wife, Raisa, along to all social engagements. The Soviet people had never seen the wives or partners of any of the previous Soviet leaders. In 1985, Gorbachev became the General Secretary of the Communist Party and Chairman of the Supreme Soviet. He planned to reform communism to improve the lives of the Soviet people and was not afraid to take bold new steps. Introducing drastic changes suddenly into a society set in its ways was not always successful. Alcoholism was a major problem so Gorbachev decided to put an end to the sale of alcohol, and replace it with mineral water. It backfired as people began to make and drink spurious liquors detrimental to health. The General Secretary was nicknamed 'mineral secretary' and had to abandon the plan.

Gorbachev was eager to cooperate with other superpowers of the world to reduce the arms stockpile and eliminate the threat of a nuclear war. He introduced the terms *perestroika* (restructuring) and *glasnost* (openness). The world leaders held Gorbachev in high regard. The British Prime Minister, Margaret Thatcher, once remarked of him, "I like Mr Gorbachev. We can do business together."

The author Victor Sebestyen in his book *Revolution 1989: The Fall of the Soviet Empire* writes:

> Gorbachev never wanted to abandon communism. He thought it was his destiny to save communism and purify it. In its early days, 'perestroika' meant a process of fairly modest reforms to improve workplace discipline. He launched measures to allow enterprises to show more initiative. He replaced incompetent and corrupt bureaucrats. Gorbachev also introduced some freedom in elections, but elections were still conducted within the one-party system. People could choose which communists would be elected to specific positions. But none of this was revolutionary. He had no intention of abandoning central planning, introducing a market economy or abandoning the communists' monopoly of power. He wanted to 'restructure' everything but without touching the foundations.

Gorbachev writes in his autobiography, 'Our system, supposedly built on scientific premises, a planned, systematic approach as well as scientific management methods, spurred innovation and prevented progress.'

Glasnost was based on the moral principle that 'the public had a right to know'. This was revolutionary in a state that had been run for decades by a governing class paranoid about secrecy. On 26th April 1986 the nuclear reactor at Chernobyl power station exploded, killing several workers and sending up into the atmosphere radioactive clouds that spread far and wide. There was a complete news blackout in the USSR. It was two days before any mention of this disastrous explosion was made on Soviet TV. Gorbachev used the tragedy and the embarrassment it had caused the Kremlin to press home the need for greater transparency and openness.

The state owned all the media and press and the entire distribution network. With perestroika and glasnost, gradually things began to change. Exciting new programmes including debates expressing diverse opinions appeared on TV. Books by Russian authors like Solzhenitsyn and Pasternak, previously banned, started to be published in the Soviet Union.

As time went by, two political groups emerged, putting pressure on Gorbachev's policies. The old school of hardliners wanted him to apply the brakes on perestroika, while the liberals, headed by Boris Yeltsin, called for an acceleration of the radical reforms. Gorbachev's middle course seemed to satisfy no one, and he was trapped in the middle.

Yeltsin became popular as the common man began to see him as one of them. He travelled by public transport and insisted on abolishing the privileges enjoyed by elite party members, despite being one of them. There were 'special shops' where only the elite Communist Party members could shop, but Yeltsin wanted these abolished. He said that there should be no 'special shops' as there were no 'special communists'.

Gorbachev's image on the international stage grew. He helped end the Cold War between the East and West. In 1990, he was awarded the Nobel Peace Prize. However, his popularity at home soon dived.

In 1991, there was a hardline coup against Gorbachev. He had agreed to give more powers to the individual republics of the Soviet Union and proposed a new union treaty known as the Union of Soviet Republics. The word socialist was taken out of the name Union of Soviet Socialist Republics. This treaty would allow the republics full national autonomy, control over their natural resources, including oil, gas and mineral deposits, and a guarantee that republican laws would take precedence over Union legislation. The treaty was to be signed on 20th August 1991, and Gorbachev went on a family holiday to the Crimean resort of Faros on the Black Sea before this date.

Gorbachev's enemies, the hardliners in the party, took advantage of his absence from Moscow and seized the moment to stage a coup. Gorbachev and his family were put under house arrest in the Crimea. Tanks were sent out into the streets of Moscow. A radio broadcast by the state emergency committee formed by the anti-Gorbachev hardliners declared a state of emergency and said it would last for six months. The reason given was that the motherland was in mortal danger. They promised to revive the economy, end the shortages of essential goods and re-establish the USSR as a world superpower. Although tanks surrounded the White House (the Russian parliament), the orders to attack it did not come as the organisers chickened out and did not have the guts to issue orders to shoot. Yeltsin, who was in the parliament house, chose the right moment to seize the initiative. Emerging dramatically from the main entrance of the parliament building, he walked down the steps towards the first tank. He climbed onto it and shook hands with its crew. Standing there, with a smile on his face, Yeltsin, in a firm voice, urged the Russian people to unite against the coup. He proclaimed the army was on the side of the people and appealed to the people to rebuff the reactionary coup. This timely, brave action by Yeltsin galvanised the resistance against the coup. The tanks turned and left, and people began to gather around the parliament building, determined to protect it. Yeltsin appealed to the people to defend freedom and democracy, and they did. The coup failed.

The Russian poet Yevtushenko, who was with Yeltsin in the parliament building, wrote a poem that summed up the feelings of the Russian people at that time. In it he pointed out that the great Russian people had been fooled long enough and they had woken up, ready to defend their liberty and freedom at all costs.

On 22nd August, Gorbachev returned to Moscow. He still believed that the coup against him was defeated because glasnost and perestroika had taught the people to think for themselves. Gorbachev could not believe that the coup had been organised by the very men whom he had personally promoted, believed in and trusted. However, he continued to believe in the Communist Party. He could not accept that it was the core of the Communist Party that organised the coup. Finally, Gorbachev was forced by Yeltsin to sign a decree banning the Communist Party. After seventy-four years in power, the Communist Party of the Soviet Union was dissolved.

Following the coup, all the fifteen republics of the Soviet Union declared their intention to leave the Union. On 25th December 1991 Gorbachev announced the dissolution of the Soviet Union.

At midnight on 31st December 1991 the Soviet hammer and sickle flag was taken down from the Kremlin towers, signalling the end of an era, and replaced by the white, blue and red tricolour Russian flag.

Yeltsin was elected President of the Russian Republic and occupied his seat in the Kremlin, ready to guide Russia into the new era of Western-style democracy, freedom and free-market economy. With help and advice from American economists, he planned to do this in the shortest possible time using 'economic shock therapy'. It aimed to propel Russia from the stagnation of communist central planning to an economy where competition and private enterprise would facilitate a giant leap forward. The reformers were aware it would cause short-term pain but argued that long-term gain would make it all worthwhile. The prices for all but essential goods were freed, and the vendors could set the price. As a result, prices rocketed. Inflation went through the roof. A friend told me this was hardly surprising as some goods that appeared in stores still had price tags in American dollars. Beggars began to appear on the streets in Russia.

Yeltsin viewed the privatisation of state property as a priority and believed it would unleash enterprise and energy and encourage the development of a market economy. However, he was determined it should not be sold to foreign buyers. It was a wise move. Otherwise, Russia would have become the property of wealthy foreigners. However, there were no Russians rich enough to buy the massive industries of the former Soviet Union that were being sold off. Hence, a 'voucher scheme' was introduced by the government. Every citizen was given a voucher worth one thousand roubles (equivalent to sixty US dollars). Each voucher represented a small stake in the country's economy. This move was a total failure, as the few people with inside knowledge, connections, cunning and clout bought up all the vouchers using every means fair and foul. A new class of modern-day tsars with unlimited, unimaginable wealth, known as oligarchs, emerged. They became immensely powerful, craved political power and began influencing the government.

Years of turmoil followed. Russia plunged into crisis. It did not get the help it expected from Western countries. The brutal separatist war in Chechnya made the situation worse. Russia went deeper into crisis.

My Russian friends told me that the nineties were, for them, the most challenging decade ever. People feared for their lives and were uncertain about what was going to happen next. They had many questions: Will there be a war? Who will stop the thugs from plundering and looting? Will we have jobs and will we get paid? Will we be able to put food on our tables?

Will we have water and heating in our homes? Will the hospitals function to look after the sick? Will there be schools for our children to go to?

Russians told me the outside world would never understand what they went through during this period. Everyone saw the historical events leading to the collapse of the Soviet Empire as Pasternak's Dr Zhivago saw the events of the October Revolution – "Freedom dropping from the heavens."

Russia needed a strong leader to pull it out of the crises, solve its problems, restore normalcy to life and regain its lost image in the world as a truly great superpower. Only then could it earn back the respect of the rest of the world. The old saying goes, 'Cometh the hour and cometh the man.' Yeltsin, the leader of Russia, gave his farewell speech to the nation on New Year's Eve, 1999. By then, he had become the joke of the world with his irrational behaviour and alcohol-fuelled antics. Yeltsin admitted he was a failure and apologised to the nation. He introduced his successor, Vladimir Putin, and handed over the reins of power to him.

Putin started his career in the KGB. He once said, "A KGB officer never resigns. You can join, but you can never leave."

His passion for martial arts had taught him the need for discipline and hard work.

Over two decades have gone by since Putin came to power. Today, Russia is once again a stable country and a superpower that is feared by foes and respected by everyone alike.

## *Chapter 36*

# RETURN TO MOSCOW

Russia! Russia! What is the incomprehensible, mysterious force that draws me to you? Why does your mournful song, carried along your whole length and breadth from sea to sea, reach and re-echo incessantly in my ears? What is there in that song? What is it that calls, and sobs and clutches at my heart? What are those sounds that caress me so poignantly, that go straight to my soul and twine about my heart? Russia! What do you want from me? What is that mysterious, hidden bond between us?

– *Nikolai Gogol, Dead Souls*

It was 5 a.m., and the announcement came in Russian: "Ladies and Gentlemen, please remain seated and fasten your seat belts as we are beginning our descent into Moscow's Sheremetyevo Airport." My heart started beating faster. I was anxious and apprehensive. Arriving in Moscow this time felt like Rip Van Winkle's homecoming. There was the excitement of the unknown as Moscow, today, was the capital of a different country. Capitalism had replaced socialism in Russia. I felt goosebumps. The Beatles song 'Back in the USSR' kept ringing in my ears, but the USSR was confined to history. I could not wait to set foot on the land and walk the streets where I had spent the best years of my life, my youth.

The TU134 flight from London landed smoothly. No sooner had the plane touched the ground than all the passengers were on their latest iPhones. The aircraft came to a standstill. Before the 'unfasten seat belt' signs came on, the passengers were up on their feet, opening the overhead racks to pull out the luggage. Everyone was in a rush.

Sheremetyevo had changed beyond recognition. It was a different world from what I had imagined. This was an airport as modern as any other airport in the world. McDonald's, Burger King, Baskin Robbins and countless designer shops were all there. In London's Heathrow airport, before leaving, I saw a Ferrari on display. It was a raffle prize. At Sheremetyevo, too, I spotted a shiny motor from a distance. Curiosity took me closer to have a look. *Was it a Rolls Royce or a Lamborghini?* Russia, today, has one of the largest numbers of billionaires in the world. I was surprised. The car was the latest model of the Skoda. Skoda was made in Czechoslovakia and imported to the USSR during Soviet times. It was considered superior to the only small car made in the USSR, the Moskvitch. Skoda had come a long way with the German carmaker Volkswagen buying the company and giving it a complete makeover, but retaining the name and badge for nostalgic reasons.

Jima had agreed to meet us at the airport. Shyam, with whom I had shared a room for five years in the hostel, was due to fly in from New Delhi. His flight was to land at 10 a.m. I grabbed a coffee and chose a good spot to sit and take in the sights and sounds of today's Sheremetyevo while waiting for Jima. People were more elegantly dressed, especially the women, in comparison to Soviet times. A group of Russian teenage girls sat in the row opposite me. I could not help comparing them with those in my youth in Moscow. In those days, beauty was more natural. There were no beauty pageants in the Soviet Union. After the fall of the USSR, Russian women had access to the latest fashion in clothes, the best beauty salons and the finest makeup in the world. The best features of girls got highlighted, and beauty amplified. The world noticed that Russian women were some of the most beautiful in the world. They began to make their presence felt in the famous catwalks around the world, appeared on the cover of *Vogue* and paired with James in Bond movies. Countless hot Russian women tennis players like Maria Sharapova and Anna Kournikova stole the hearts of millions of tennis fans around the world.

Seated next to me was a priest with his young family. During Soviet times you would not see a priest, as religion was banned. After the collapse of the USSR, religion was back with a vengeance and became big business. It began to play an essential part in people's lives once again. The majority of Russians are Orthodox Christians, but many religions are practised today in Russia.

I had not got a wink of sleep on the flight. The excitement and anticipation of meeting old friends after three and a half decades kept me awake. While at medical school, we could not wait to finish studies, throw away our books and get out into the wide world. The world was our oyster. Looking back today, we sadly realised that those student days were the best days of our lives.

I dozed off and was woken by a tap on my shoulder. I opened my eyes. Standing in front of me was my good old friend Jima. Thirty-five years had only placed the odd wrinkle on his face and changed the colour of his hair from light brown to a distinguished grey. After a hug, we sat down to catch up on the bygone years. It was hard to know where to begin. We exchanged life's summaries in forty-five minutes. Jima told me proudly that he was already a grandfather.

Shyam and Carlos joined us shortly afterwards at the airport. Carlos was a successful ophthalmologist, running his private clinic in La Paz, the capital of Bolivia, in South America. Shyam worked for the health services in the state of Jharkhand in north India and had risen to the position of Chief Medical Officer.

Jima had booked rooms for us in one of the old hostel blocks. It was just what we had wished for. *What could be more nostalgic than staying in a hostel where years ago we had lived life as poor students?* Jima had taken his Masters in Public Health and joined our alma mater as a lecturer. He was now a professor and head of the department. Hence, it was easier to arrange the reunion at our alma mater itself.

We took the airport express train to the city. Jima had purchased a week's season ticket for the entire group to travel by bus or metro in Moscow. He had also made photo identification badges for every one of us. During our student days, Jima had the reputation of a Good Samaritan. He had not changed at all.

The airport express was the most modern train – clean, comfortable and fast. We were loudly chatting and catching up, remembering the good old days. Fellow passengers were wondering who we were, speaking rusty Russian with different accents but understanding each other perfectly well. Before we knew it, we had arrived at the *Belorusskiy vokzal* (Belorussian railway station) in the centre of Moscow. It was one of the main stations from where trains set off to different parts of Russia and many of the former Soviet Republics. We had all been there numerous times. The station and its surrounding areas had changed beyond recognition. In front of the station was a new statue, the statue of a soldier returning home from war. During our student days, statues in Russia were mostly about the Great Patriotic War. The world had changed, but unfortunately wars continued to happen around the world. For the Russians, first it was Afghanistan and then it was Chechnya, followed by Ukraine.

I remembered a moving Russian story that portrayed the feeling of loss and solitude of a mother. An elderly woman steps out of her little cottage every morning and stares down the road at the horizon. A few years before her only son Alyosha had gone down this road to join the forces to fight in the Second World War. Looking down the road became her daily routine, in the hope of seeing him return one day. But he never did. The mother's eyes would fill up, and after a long wait she would retreat into her cottage. Hope that her son would return one day kept her alive and made her carry on with this ritual.

It was time to convert some money into the Russian roubles for use in Moscow. In the olden days, it could be done only in banks. Now one could do it at any one of the many kiosks at the station. The exchange rate was the same as in the banks.

Skyscrapers had sprouted like wild mushrooms all around and dwarfed the old buildings. Today, Moscow is a big concrete jungle. Taxi drivers waited outside the station, coaxing you to get in, just as you would see in any developing country in the world. The majority of the taxi drivers were of non-Russian origin, from the Caucasus region. When the Soviet Union collapsed, a lot of people came over to Moscow from those parts hoping to find a better life. We hired a minivan to take us to the People's Friendship University hostel campus. Jima instructed the driver to take the route through town to show us today's Moscow. It would also jog our memories of the city that we had known inside out in our youth.

The variety and number of vehicles on the road had grown exponentially. We saw every car from Fiats to Ferraris. In the USSR, you could count the different makes of cars on the fingers of one hand.

We travelled down Leninsky Prospect (Avenue). This big street, running from the heart of Moscow towards our university, was unrecognisable because of the tall buildings that had sprung up on either side. Some of the old landmarks, like Havana, the hotel near our hostel, still stood there. It was the only place one could go for a drink and a bite after 8 p.m., as the university canteen and the little café in our hostel would close. Havana had survived the political changes, but no one recognised it until Jima pointed it out. Four miles before our hostels, the tramline cut across Leninsky Prospect. To get to the main building of our university, we had to travel by bus from our hostel up to this point and cross over to catch the tram, which took us straight up to the main university campus.

It was at this junction that one day, on my way to the university, I decided to stop for a few minutes amidst the crowds lining the sides of the streets. They were waiting to greet the American President Richard Nixon's motorcade. People were holding placards, welcoming the president. As I stood in the crowd, I felt a firm tap on my shoulder and turned around. It was a stranger in a grey suit and tie. He asked me if he could have a word with me in private. I moved back out of the crowds with him.

In a firm tone, he asked, "Are you a student?"

"Yes," I replied.

"Where do you study?"

"In Lumumba University. Why?"

"Did your Rector, Comrade Stanis, not tell you that you are not supposed to come to meet President Nixon today?"

"No," I replied.

"He must have forgotten," he said, and added, "I am telling you on his behalf that you should not be here," and he showed me his identity card. It had the man's photograph and the words 'Committee for State Security' (KGB) printed on it. He said this very firmly, and I got the message. I dared not argue and crossed the road to catch the tram to the university. As I waited for the tram, I looked across to see if the man in the grey suit was still there. He was not to be seen. He had dissolved into the handpicked group waiting to wave the flags of the USSR and the USA as President Nixon's motorcade went by. I had to be content with watching President Nixon on television that evening. Looking back, I felt it was the invisible eyes of the state, like the man in the grey suit, who ensured that life in Moscow was absolutely safe. They would become visible only if trouble was anticipated.

We reached the end of Leninsky Prospect and looked for the familiar landmark, the artificial lake and woods before the intersection of Leninsky Prospect and Miklukho-Maklaya (MM) Street. The nine blocks of our hostels stood to the left side of the street. Behind our hostel blocks were woods that backed on to the lake. A short walk through the woods would bring us out to the lake. There was a footpath all around it. In winter, when the lake froze completely, youngsters would be ice-skating on it. Today, the lake had shrunk into a little pond, and its place was taken up by sizeable concrete office blocks.

As we turned into MM Street, I was expecting a feeling of déjà vu. There was none of it. Tall buildings had sprung up in between and around the old hostel blocks, dwarfing them and making them almost invisible. The supermarket building still stood there. It had been extended beyond recognition. Today, it housed a couple of restaurants and a bank. Adjacent to this was a small building with a lovely coffee shop and a Middle Eastern takeaway. The strong aroma of real coffee and freshly baked pizza grabbed your senses from a distance.

## *Chapter 37*

# BACK AT THE ALMA MATER

The Peoples' Friendship University, Moscow, is now known as the Russian University of Peoples' Friendship (RUDN). It adapted well to the new realities after the collapse of the Soviet Union. Today, it is a popular private university with students from over 158 countries studying in its different departments. Over 100,000 students from all around the world have graduated from the university. Among the graduates are the presidents of Guyana and Honduras, doctors, engineers, solicitors, physicists, mathematicians and specialists from every other walk of life working in 170 countries around the globe. The university is very popular with students across the world because of its history and high standards. It provides all courses in both Russian and English languages.

The main university building across the road had not changed but looked a lot more appealing because of the beautiful landscaping and fountains in front of it. On either side of the road, between the hostels and university buildings, were rows of parked cars of all makes, from Mercedes to Micras. There was not a Moskvitch or Lada, the most common cars in the USSR, to be seen. We were put up in the old Block 3. The security to all the buildings was much tighter than in our university days. One could only get in through the security barrier after showing passports or identity cards to the guard at the door and passing through metal detectors. Inside the block was a small corner shop that sold everything you needed for day-to-day living. A small café within the shop served coffee and snacks. We went up to our room on the third floor. It took us back in time. The room looked and smelt the same as in our student days. A lick of paint on the pink walls would have made it more appealing. A small table with two chairs and two small cupboards were the only pieces of furniture. It was not a star accommodation, but we felt a certain warmth about it, and pleasant memories came flooding back. Shyam and I shared a room, as we did all those years ago.

While freshening up to go out for the meal, there was a knock on the door. A scholarly looking gentleman with streaks of grey hair and a pair of golden-rimmed 'John Lennon style' glasses stood there. He looked at us carefully over the rim of his glasses and said, "Hello, Hari and Shyam." We recognised the voice. It was our old pal, Dr Ali from Bahrain. Appearances change with time, but voices seldom do. Ali was travelling with his brother-in-law, Dr Jaffar, a veterinary surgeon. Ali was heading a large family practice in the capital city of Bahrain, Manama. The pair of them had combined our reunion with an extended European holiday.

"Are you going to London, Paris or Rome?" I asked.

"No," replied Ali with his old cheeky smile, "Minsk."

Minsk is the capital city of Byelorussia, the only other country left from the former Soviet Union with remnants of Soviet-style socialism. Ali's logic was that the nostalgic trip would be incomplete without seeing the leftovers of socialism in Europe.

We went out to a new restaurant in the building past the old ninth block. On the way, we passed many cafes. Capitalism had brought a café to every block. Each building was now self-contained. In the biting Moscow winter, one hardly needs to step out of the building, except to go to classes.

At the restaurant, we met up with the rest of our group who had come for the reunion. Each one of us had interesting stories to tell from our lives after medical school. Shyam went back to the state of Bihar in India and started work in the poorly funded government health services of the state. He was surprised by the volume and variety of work and came across infections he had only read about in textbooks. In Moscow, a lumbar puncture (drawing fluid from the spinal canal by inserting a needle in the back) was performed as a major surgical procedure under very strict aseptic conditions. In India, he had to do it at the patient's bedside with minimal aseptic precautions. Furthermore, it had to be done quickly as there would be three more patients waiting to have the same procedure done.

As medical students, we had seen a couple of autopsies done but never performed one ourselves. When Shyam started working in India, he had no choice but to do them. The dictum 'see one, do one and teach one' applied there. At times he had to do three or four autopsies a week, and gradually it became second nature to him.

Ali owned a GP practice in Manama, the capital city of Bahrain, and was doing well. The story of his arrival and departure from the USSR was a strange one. USSR was not listed among the countries a citizen of Bahrain could travel to in the seventies. He took the secret long route by going to Lebanon, a neutral country, first. After staying there for a few days, he travelled to the USSR. The Soviet Union did not put its stamp on arrival on the passports of people coming from such countries. Similarly, after completing the degree, he had to take the long route back. Ali never imagined he would ever be able to come back to Moscow. After arriving back in Bahrain with a medical degree from the USSR, he could not find employment for months. Instead, he was called to the internal affairs ministry and questioned about where he had been all those years. When he was still unable to find a job, Ali wrote to the Emir of Bahrain explaining his plight. The Emir was a kind person. He understood the situation and instructed the ministry to employ Dr Ali. Once Ali got the job, he proved himself and there was no looking back. Today, he is a highly respected senior doctor in Bahrain. Ali has led the team of doctors sent from Bahrain to treat patients arriving for the Haj in Mecca many times. Travelling to the

Russian Federation from Bahrain is not at all a problem today as Bahrain has a good relationship with Russia and has an embassy in Moscow.

Carlos was fortunate to do his post-graduation studies in ophthalmology at one of the leading institutions the world – the Moscow Research Institute of Eye Microsurgery. The renowned Soviet ophthalmic surgeon, academician Professor Fyodorov trained him in techniques like intraocular lens implantations and refractive surgeries. He was the first in South America to introduce these surgeries in the capital of Bolivia – La Paz – and restore vision to thousands of patients. Today, the ophthalmology fraternity of South America holds him in high regard.

It was nice to see Raga, our old friend from Yemen. Yemen, a small country in the Middle East, had been plagued by war for many years. Her voice choked when she told us about the terrible suffering the war between religions factions has inflicted upon her country. Luckily, she lived in a safe area of the capital city of Sanaa. Raga had worked as a general practitioner, retired and was now leading a quiet life, looking after her grandchildren.

Valentine had become a forensic expert with the police department of Moscow. It is a well-paid and highly respected post. During the troubled times after the collapse of the USSR, when there was a shortage of commodities, he never felt the pinch as the supply chain to the police department was seldom affected. Even if there was a shortage of anything, the officers made sure their doctor got it first.

When the Soviet Union collapsed in 1991, and later in 1993 when the Russian parliament building was shelled by the army, the administration anticipated a lot of casualties (a mountain of corpses requiring autopsies, as he put it). Fortunately, fatalities were minimal.

Valentine also explained to us that if during socialism alcoholism had been rampant, following the collapse of the USSR it was replaced by drug addiction. Today drug addiction is a major problem in Russia, just like in the other countries of the capitalist world.

Romaan became a rheumatologist. He did his post-graduation and started working in a Moscow hospital. He wanted to do a doctorate in rheumatology but by then the USSR had collapsed. In the USSR doing the doctorate would have been free, but in the Russian Federation he would have to pay for the course and could not afford it. As the salaries were low he went abroad and worked in Angola for one year. Today, he is the head of rheumatology in one of Moscow's district general hospitals.

Romaan could speak a little English and told us about an embarrassing incident that occurred at an international conference in Edinburgh. There was a gala dinner after the conference. Many of the delegates came to dinner in kilts. Foreign delegates were asked to say a few words. Romaan got up to give a thank you speech in English but was suddenly lost for words. He just about managed to say "Thank you" and sat down, red faced. But the worst was yet to come. A professional group performed Scottish folk dances. The leader of the group then invited the delegates to come out and join them as the names of their countries were called. First it was France. Two French delegates stepped out. They were shown the steps and joined in the next dance. It went well. Then it was the turn of the Germans. They too managed reasonably well. Next, he announced Russia. Romaan was the only Russian delegate and tried to wriggle out of it, saying he did not have a kilt. Besides, he knew full well that he could not dance to save his life. The delegates sitting around him, including many women delegates, started chanting "Go, Romaan – go, go!" He was left with no choice but to step out. He could not remember any of the steps. During the dance, when the group of dancers turned right Romaan turned left and vice versa. It was comical. He felt very embarrassed and left after the dance and skipped the gala dinner.

Galya worked as an emergency doctor with the ambulance services. She was on duty that evening till seven o'clock, and the ambulance dropped her off at the restaurant. She was a private person during our student days and remained so. She said she loved her job and was very happy to meet everyone again after all these years and nothing more.

Tanya worked as a GP in a polyclinic. Our group had met up in her flat on many occasions. Her mother was a good hostess and loved to entertain. Tanya's mum was no more, but being the kind person she was, she told us, "If anyone of you is in Moscow at any time, you are more than welcome to come and stay with me."

Jima mentioned something that many of us felt. Although we were all together for six years, today it felt we had not spent enough time with each other. Then we were all young, energetic and had our own interests, like meeting up with our countrymen, doing sport, art, chasing girls, travelling and so on, and did not spend enough time with friends from our own class group outside working hours.

Jima told us an interesting story about the value of money, after the change of the social system in the country. His in-laws had left a sum of money in the bank for the grandchildren to use on a rainy day. Unfortunately, after the collapse of the USSR, the value of money changed so much that it reached a level where it was not even worth the trip to the bank to collect it.

After specialising in public health, Jima worked for a period in Laos for the World Health Organization. He was surprised by the respect most international experts had for the well-organised and efficient public health system of the USSR. People regretted the loss of such an excellent health care system with the collapse of the Soviet Union. However, they soon realised that it had laid such solid foundations that a new system could be built upon it if necessary with ease.

I mentioned an incident that occurred when I started working as an orthopaedic surgeon in Kerala, which my friends found amusing. A patient who came to consult me owned a little restaurant by the sea about forty miles from my house. Before leaving he asked me if I liked crabmeat. "Yes, why?" I asked. "I just wanted to know," he replied. Three weeks later, he arrived for the follow up with a big bucket in his hand. "Doctor, I brought you some crabmeat," he said. "Do you have a maid?" We had the luxury of a maid then so I called her out. The patient lifted the lid to show her the contents when a big crab jumped out of the bucket. It ran into the house and the screaming maid ran out of the house. The bucket was full of live crabs. The maid was terrified of spiders. She had never seen a crab and thought it was a giant spider. The patient picked the crab up with his bare hands and killed it with a knock at the critical spot, using a little hammer. He then killed and took the meat out of all the crabs in the bucket and explained to the maid how best to cook it. The crab dish was delicious.

The restaurant where we met was owned by one of the Lebanese graduates of our university. The delicious food served was a combination of Mediterranean and Russian. The tradition of toasting with shots of vodka had not changed. Jima had prepared a little surprise. He had arranged for two beautiful belly dancers to entertain us. It would have been unthinkable in Soviet times. Everyone got up and danced on their aching bones and creaky joints, making the first day of the reunion a memorable one.

The following morning, a visit to the medical faculty was planned. We could not wait to see how time had changed things there. The building looked the same, but the security arrangements had become strict. When we were students, there would be an elderly lady or gentleman (keeper) at the door just to keep an eye on everyone and make sure that only students entered the building. Now, the young, burly guard at the door carefully verified our documents. After a thorough search of our bags, we had to pass through the metal detectors to enter the building.

Professor Jima led us into the Russian language class that was in progress. The class stood up, on seeing him. Jima introduced us to the class. The teacher kindly allowed us to join the group, and we sat in for the last few minutes of the lecture. We remembered the days when we had sat on those very same benches, and it brought back many pleasant memories. The teacher told us that they still conduct the 'We Speak Russian' concerts regularly. They remain a popular and eagerly-awaited event in the calendar of the department.

Outside the lecture theatre was a notice board with photos of some of the renowned professors of the medical faculty and their list of achievements. Our microbiology professor, Dr Kiktenko, was an expert on leptospirosis. He had been bold enough to inject himself with the bacteria to personally experience the symptoms and learn the natural course of the disease. We felt lucky and proud to have been taught by such eminent people. Many of them had passed away, but they continued to live in the memories of thousands of students from across the globe.

The next part of the programme was meeting an amazing person, Professor Frolov. He was still the head of the Department of Physiology and, as ever, a bundle of energy. It was great meeting our beloved professor after all those years. He looked well, and even at ninety years of age he carried on teaching.

"Professor, what is the secret of your health?" I asked.

"Hard work, exercise and doing what I enjoy," he replied.

"What exercise do you do?"

"I walk," was his reply.

He lived three miles away from the university and walked to work. Be it sunshine, snow, rain or wind, Professor Frolov walked to and from work.

"God gave us a pair of legs to walk. There is no exercise better than brisk walking and no tonic better than fresh air," he said with a smile.

Outside the physiology department was a notice board with photographs from Shakespeare's play *Hamlet* that had been staged by the dramatic society of the university. It was difficult to believe that Professor Frolov, even at the ripe old age of ninety, was chairman of the drama society of the faculty and played the role of the Ghost. That was genuine passion!

We walked into the old café for some tea and biscuits. It was full of medical students. They were all in a hurry to get a bite before the next class. While enjoying tea, we had a strange feeling that our Latin teacher might turn up at any minute to join us and make sure no one disappeared before his class. It was not to be. Sadly, he had passed away a few years after we completed our course.

Carlos was carefully observing the female medical students. During our student days, he had the reputation of a ladies' man.

"Are you thinking of going back to medical school?" I asked him.

"No," he replied with a smile. "I wish I could! My son wants to do medicine. I was considering sending him to RUDN to study medicine. Now, I've changed my mind. There are too many beautiful girls around. The Russian girls look even prettier than in our days." He tried to explain it. "They are naturally beautiful because of their ethnic diversity. The USSR was made up of multiple nationalities, and most girls were of mixed ancestry. Girls of mixed ancestry are prettier because of a wider choice of genes available to the maker. After the collapse of the USSR, girls have become more fashionable and health-conscious. They look after themselves more and dress better. On the whole, Russian girls are more confident today, and with the latest in fashion and makeup, they present themselves better. I am convinced after seeing the girls around that my son will not return to Bolivia if I send him to RUDN to study."

Jima had another surprise in store for us. We were joined in our rounds of the university by another familiar face, Dr Pautkin. He was our first tutor in surgery. The young and energetic Dr Pautkin had just finished his training in general surgery and joined the department as a tutor. His nickname was 'Inflammation Pautkin', as his favourite word was inflammation. According to him, most if not all surgical pathology could be summed up by the word inflammation, as is represented by terms ending with the letters 'itis' – for example, inflammation of the appendix is appendicitis and inflammation of the pancreas is called pancreatitis. Dr Pautkin was unbelievably passionate about surgery and put his heart and soul into every class. His love of surgery and dedication to the subject made several surgeons from our group.

He was kind and caring and would do anything for his patients. Dr Pautkin continued working in the department, became a professor and was still operating until recently. As age gradually caught up with him, the dexterity of his fingers diminished, and he finally had to give it up. However, he carried on teaching medical students. We could feel the sadness in his voice when he told us how much he missed operating.

"Well, nobody can carry on forever," he continued with a smile. He looked well for his age and appeared content with life.

"How do the present-day students compare to us?" we asked Dr Pautkin.

"Different," he replied. "The hunger and motivation to learn are sadly lacking today. Modern-day kids have everything given to them on a platter. That takes away the 'drive'. Look around," he told us, pointing to the cars parked outside, "All these expensive, latest-model cars belong to our students. What do you expect then?"

This conversation reminded me of an African student from our year group. He was the son of a chief. We heard that when he left the country to study medicine, his father had already built a massive villa ready for him to live in when he returned as a doctor. The guy was loaded with money and lived the life of Riley, hosting lavish parties in his room daily. It was no surprise that at the medical exams when the teacher asked him how many chambers the human heart had, he had no clue.

We strolled around the medical faculty building. Each one of us had stories to tell and friends to remember. The anatomy museum still existed on the floor above the café. The numerous exhibits in the formalin-sealed jars did not arouse the same curiosity or awe as they did all those years ago.

After the tour of the medical faculty, Dr Pautkin took leave of us. We crossed the road and stood in front of Block 7. It had been our home for what then seemed to be six long years. The building looked the same, but with the tall buildings around it, appeared small. The hostel block also had the same airport-style security arrangements.

The buffet (small canteen) in the hall next to the staircase was no longer there. It was the only buffet in all the seven hostel blocks. During the cold evenings and lazy weekends, it was a blessing as we did not have to go out. The only hot food served there was an omelette with whatever extras you fancied adding to it – cheese, ham, sausage or tomato. The coffee was excellent. The round, middle-aged Russian lady with the pink face who worked in the buffet had a wicked sense of humour.

I remember one of my friends asked her one day, "Do you have kefir?" (a variety of liquidy yoghurt).

"No. Do you?" she asked, keeping a straight face.

It took a while for my friend to understand her humour (a crude reference of kefir to sperm) before he burst out laughing.

We went up the stairs to the fourth floor where we used to live. Shyam and I stood in front of room number 411, our home for six years. At the end of the corridor was the same old kitchen with two washbasins and eight hot plates. Someone recalled an incident one evening when the corridor smelt of urine. Everyone thought there must be a crack in the toilet pipes. Later we found out that the smell was coming from the kitchen and not the toilet. One of our classmates, David from the Ivory Coast, was cooking lamb kidneys. He explained that lamb kidneys make a very tasty dish. Someone had to politely tell him, "At least wash the kidneys properly before you cook them next time, as the whole corridor smells of urine."

The views through the windows had changed. Tall buildings had been put up along the stretch of open land seen from the kitchen window in the past. Today it felt claustrophobic.

It was around noon. Jima knocked on the door of our old room. After a delay, it opened slowly and hesitantly. A young man, still in his pyjamas, stood at the door, rubbing his eyes. He was having a lie-in as most youngsters do on the weekend. He was about to tell us off for waking him up early, but as soon as he saw Professor Jima, he woke up fully, became alert and said,

"Good morning, sir." Jima introduced us as his classmates and added that Shyam and I had lived in that room many years ago.

"Can we come in?"

"Sure," he replied, and there we were, standing in the room where we had lived for six long years over three and a half decades ago.

Very little had changed in the room. The young man apologised for the mess. We said it was perfectly understandable as it was no different when we lived here. This student from Tanzania informed us that the only change that had happened to the rooms over the years was that the previously wooden single-glazed windows were replaced by double-glazed UPVC Windows. We stood for a few moments, remembering the good times and old friends. Shyam and I wondered where our third roommate, Fis, was. Did he end up in Eritrea, the country he hoped to see free one day, or was he treating STDs in some other corner of the world? God knows! Even in the age of Facebook, Twitter and WhatsApp, we were unable to track down our old friend Fis.

After spending some time in our old room, we went for lunch at the restaurant in the medical building. A former student of our university owned this restaurant. It was a cosy place with romantic, low lighting and comfortable seating. The menu had plenty of choices. Next to the lady at the till stood a well-built, tough-looking guy with a face resembling a bulldog. He stood still as a statue and never spoke a word. Only his eyes rolled around, surveying every movement in the restaurant. Was he a bouncer? It was an unusual sight. Why does an ordinary restaurant inside a university building need a bouncer? While paying at the till, I managed to strike up a conversation with him. He decided to have a chat as he saw Professor Jima with us, and gathered we were his classmates. With the semblance of a smile, he told me that he too had completed medicine at our university. His brother owned the restaurant and he had joined his brother in business as in the nineties it was much more lucrative than practising medicine. Jima told us that during the transitional period from socialism to capitalism, trouble could erupt anywhere and at any time. Bouncers were necessary to maintain order and protect the property. This restaurant merely continued the tradition after things normalised.

Jima had booked five tickets for the ballet *Swan Lake* at the Bolshoi Theatre that evening. No trip to Moscow would be complete without going to the iconic Bolshoi. Six of us wanted to go. We only had five tickets and wondered who would have to give it a miss. Jima confidently said all six of us were going. We could buy an extra ticket there. During Soviet times, the tickets would be sold out months ahead, and there was not a chance in hell of getting one on the day. It was a bright sunny day, and the Bolshoi looked majestic with its pillars and the statue of the horse-drawn chariot above it. The big beautiful fountain in front enhanced its beauty.

The pillars of the Bolshoi reminded me of a story. There is a saying in Russian 'Meet you at the ninth pillar of the Bolshoi.' At the end of the first date, the boy asks the girl, "When and where shall we meet again?" If the girl did not enjoy the date, she would tell him, "Next Saturday at six by the ninth pillar of the Bolshoi." Unaware of the saying, the poor boy turns up. He waits and waits until his patience runs out. Then he counts the pillars to make sure he is waiting at the right spot and realises that the numbers fooled him. The Bolshoi only has eight pillars.

Across the busy street, in front of the Bolshoi Theatre, stood the lonely statue of Karl Marx. His revolutionary ideas have influenced every corner of the world. The Bolsheviks, led by Lenin, first put his ideas into practice in the Soviet Union. His idea of a communist state where everyone was equal had almost come to fruition here, but eventually it failed. If statues had emotions, this one would have shed many tears. No one took any notice of the great thinker whose statue was looking across the busy street at the Bolshoi. Birds found his head a convenient place to sit and dirty while watching life pass by in modern-day capitalist Moscow.

Looking at Karl Marx's statue, I remembered an interesting fact about Marx, Engels and Lenin. The faces of these three thinkers were pictured on thousands of flags carried by demonstrators through Red Square on Revolution Day, commemorating the victory of the proletariat over the capitalists. Interestingly, none of them were from the working class. They were all from the wealthy aristocracy. Marx's father was a successful lawyer. Engel's dad was a rich businessman and Lenin's parents were landlords. Lenin never worked in his life and spent most of his time in exile abroad, living off his mother's estate. It was the first two who invented the idea of 'dictatorship of the proletariat', and Lenin put it into practice in the USSR.

Ballet is considered the sublime form of dance. I was not a fan, as I never understood it. I had been once to the Bolshoi during my student days with a Russian friend. I cannot recollect the name of the ballet I saw, but I remember the visit for another reason. We were lucky enough to get a seat in the second row. In the first row, right in front of us, sat an older couple. Everyone passing stopped to greet the gentleman and shake his hand. His face looked familiar. Clearly he was someone important.

We were chatting away loudly waiting for the ballet to begin when the gentleman turned around, looked at me and asked with a smile "Indian?" My looks and Russian with the Indian accent were a giveaway. "Yes," I replied.

He extended his hand: "Zdravstvuite". I reciprocated and shook hands. His hand felt solid, big and strong.

"Are you a student"? "Yes".

"What do you study"? "Medicine" I replied.

"Study hard! You will need to save lives," advised the gentleman with a smile and turned back to talk to his wife.

My friend, whispering, asked if I recognised him.

"No. Is he an actor?"

"Never. He is the greatest football goalkeeper the world has seen, Lev Yashin."

In his heyday, Yashin was nicknamed the 'Black Spider' due to his lightning reflexes. Even the greatest names that graced football, like Pele, Eusebio and Bobby Charlton, found it difficult to score when Yashin was at the goal. Pele called him "Forever number one". To this day, Yashin is the only football goalkeeper to have received the Ballon d'Or trophy for the world's best footballer of the year.

As soon as Jima arrived, we walked to the entrance. A man approached us and offered tickets to the show for double the face value. The tickets exchanged hands in the open. In the USSR, such trading was illegal and the police would have arrested the seller for black marketing. Today, it was considered enterprise.

The Bolshoi Theatre was beautiful inside. I could appreciate it better this time around as I had been to many theatres around the world. The seats were covered in red velvet, and the frames were golden. The massive golden chandeliers with a thousand bulbs hanging down from the ceiling made the place look big and beautiful (Bolshoi, in Russian, means big). The ballet was based on Pushkin's novel *Eugene Onegin*. The performance was breathtaking. One can imagine the amount of training and hard work that goes into the making of a ballet. The dancers' movements are graceful and for most of the performance they are standing and moving on their toes. The large orchestra providing the music was brilliant. Little wonder the Bolshoi Ballet is considered one of the best in the world. After the show, we returned to the hostel, satisfied.

## *Chapter 38*

# VISITING A MOSCOW APARTMENT AND TRACKING DOWN AN OLD FRIEND

The following day, Jima invited us to his flat. He lived half an hour's metro ride away from the university. The flat was in a concrete city of many blocks of high-rise flats. In front of the buildings was a lawn with a play area for children, with swings and climbing frames of different heights. The majority of the people living in these flats were young families. There were a medical store, a hairdresser's and a café on the ground floor of Jima's block. Across the road were a supermarket and a multiplex cinema. The residents' car park was situated behind the block of flats. Jima proudly showed us his Ford car parked there. Most families in Moscow own cars today but use them only on weekends to go to their summer cottages (dacha), as the Moscow traffic and traffic jams (*probka* or *the cork* as Russians call them) are notorious. It is much quicker and less stressful to use the metro than to drive to work during rush hour.

Jima's was a good-sized, three-bedroom flat with all modern amenities. It was tastefully decorated with little souvenirs he had picked up from countries around the world he had visited. One of the rooms was converted into a mini gymnasium.

The table was laden with all the imaginable Russian delicacies. We browsed through photo albums from university days. The photos reminded us of many classmates we had forgotten. All of us fondly remembered Kimaro, our 'wise friend', and missed him terribly.

Most of the guys we knew of had done well. One guy left medicine altogether and dedicated his life to politics. Today, I believe, he is a prominent politician in Palestine. A few others went into business and did well for themselves. The majority continued working as doctors across the globe, saving lives.

After dinner, Jima showed us a fascinating curio, a little red booklet resembling a passport. It was his Communist Party Membership Document. After the fall of the Soviet Union, it had become worthless. However, it remained a memorable souvenir and reminder of when he grew up in another country with a different political system, the Socialist Soviet Union. There was no need to keep it a secret, as the rules of the game were different then. Times have changed. We were all eager to see it and touch it. This was the first time any of us foreigners got to see this document, which we knew existed but had never seen before.

The little red booklet reminded us of our Russian classmate, Kostya. All the international students believed he was a KGB agent. We were convinced he was the reason for our classmate from Panama, Mario, having to leave medicine and go back home in the first year. We asked Jima about what happened to Kostya. He had dropped out of our group in year four as he was struggling to cope, but then rejoined medicine in the year below us and managed to complete the course with great difficulty. It turned out that he had learning difficulties and asking silly questions during lessons and putting on an air of someone important was his way of masking it. During medical school days, we had never heard of a diagnosis 'learning difficulty'. We genuinely felt sorry for the guy as he was misunderstood throughout his medical school days.

## Tracking Down an Old Friend

The following day, Jima and I set out on our quest to find my old pal and karate partner, Oleg. We had worked together in Hospital 61 in Moscow. All my attempts to contact him through the hospital switchboard had failed, and I got the same reply: "Oleg does not work here anymore." They would not give me his address or telephone number. Jima was confident we could track him down if we went there. We set off by metro at 8 a.m. It was an hour's journey. The hospital had changed beyond recognition and also had the same airport-style entry security system. A colleague of Oleg told us he was working part-time in a polyclinic and gave me his number. I later met up with him.

It was great to see Oleg and his family after so many years. He looked well as he had carried on practising martial arts. He opened the best bottle of champagne from his collection.

"How is Misha, our taekwondo instructor?" I asked Oleg, "I was very much looking forward to meeting him."

"Misha passed away ten years ago," he replied.

It was a big shock to me. Misha had not only taught me taekwondo. He was my mentor and gave me the courage and confidence to calmly face difficult situations in life. Although a master of many martial arts, Misha was the calmest, coolest and most unassuming person I had ever known. He had diabetes but did not trust allopathic medicine. He believed that all modern synthetic medicines were harmful to the system and he ended up being treated by a charlatan (a so-called natural medicine expert) with vague herbal remedies. Oleg tried helping Misha by arranging an appointment with the diabetologist in the hospital, but so great was his trust in natural medicine and hate for Western medicine that he flatly refused. Eventually, Misha went into a coma and died. We had a shot of vodka in memory of our great guru and for his soul to rest in peace.

"You remember Uri, the KGB guy, who trained with us?" Oleg asked me.

I could not remember any KGB guy training with us, but from Oleg's description it was a tall, fit chap who had trained with us. I thought he was a police officer as I saw him in uniform once. Uri was shot dead in a skirmish at a Moscow suburb during the troubles that occurred when the Soviet Union collapsed.

We remembered some of our colleagues from the orthopaedic department in the hospital. Oleg updated me on the ones he knew and still kept in touch with.

"What about Anton?" I asked.

Anton was a handsome man and resembled the actor Roger Moore. He was a brilliant orthopaedic surgeon with a good sense of humour and a great pair of hands. He taught me how to perform many operations and helped me gain confidence. Sadly, Anton had a weakness. He enjoyed a drink or two. Oleg told me that Anton finally hit the bottle big time and was thrown out of the house by his wife. He ended up homeless in his old age and met with a miserable end.

Before we knew it, it was 6 p.m. and time for me to take leave of Oleg and his family. I had to get back to the university for the concert hosted especially for our group by the arts society of the university. Diversity was the striking feature of the group. They had members from all continents and performed dances from Europe, Asia and Latin America. It was an honour to watch this exclusive concert. The group had won every dance competition in Europe over the years. The members of the group joined us for dinner and were fascinated to hear the life stories of their predecessors.

## *Chapter 39*

# BACK IN RED SQUARE, MOSCOW TOUR AND TO THE SANATORIUM

A visit to Moscow is incomplete without a visit to the most famous square in the world. Near the entrance to the square now stood the statue of a soldier on horseback. It was the statue of the most celebrated soldier of the Soviet Union, Marshal Georgy Zhukov, and was erected in 1995. Zhukov had led the country to victory in all the major battles of the Second World War, from the liberation of Moscow and breaking the siege of Leningrad to driving Hitler's Wehrmacht back to Berlin and destroying it. After entering Berlin, he passed a decree to his soldiers: 'Crush the Nazis, but respect the German people.' Marshal Zhukov rode a white stallion through Red Square after the end of the Second World War to celebrate victory over Hitler's Germany. A true soldier, Zhukov was never afraid to speak his mind. As a result, he fell out of favour with Stalin and got sidelined. Khrushchev once again brought Zhukov back to the forefront of Soviet politics after Stalin's death, and he was entrusted with the task of arresting Stalin's secret police chief, the notorious Beria. Beria was the man who orchestrated the killing of millions of innocent Soviet people in the purges, during Stalin's reign.

In the seventies, Red Square was an open square. There used to be a gate at its entrance in the seventeenth century, but Stalin demolished it to allow parading troops easier access to the square. A new gate called Resurrection Gate, believed to be a replica of the seventeenth-century gate, was built in 1995. As we walked through the gate, we spotted two old women sitting on the ground next to it, begging for alms. One could never have imagined this happening in the Soviet Union.

While walking into Red Square, the most unusual sight caught our eye – a silent demonstration by communists. There were about twenty people, men and women in their fifties and over, in it. They carried placards that read 'Down with Capitalism, Victory to Communism' and 'Long live the Revolution'. It was a pathetic sight. Tourists watched the demonstration with curiosity. The locals hardly took any notice.

How times have changed! In the Soviet Union, the Communist Party was king. Demonstrations that filled the square during the Soviet times were celebrations in support of the ruling Communist Party.

I wonder what the man inside the mausoleum thought about all the changes. I am sure he knows where his successors went wrong, but you cannot control the course of events in the country from inside a mausoleum.

It was a great feeling to be back in Red Square. The weather was bright and sunny, and the square was filled with tourists from all over the world. Newly married couples were having their photographs taken. The square itself had not changed. Lenin's Mausoleum stood to the right of the square, backing up to the Kremlin wall. The change of guards at every hour in front of the mausoleum continued as before.

The queue to get into Lenin's Mausoleum nowadays is not long. In Soviet times, people queued for hours to see and pay their respects to the architect of their country and the father of the nation. Today, people queue out of curiosity and to see a work of art.

We bought tickets and went in to pay homage to the great leader. Nothing had changed inside. Lenin appeared to be dreaming but looked paler than when we saw him years ago. The dreams could not be sweet ones today. His idea of creating the perfect communist state had been shattered. The country had slipped into reverse gear, and gone back into capitalism. Credit must be given to the team of scientists and technicians who manage to keep Lenin's body looking natural after all those years. At what cost and how this is done remains a mystery.

After Lenin's death, the authorities asked the pathologist performing the autopsy to check if the great man's brain was different from that of other people. The pathology professor disappointed them, as he found it was no different from that of other mere mortals.

From Red Square, we went into the main department store, GUM. It was now a grand Western-style department store. Most of the shops were designer ones. We spotted a queue in one corner of the store. Curiosity took us in that direction as in today's Russia, queues are non-existent. In the USSR, the dictum was 'If you see a queue, join it straightaway, as it must be for something worthwhile put up for sale. You join first, and then ask the person in front of you what the queue is for.' This turned out to be a queue for softee ice creams. They were made from an old Soviet recipe without any additives or preservatives and tasted as good as ever.

As we walked past the Kremlin wall, we remembered our visit to the Kremlin during our first year. We were shown the palace of congresses. The massive hall inside was the venue for the annual Communist Party Congress of the USSR. The entire proceedings of the Congress were shown on TV without fail. The party General Secretary Comrade Breshnev's policy speech was the main item of the Congress. He read out his speech and it went on for hours. In the copy of the speech distributed to delegates, it would be highlighted when to clap. When he reached that point, someone who was awake and noticed it would start clapping. This would wake up the entire hall and everyone would join the clapping. When the speech resumed, most would go back to sleep with their eyes open. Someone told me a story that Breshnev was once about to fire his speech writer when he noticed that most of the delegates were asleep during the afternoon session.

"Why did you write a hundred page speech?" he shouted at the speech writer. "I asked you for a twenty page speech." The man replied, "Sorry, comrade. I gave you a twenty page speech. If you remember you asked me to give you five copies, which I did."

I could not help but wonder at how the times had changed. Deep Purple, the popular American band whose songs on bootleg tapes got me hooked on to rock music in Sergei's house years ago, had played a sell-out concert at this very palace of congresses. It was difficult to compare the contrasting scene in the hall during the sleepy Party Congresses of the USSR with the same hall today packed with thousands of rock music fans screaming to the popular Deep Purple anthem 'Smoke on the water, fire in the sky'.

From the Kremlin, we went to the nearby shopping mall. At the entrance to the mall stood two familiar characters, the spitting images of Lenin and Stalin. Lenin wore his characteristic goatee beard and Stalin, in his military uniform, was smoking a pipe. People were taking selfies with them. In return, the 'leaders' demanded money. Stalin, in his gruff voice, said, "Only dollars or euros please." For the effort they had taken to become the spitting images of the two great leaders, they certainly deserved a few pennies.

## Tour of Moscow

The Moscow Metro had expanded significantly in every direction. Many new, modern stations had been added. Over nine million people use the Moscow Metro daily, and it remains the fastest and most reliable mode of transport in Moscow. I could not recognise the names of a lot of old stations on the metro map. Twenty-six stations had their names changed after the fall of the USSR, in an attempt to erase memories of the communist past. The metro station closest to the Red Square, which we had regularly used – Marx's Prospect – was now called Hunter's Row.

Ali, Shyam and I went on the hop on and off open top city bus tour of Moscow one afternoon. We boarded the bus near Red Square and got off at the Sparrow Hills stop. It was where I came on my first outing with my friend Thomas all those years ago after escaping quarantine. It used to be called Lenin Hills. After the fall of the Soviet Union, the hill was renamed Sparrow Hills in 1999 and the metro station Sparrow Hills Station. From here, you get a bird's eye view of the whole of modern Moscow. The Lenin Stadium had been renamed *Luzhniki*. The word means meadows, and it was so called because it was built on flood meadows. This stadium was the central venue for the most successful World Cup football competition held in Russia in 2018.

The tallest of Stalin's Seven Sisters, the imposing Moscow State University building, stood at the top of the hill, unchanged. This monument to Stalinist architecture is a beautiful building, even by today's standards. Looking down from the Sparrow Hills, one can see how Moscow had changed. Countless modern skyscrapers could be seen in the distance in the centre of Moscow, but the Seven Sisters of Stalin still stood out with a majestic charm of their own.

From the observation platform on the Sparrow Hills, one can see the Luzhniki Metro Bridge. The two-level Metro Bridge across the Moscow River has the metro going over the river, and the motorway runs above it. We could see the trains arrive at and leave the station at regular intervals of one to two minutes through its glass walls.

The hopper bus then dropped us off at the Cathedral of Christ the Saviour near metro station Kropotkinskaya. I remembered my trips with Carlos to swim in the massive open-air heated swimming pool complex right next to this station. There was no pool to be seen. I was a little disappointed. The big cathedral had replaced it after the fall of the Soviet Union. Standing tall at 103 metres it is the tallest Orthodox Christian church in the world. The history of Russia from the nineteenth and twentieth centuries is mirrored in the history of the cathedral. It was first built in picturesque surroundings on the banks of the Moscow River to thank the Lord for saving Russia from Napoleon. Stalin ordered the cathedral to be demolished in 1931 and wanted a magnificent, big palace, the Palace of the Soviets (parliament building), to be built in its place. However, the plans had to be shelved due to the start of the Second World War. After the war, Stalin changed his plans and ordered the building of the world's largest open-air swimming pool complex. The complex was demolished after the fall of the USSR and the Cathedral of Christ the Saviour was built in its place. Situated on the banks of the Moscow River it is only a stone's throw away from the Kremlin.

We went into the cathedral. It looked impressive, with numerous paintings and icons decorating its walls. Hundreds of candles were lit in different parts of the main hall and groups of devotees were chanting hymns. Ali asked me a question that took me by surprise. Is this cathedral as beautiful as the Taj Mahal? I told him that there can be no comparison as Taj Mahal is regarded as one of the seven wonders of the world. However, I could not help comparing this cathedral with the famous cathedrals of Europe like St Peter's Basilica in Rome or Notre-Dame in Paris, where sublime art meets superb architecture and astonishing craftsmanship. This modern cathedral was different. In spite of all the modern technology, I guess it is impossible to build cathedrals to match the ones designed by divinely gifted masters of the past like Michelangelo.

Our classmate Yuri, a psychiatrist, told me an interesting story about the cathedral. He was certain there was something very special about it. Although not a believer, Yuri came here occasionally to spend some time in the cathedral. After standing still for a minute, with eyes closed, under the dome of the church (where the roof is high), he went into a state of levitation. This was followed by an incredible feeling of physical wellbeing and inner calm and he noticed all the stress bottled up in his body gradually melt away. He walked out from the cathedral a very relaxed, re-energised and different man.

A pedestrian bridge spans the river from one side of the cathedral. We stood on the bridge for some time, enjoying the views and watching the boats sail by.

At a distance we could see a big, dark statue on the Moscow River. A passer-by told us it was the statue of Peter the Great, and added, "There is nothing great about it." Since it was built after our time in Moscow, we decided to go and see it up close. It was located a fair distance away and looked tall as we approached it. A guide told us it was taller than the Statue of Liberty. The statue stands on a pedestal on the artificial island in the middle of the river and was built to commemorate 300 years of the Russian Navy that Peter the Great built. The statue depicts Peter holding on to the wheel of a ship with his left hand. In his right hand, he is holding a rolled-up sheet of paper. From the column on which the vessel is standing, bits of other ships seem to be weirdly sticking out. Although symbolic, the statue was not very pleasing to the eye. No wonder it was unpopular with the Muscovites, who appreciate good art.

Our next stop was VDNKHA, the permanent Exhibition Centre and an amusement park. Crowds of people were having a good day out. Many youngsters were roller-skating, while others were on their bicycles. Dotted along the sides of the long footpath were various performers. People were listening to a band playing Russian and English Rock music. A juggler, a clown and a magician entertained children. There were numerous stalls by the wayside, selling ice creams and snacks.

Sadly, it was a Sunday and the exhibition was closed. In front of the main entrance, we bumped into a statue of a character we missed on this trip. It was the forlorn statue of a certain Vladimir Lenin. During our medical school days, he was omnipresent. There were over eighty statues of Lenin in Moscow itself. This was the only statue of Lenin we had seen this time around. I remembered a joke about this statue. Alexei Kosygin, the Foreign Minister, was walking by one day when he heard the statue talk: "Alexei! Get me a glass of vodka." Kosygin went to the Kremlin and brought his boss Leonid Brezhnev to listen to the talking statue. The statue spoke again in a loud, angry voice: "Alexei! I asked you for a glass of vodka and not for an ass."

After Stalin's death, his memory was completely wiped out by Khrushchev, who followed him to power. Martin Sixsmith, in his book *Russia: a 1,000-year Chronicle of the Wild East*, writes:

Russian historiography continued to revere Lenin even as it denounced Stalin for the crimes of the Soviet system, but those crimes originated with the first Bolshevik leader. Lenin seemed to care more for ideas than for people. He pursued the cause of the revolution exclusively, single-mindedly, whatever the cost in human suffering. It was he, not Stalin who founded the one-party state; he who created the feared secret police and the system of forced labour camps later known as the Gulag; and he who first gave the order for summary executions of suspected opponents.

We assumed all other statues of Lenin and the other Soviet leaders would have been destroyed after the collapse of the USSR. A friend told me that the statues of former leaders were not destroyed, but moved to an open-air museum called Muzeon Park, by the side of the Culture Park (formerly Gorky Park) not far from the city centre. We would have loved to go there to see some familiar old faces but sadly were short of time.

Talking about statues, I must mention one man whose statues appeared not only in many cities of Russia but also in other parts of the former Soviet Union after its collapse. It is the multi-talented actor, singer and songwriter Vladimir Vysotsky. Streets have been named after him in many cities, and he is popular even with the younger generation. After the fall of the Soviet Union, Vysotsky's talent began to be appreciated. His works were published in Russia. Every year, on 25th July, the anniversary of the poet's death, concerts are held in Russia, where modern-day poets and singers gather to recite his poems and sing his songs. "Vysotsky saw life as it was in reality. What he sang and wrote has meaning for us even today," said a modern-day poet at one of the anniversary celebrations, after reciting Vysotsky's poems.

Here is my translation of one of Vysotsky's popular poems.

## 'The Giraffe'

*In hot and sunny Africa,*

*in its central region,*

*something unusual happened.*

*The elephant predicted,*

*"Looks like the deluge is coming."*

*It happened that*

*a 'Giraffe' fell in love with an 'Antelope'.*

*There was a lot of loud chattering and barking;*

*the old parrot shouted from high up in the branches,*

*"Giraffe is big and knows what is best!"*

*"What if she has horns?" shouted the love-stricken Giraffe.*

*"These days, all are equal in our animal kingdom.*

*If relatives are unhappy with my choice,*

*don't blame me. I will leave the herd."*

*There was a lot of chattering and barking;*

*the old parrot shouted from up the branches,*

*"Giraffe is big and knows what is best!"*

*Of what use is such a son to the father-in-law;*

*he is as thick as thick can be!*

*Giraffe left his in-laws and went to live with the 'Bisons'.*

*There was a lot of loud chattering and barking;*

*the old parrot shouted from high up the branches,*

*"Giraffe is big and knows what is best!"*

*In hot and sunny Africa,*

*there are no ideals anymore.*

*The Giraffe's parents shed crocodile tears,*

*being sorry will not help.*

*There are no laws anymore.*

*Giraffe's daughter married a Bison!*

*The Giraffe is not guilty.*

*The really guilty one*

*is the one who sits high up in the branches and shouts,*

*"Giraffe is big and knows what is best!"*

Many of Vysotsky's poems are deeply symbolic. In this poem, the old parrot perched on the treetop shouting "The Giraffe is big. He knows what is best" is a reference to the ageing ruling Politbureau of the Communist Party of the USSR. Who the other animals are is left to the reader's imagination.

Our next destination was Arbat Street. It is one of the oldest streets in Moscow and was once the most desirable address to live at. A lot of the nobility lived here. The cafes and bars of the Arbat were the favourite hangouts of the artists, poets, musicians and writers in olden days. In the 1960s, a new six-lane highway was built parallel to the old Arbat, and the street lost its importance. However, after the pedestrianisation of the street in the 1980s, it became popular once again. Ancient buildings lining the street maintain old Arbat's charm. Today, it is a lively street filled with portrait painters, buskers, souvenir stalls and tattoo artists.

The majority of the people there were tourists. As we carried on, we came across the statue of another famous Soviet bard, Bulat Okudzhava. He lived on Arbat Street and wrote many songs about the world around him. One of the popular ones was about his favourite street, the Arbat, which he calls his Fatherland. Okudzhava fell out of favour with the authorities, and the reason is evident from his famous poem, 'Song of the Black Cat'. There can be no doubt about the theme of the poem, although he never mentions the leader's name. Here is my translation of the poem.

## 'Song of the Black Cat'

*From the courtyard, there is a famous entrance*

*called the 'Black door'.*

*In this entrance, like his own estate,*

*lives the Black Cat.*

*A smirk hides behind his whiskers,*

*and darkness is his shield.*

*All cats sing and cry,*

*but this one, not a sound.*

*He has long given up catching mice,*

*just smirks under his moustache.*

*It's us he baits with noble words;*

*on a bit of sausage,*

*he doesn't demand, doesn't ask.*

*His yellow eyes are fiery;*

*every cat brings him offerings,*

*and thank him too.*

*He does not say a word;*

*just eats and drinks.*

*His paws scratch the dirty ground,*

*as if he could tear your throat with them.*

*One wonders why*

*it's so dark and gloomy in our home.*

*Must fix a lamp here,*

*but money for it we cannot collect.*

## The Sanatorium

The following morning, we were to set off to the sanatorium in the suburbs of Moscow. The coach that was to take us did not turn up. The driver informed Jima that it would not start due to engine trouble. Jima managed to get a replacement at the last minute, a minibus. It turned out to be an old banger and looked like a leftover from the Soviet times. It was the most befitting mode of transport to rekindle nostalgic memories. The journey that took an hour was fun, even though the weather was sweltering and the bus felt like an oven, as it did not have air conditioning. It reminded us of the minibus that used to take us to one of the faraway hospitals for our surgery posting.

Driving in today's Moscow is notoriously bad. A colleague who had been to Moscow on holiday recently showed me the photograph of a Ferrari parked on a zebra crossing. The drive started well, but at one point the driver missed a junction off the motorway. He realised it only half a mile later, and what did he do? He slowly reversed on the hard shoulder of the motorway until we got back to the point where we should have come off. Our hearts were in our mouths. All this while, vehicles were speeding past us. Some drivers gave us an angry look, others honked, and a few others put up their index finger to the corner of their forehead and did the semi-circular movements which in Russian meant 'Are you bonkers or what?' Yet others showed our driver the 'V' sign ('V' not for victory, but 'up yours'.) The man was made of steel. He was least bothered and remained cool as a cucumber. Once we were back on the right road, the entire group heaved a massive sigh of relief and applauded.

The sanatorium, situated in the middle of the woods, was built during Soviet times. This was evident from the artwork on the walls. A large painting pictured a man and woman heading a march, holding the red flag with the hammer and sickle sign on it. The director of the sanatorium was a graduate from the Peoples' Friendship University and, as Jima told us, a useful connection to have. We got the best rooms. They were spacious and comfortable, although a little outdated. It was the ideal location to reminisce and relax. There were scenic walks in the woods, a small cinema, a games room and a computer room with Wi-Fi to keep us entertained. We were given a private dining room with a personal chef. The meals were delicious, and the beer was on the house. The waitress smiled when she heard we were doctors. She was a qualified dentist but decided to do the job of a waitress instead. After the breakup of the Soviet Union, most of the hospitals and clinics became private. Private institutions need to make money and retained only the essential number of staff. Redundancies followed, and there was a surplus of doctors and dentists. Many of them were forced to take up other professions that were in demand, like pharmaceutical company representatives and surgical assistants and in the service industry as chefs, receptionists and waitresses.

There was still so much to catch up on. Jima showed us the video of his son's wedding. The group went out together for refreshing walks in the woods and kept on chatting continuously, just as in our student days.

On the final morning, the weather was sunny and hot. The sanatorium arranged a barbecue with plenty of cold beer. The general mood, however, was sombre as we had to leave Moscow after the barbecue. We hugged, said our goodbyes and made promises to meet up again, and as someone put it humorously, “On our walking frames and wheelchairs.” We left for the airport in time to catch our flights. Valentine agreed to drop us off at Sheremetyevo Airport in his brand new Mercedes 4x4. The most memorable week in our lives had ended. As we set off to the airport, nature summed up our feelings. After six days of glorious sunshine for the reunion, dark clouds gathered and the heavens opened up. Full credit to our friend, Jima, for organising this remarkable reunion and let us all experience a different Moscow after three and a half decades. This ‘once in a lifetime’ reunion in the alma mater will remain etched in our memories forever.

## *Chapter 40*

# COMPARISON OF LIFE IN RUSSIA DURING SOVIET TIMES AND TODAY

Andrei Schleifer, an economics professor from Harvard University, was one of the advisers to the Russian government and the primary engineer of Russian privatisation in the early nineties after the collapse of the Soviet Union. He published a book, *A Normal Country: Russia After Communism.* What is a normal country? How do you define a normal country? By changing from a communist dictatorship into a multiparty democracy, from a centrally planned economy into a capitalist order based on markets and private property, does a country necessarily become a normal country?

I was eager to find the answer to a seemingly simple question – was life better for the people in the Socialist Soviet Union or in today's capitalist Russia? Had freedom, with fast cars, skyscrapers, massive malls and fast-food outlets, brought real happiness to the people? Comparing life in the Soviet Union to life in today's Russia is like comparing apples and oranges. If you ask a Russian oligarch this question, the answer would undoubtedly be "In Russia today." Put the same question to an old age pensioner who is struggling to make ends meet and their reply without any hesitation would be "Back in the USSR." How do you decide if the historical changes that happened in 1991, leading to the collapse of the Soviet Empire, genuinely improved the quality of life of the ordinary people in Russia?

I asked friends from different walks of life who lived in the USSR, including many of our classmates, this question and got the same diplomatic answer: "Some things were better then and others now." To get a clearer idea of what it meant, I decided to delve deeper and asked three specific questions. Here are their answers:

1. **How does life in Russia today compare to life in the USSR?**

   The standard of living is undoubtedly higher in Russia today, but the problems are also bigger. In the USSR, fewer goods were available in the shops, and choices were limited, but what was available was affordable. Today, everything is available in the shops, but only a few can afford it.

2. **What were the positives and negatives in the USSR and in Russia today?**

   **Positives in the USSR** – Life was stable, predictable and less stressful. Jobs were guaranteed. Free medical care and subsidised holidays were available to every citizen. Education in schools and colleges was free for all. People received a reasonable pension at the end of their working lives. Everyone felt that the future was bright and that they had something to look forward to.

   **Negatives** – People could not travel abroad and see the world. They had only limited access to world news, developments in the outside world, music, art and literature. The choice of luxury items was limited. Religious beliefs were actively discouraged. When everyone doing the same job gets paid the same, initiative and incentive are lacking, and that affects productivity.

   **Positives in Russia today** – People earn more. They can travel the world, invest their earnings and buy a car and house. They have easy access to modern technology. Young people have become more confident and ambitious. Absence of guaranteed jobs stimulates creativity and hard work. Qualified people can travel far and wide to sell their skills and improve their standard of living. People are free to practise any religion.

**Negatives** – The cost of living is very high. Most of the medical care is private, and only a few can afford it. Medical care is of a high standard in the big cities, but is poor in the villages. Education is expensive. There is massive inequality between the rich and the poor. People who are struggling to make ends meet form the majority.

3. **Given a chance to live your life again, would you choose to live in the socialist USSR or today's capitalist Russia?**

   Possibly in the USSR. There was far less stress, fewer worries and life was predictable. True, we had to sometimes stand in queues but we would get what we were queueing for in the end. People had a sense of being part of something great and were generally happier.

The opinions of a few friends may not fully reflect the views of the general public. I looked at some of the results published by the Levada Centre in Moscow, which conducts sociological research. This Centre has been regularly conducting public opinion polls, first across the USSR and later in Russia, since 1988. The data of the mass surveys it conducted was taken from nationally representative samples. It was supplemented by the results of interviews with qualified experts, representatives of the new elite, entrepreneurs, farmers, the unemployed and many other population groups (levada.ru – about us).

The Centre did a survey on the collapse of the USSR. The survey took place between 24 and 28 November 2018 and was conducted throughout Russia in both urban and rural settings. It was carried out among 1600 people over the age of 18 in 136 localities of 52 of the country's regions. It was conducted as personal interviews in residents' homes.

One of the questions asked was "Do you regret the collapse of the USSR?"

Of those surveyed, 66 per cent replied "Yes," 25 per cent "No" and 9 per cent answered, "It is difficult to say." It is hardly a surprise that the majority of the people who replied "No" were people who were born after the collapse of the Soviet Union and had heard of it only from their parents or elderly relatives. What stuck in their minds about the USSR were the queues, scarcity of luxury goods and limited freedom.

The *Moscow Times* newspaper conducted a similar survey. In an article published on 24th June 2019, after the survey, the paper states:

> Most Russians say that the Soviet Union took care of ordinary people. Fifty-nine per cent of the people interviewed were of this view. The absence of ethnic conflicts during the Soviet period (46%) as well as economic growth and universal employment (43%) were the second and third most common responses given for supporting life in the Soviet Union.

I could now understand why it was impossible to get a straight answer to my seemingly straightforward question, and I will leave it to the readers to make up their own minds as to which is the right answer – if there is one.

A conversation I had with a wise old friend, Professor Nikolai (Nick), stands out in my mind. He was in his early seventies and retired as a professor of economics. Professor Nick was in good health and joked that the seventies are the new fifties. He remained an avid reader. The professor insisted on making me a cup of tea.

"How do you spend your time?" I asked.

"I read and I walk. Reading keeps my marbles in place, and walking keeps me above the ground rather than six feet below," he replied with a smile.

Professor Nick had been witness to the changes in Russia and had his views as to what would be the best social system for a country.

He explained, "Greed and jealousy are two negative qualities that every human being is born with, along with a hundred virtues. There is no denying that. A poor man aspires to be a rich man. All rich men want to be millionaires. Every millionaire aims to become a billionaire. All billionaires dream of becoming Bill Gates or whoever is the richest man in the world today. [Bill Gates' name was the first that came to his mind.] Every social system, be it capitalism, socialism or communism has its pluses and minuses." He paused to gauge my reaction.

"I am sure you remember socialism well," he said to me, and carried on. "There was no incentive to work hard, as you would be paid if you worked hard or not. A lazy man who dodged work got the same pay as the guy who worked his socks off. The drive to do better was lacking. Talent and hard work were not properly rewarded. A little competition is undoubtedly helpful to bring out the best in man."

Professor Nick continued airing his views. "I am sure you remember the handful of private markets that were allowed during the Soviet times. They were profitable, whereas the state markets nearby were not. It is ridiculous to argue that physical labour and mental labour should be paid equally. How can you say that a specialist doctor who spent ten years training to become one should be paid the same as a manual labourer who needs very little training to do his job?" After that, the professor returned to the present-day situation in Russia. "In tsarist Russia, there was only one tsar. Today in Russia there are at least five dozen. They call them oligarchs. There is a saying in Russian, 'Empires are built by giants and destroyed by pygmies.' The USSR was sold off for kopeks [Russian pennies] by one man called Boris," he said with a sad expression, and paused to sip his tea.

The professor then carried on, "Boris Yeltsin sold off all the natural wealth of this great country to crafty devils. They became the modern-day tsars. The majority of the population became poorer. Have you seen a beggar on the streets of Moscow when you lived here? Now they are not uncommon. If all the oil, gas, minerals and other natural resources that

Russia is blessed with were not given away for peanuts to individuals, Russia would have been a much happier place. All the small-scale industries, businesses and farming should have been left to private individuals to bring the best out of them."

To summarise, in the professor's view, a hybrid social system where the state owns the natural wealth of the country and heavy industries but encourages private enterprise to run smaller businesses would be ideal. It would give the country the best of both worlds. However, it needs a strong, selfless leader interested in the welfare of the people and not one aspiring to become a billionaire.

"Would you say China is going down this route today?" I asked.

He gave me a diplomatic reply with a smile, "Honestly, I cannot say. I have never been to China."

It was time for me to take leave of my old friend. We shook hands. During our short meeting, the wise man had given me a lot of food for thought.

On my way back to the hostel, I remembered an interesting lesson with Comrade Dimitry, the history teacher in the first year of university. Dimitry spent the entire lesson explaining the evolution of society and how and why 'capitalism' gets replaced by 'socialism' and 'socialism' by 'communism.'

At the end of the lesson, he asked a lazy, disinterested backbencher who regularly slept through the history lessons, "Which system of society evolves from socialism?"

"Capitalism," he replied with confidence, conviction and a naughty smile.

The class laughed.

"No, communism," Dimitry corrected him with a degree of annoyance in his tone and once again summarised what he had been explaining for the last forty-five minutes.

"It sounds like Utopia to me," came the reply from the backbencher in a hushed voice, and the whole class laughed again.

Comrade Dimitry did not hear or pretended not to hear the last reply, and the class was dismissed.

History has proved the lazy backbencher right. Who would have imagined then that the largest, most powerful and stable empire in the world, blessed with all the natural resources and talented, hardworking people, the USSR, would collapse like a pack of cards and slide back into capitalism?

On 5th December 2019, the Russian Prime Minister Dimitry Medvedev, in an interview with the Russian media, was asked by a correspondent about what he thought of the results of their survey.

Over three decades after the collapse of the Soviet Union, in a question and answer session with the public, our news channel found an overwhelming nostalgia for the Soviet Union. When asked if they would have liked to live in the USSR, 92 per cent of the participants replied "Yes". Interestingly, many of them were in their twenties. The reasons they gave were as follows:

1. The certainty of the future. No one had to worry about becoming jobless
2. Universally accessible medical care
3. Free education for all
4. A happier population as there was a better relationship between people when the income inequality and wealth disparity in society was significantly less.

Medvedev's answer was:

> It is the quality of the human mind to remember the good things from our youth and forget the bad things. If bad things are retained in memory, it will destroy us. Over time, we begin to idealise the good things from our past. No doubt, there were good things in

> the USSR, but it is pointless idealising it. True, there were more guarantees in life, but one should not forget the empty supermarket shelves and the queues to buy shoes. It is easy to romanticise the past, but I am certain that today's youth would have found living in those times extremely uncomfortable and would not survive. The education system in the USSR was good, and there are lessons to be learnt from it. Medicare was universal but primitive. All I remember about medical check-ups in school was my height and weight being recorded. Idealising the Soviet Union is pointless. It was a very complex country. It is impossible to return to the past. We need to look to the future.

Last year, Russia and the world celebrated the seventy fifth anniversary of victory over Fascism. A journalist interviewed an amazing ninety-five-year old Soviet war veteran Maria Rochlina to find out her views about the USSR and Russia today. Maria had participated in the battles of the Second World War, including the fiercest of all – the battle for Stalingrad. To this day, she remains very bitter about the fall of the USSR. Maria says that even in her wildest dreams, she did not imagine it happening to her country. She strongly disagrees that Russia is the same as the USSR. Maria does not feel Russia is her country although she lives in it as a law-abiding citizen. "In the USSR," says Maria, "we had free housing, free education, zero unemployment and free holidays. We never differentiated one another by nationalities. There was only one nationality – Soviet nationality. The whole world respected us. Many wanted to emulate us." Maria believes the Soviet Union was robbed. Even at her age, she says that she is prepared to go to war if it were for the Soviet Union. The commitment to her beliefs and the clarity of thought of the ninety-five-year old war veteran are admirable.

The biggest experiment in history, which took place in the largest country of the world with the greatest natural resources, the Soviet Union, eventually failed. Could it be that Marx, Engels and Lenin's dream of creating a communist society is bound to remain pie in the sky forever?

But it is not over yet. There is another empire in the world today that learnt some lessons from the Soviet experiment and avoided a few of the pitfalls to become the fastest growing economy in the world – the People's Republic of China. It implemented perestroika but avoided glasnost.

China today operates an economy which is a mixture of plan and market. The state mostly owns the strategic industries in the energy sector (oil, gas, coal and power). The economy has done very well, and become the envy of the world.

It makes one wonder if democracy is the best form of government for all countries of the world. Looking back at the history of the USSR, the Bolsheviks under Lenin seized power in 1917. From then on, his successors – Stalin, Khrushchev, Brezhnev, Andropov, Chernenko and Gorbachev – came to power by *selection* rather than a democratic *election* as we understand it. After Gorbachev was overthrown and democratic elections were first held in the USSR in the early nineties, Boris Yeltsin came to power. Under Yeltsin's rule, the mighty Russian empire became weaker by the day. After Yeltsin handed over the reins of power to Vladimir Putin at the turn of the century, Russia once again rose to become a force to be reckoned with and has remained so ever since.

Let us take a look at countries of the Middle East like Iraq and Libya. Dictators in these countries were removed from power with significant help and intervention from outside. It was all done in the name of freedom and democracy. One wonders whether the ordinary people of these countries are any better off today than under the dictators. Nobody likes dictators. However, the majority of people in these countries today would agree that life was better for them under those dictators. Unless the people are educated and mature enough to understand democracy fully and know their duties and not only their rights, no country is ready for democracy. The imposition of democracy from outside only compounds the situation. A good dictator (if there is such a thing) in such circumstances is probably better than a bad democracy.

At the end of February 2019, I visited Moscow again to lecture at an orthopaedic conference. It was the tail end of winter and the thermometer in the morning read minus twelve degrees Celsius. The temperature was the only thing that had not changed in Moscow. The city centre was unrecognisable. It was completely lit up in the evening with decorative lights, giving it a magical feel. The illumination is on throughout the year. The town centre has been fully pedestrianised for people to enjoy the city. Modern underground cables have replaced the ugly overhead ones. It looks pleasing to the eye and has created the feeling of open spaces. The streets have numerous restaurants catering to every taste. Shops are selling all international brands of goods. We went into a popular, typical old-style Russian café for a meal. The paintings on the walls were reminiscent of Soviet times. On one wall was the picture of a worker with the inscription, 'Factories to workers and land to the peasants.' On the opposite wall was a historical painting of Lenin addressing the workers. These pictures will continue to evoke nostalgic memories in the minds of generations that grew up in socialist times.

There is something about Moscow that tends to attract you back like a magnet. It must be the warmth and genuineness of the people. Russians who live all over the world today feel the longing to be back. There is a saying, 'You can take a Russian out of Russia, but you cannot take Russia out of a Russian.' Alexander Solzhenitsyn, the Russian dissident writer and Nobel Prize winner who was exiled from the USSR, returned from the US to his native Russia to spend the last years of his life.

Looking back on life, I feel greatly blessed to have been a student in the heart of the mighty USSR, Moscow, during the times of the great 'social experiment' which, today, is remembered by many Russians as 'the lost paradise'. Over the years, I have travelled the world and got to know people from across the globe. I am yet to meet people who are so rough on the outside, but as simple and sincere, honest and humble, likeable and loving on the inside as the Russian people.

**The Alma Mater – RUDN**

**With Surgery Professor Pautkin (Third from the left)**

**Lady begging in the Red Square!**

**A demonstration by the communists in the Red Square!**

**View of the Red Square from the far end.**
**Lenin's mausoleum is on the left. GUM supermarket is seen on the right**

**Statues of Minin and Posharsky in front of St Basils cathedral**

**The beautiful Bolshoi with its eight pillars**

**The statue of Karl Marx with the inscription "Proletariat of the world unite"**

**A solitary statue of Lenin at the VDNHA**

**The beautiful Friendship of Nations Fountains at the VDNHA. The sixteen golden statues of women represent the different republics of the USSR**

The great guitar poet Vladimir Vysotsky

The cathedral of 'Christ the saviour'

Farewell to Moscow and off to the airport!

**Moscow by night! Red square and Kremlin seen illuminated in the background**

**Hari's parents and extended family**

# REFERENCES

Gorbachev, M. (1995) *Memoirs*. Bantam Books.

Levada.ru (2018) Survey report – The collapse of the USSR.

Lenin V, I. (1902) *What is to be done? Burning questions of our movement*. Stuttgart.

Schleifer, A. (2005) *A Normal Country: Russia After Communism*. Harvard University Press.

Sebestyen, V. (2009) *Revolution 1989: The Fall of the Soviet Empire*. Phoenix.

Sixsmith, M. (2011) *Russia: A 1000-year Chronicle of the Wild East*. BBC Books.

Hari Kumar is a Consultant Orthopaedic Surgeon working in Doncaster in the United Kingdom. He did his basic medical training in Moscow, USSR. In the memoir, he takes the reader along with him in this unusual, fascinating and hilarious journey through medical school in the Soviet Union and simultaneously opens a window to life as it was behind the iron curtain.